Psychoanalytic Theory and Methodology Today:
Selected Papers of Charlotte Schwartz

Psychoanalytic Theory and Methodology Today

Selected Papers of Charlotte Schwartz

IPBOOKS.net
International Psychoanalytic Books

International Psychoanalytic Books (IPBooks)
New York • http://www.IPBooks.net

Psychoanalytic Theory and Methodology Today

Published by IPBooks, Queens, NY
Online at: www.IPBooks.net

ISBN: 978-1-956864-81-6

Table of Contents

BOOK REVIEWS:

THEORY

CHAPTER 1

COMMUNICATION IN PSYCHOANALYSIS— DEVELOPMENTAL ANTECEDENTS[1]

[(1982). *Psychoanalytic Review* (69)(2):267–281.]

From the point of view of psychology, the unit of the function of speech is the word, a complex presentation which proves to be a combination put together from auditory, visual and kinaesthetic elements. (Freud, 1891).

I should like to draw your attention to the kinaesthetic element of the word *configuration*. It is not my intention to show how it is possible that a kinaesthetic sensation is reproduced in a sound image that finds final expression in a word presentation. What I am expressly interested in is by what agent or means kinaesthesis transmits communication from the external world to the nonverbal infant. *The Oxford University Dictionary of Historical Principles* defines communication as "to have a connection or passage from one to another," or "an interchange of thoughts."

During the first months of life, there exists no verbal communication from the infant to the mother, unless we wish to recognize crying, a global response, as a specific verbal communication. The mother's capacity to understand the needs of the young infant has, in all probability, a phylogenetic origin that ensures the continuity and survival of the human species. The

---

1 Paper presented at the University of Connecticut, Stamford Campus, seminar series on Communication, February 4, 1977.

3

psychological counterpart of the most basic of human instincts we recognize as "empathy." The studies of Spitz, Provence, Solnit, and others have shown the crucial role of empathy for the maturational development of the child. The failure of this mechanism in the mother can result in retarded physical and mental development, as well as disturbances in drive development and object relations (Spitz, 1950).

Empathy implies the ability to perceive the affects and experiences of another. In regard to the mother, we anticipate the capacity to experience affective regression (A. Freud, 1936, pp. 43–44), the ability to reexperience various infantile states without the behavioral manifestations. The experience is understood in mentation, in bound affects, not behaviorally. We regard this aspect of regression as at the behest of the ego and certainly in the service of the infant.

As an affect, i.e., an aspect of emotion, empathy is a drive derivative, capable of mobile cathexis. As a mental mechanism, it is comprised of a synthesis of various defense mechanisms. Perhaps we should note here Waelder's (1936) Principle of Multiple Function; we observe the affect, the displacement and projection of the affect, and the mechanism of primary identification (Bak, 1956, pp. 231–240; Brenner, 1976).

To refer to cathexis as simultaneously in a bound and mobile state only gives the appearance of a contradiction. Cathexis may be both bound and mobile. In an unbound state, primary process dominates, the cathexes are easily displaceable and give way to condensations. In a bound state, the dominance of secondary process prevails and the reality principle is operative, there is less displaceability of cathexis. In mobile affects, what is operant is the displaceability of cathexis wherein the sensations derived from the drive seek discharge (Glover, 1938). Mobile cathexis maintains a necessary role in secondary process (Hartmann, 1950); otherwise, an intensification of fixation to early objects and aims which ultimately impede human development would result (Freud, 1933).

The vehicle through which the infant communicates his needs is empathy in the mother. It must be remembered that the infant's communication reflects a physiologic process, an act of tension- increase and discharge (Glover, 1938). No meaning is as yet given by the infant to his behavior. He is expressing organic displeasure. Behind all psychological mechanisms rests a physiological psychological regulator, the pleasure-unpleasure principle (Freud, 1912). When physiologic tensions reach a level of discomfort (initially it is a question primarily of quantitative factors—how early to introduce the qualitative factors is indeed the question) the organism reacts with discomfort. This is observed in response to hunger, pain, and changes in body temperature. When the body's homeostatic balance is redressed, a state of pleasure results in a reduction in tension. Later psychological factors such as anxiety, love, panic, hate, will influence the pleasure and unpleasure principle.

The infant's "cries" to the mother are nonverbal. If he is in a state of equilibrium, longer periods of sleep are anticipated; if he is in a state of tension, often crying of varying intensity will communicate the discomfort. There is nothing purposeful or ideational in these messages. Certain kinaesthetic behavior may also communicate a global message by the form of the body posture such as a quality of stiffness or flacidity, atonicity or spastic movements.

Since the infant is incapable of empathetic responses and mentation is only developing (despite the claims of Melanie Klein and her followers), what can explain the infant's nascent comprehension of the mother's verbal and nonverbal communications?

Organized phonology will take on meaning only by the 6th month (White 1978, p. 25), though very early the infant seems to recognize and prefer the mother's voice (Bower, 1977, p. 31). This discrimination is based upon the pitch, timbre and rhythm with a preference to the high pitch sound (MacFarlane, 1977, pp. 76–77). To what degree the infant's equilibrium is disturbed by affect changes that reflect in the pitch and rhythm of the voice is unknown. I would suspect that these subtleties of sound cannot be communicated until a later stage when vision and sound are more finely organized and coordinated. That loud sounds can penetrate the stimulus barrier and cause sudden upset is well established. Infants subjected to continuous eruptive screaming may indeed be aversely affected by the excessive stimuli causing tension increase and trauma. This traumatic state does not at this early stage communicate the nature of the external world but effects organismic chaos and disorganization of the sensorium.

Vision is another sensory mode that will eventually refine and develop into the most complex source for human intellectual development. The relationship between vision and thinking is exemplified by the role of metaphor in abstract thinking, i.e., the degree by which thought relies upon a visual idea expressed in language. Vision is only gradually developed; the infant can see early in prenatal life but sight is responsive to contrasts of light in motion (MacFarlane, 1977, pp. 76–77). Studies show that the infant by the second week prefers the face of the mother (MacFarlane, 1977, p. 79), yet a gestalt can only be recognized by the third or fourth month.

Focusing is possible at approximately 8-inch distance both for nearness and farness. The face of the mother in the feed position can be focused upon. It would appear to represent an almost innate selector in order to ensure survival through the human rapprochement—since 8 inches is the distance of the mother's face during the feeding. The face, particularly the eyes, attracts the greatest attention, for the contrasts of the whites of the eye with the darker pupils and irises provide the source of contrast. (MacFarlane, 1977, pp. 76–77). Sight, in the early postnatal phase until the third month of life, is largely dependent upon movements, i.e., rhythmic movements and contrasts. Whether these visual perceptions can produce nuances of meaning for the infant in terms of mood and affect content is highly questionable.

It is possible that retroactive meaning can be given to early, archaic visual memories.

Since rhythm features so prominently in the auditory and visual receptors of this early stage, it is a more probable hypothesis to assume that sound and vision are made meaningful by association, or in sensory coordination with, the kinaesthetic or "proprioceptive" senses. Bower's (1977) study of the sequential development between the visual and proprioceptive senses indicates that the younger infant responds first by proprioceptive means, and only with later development does the visual field gain supremacy.

An infant shown an object in a lighted area will accurately reach for that same object when the room is darkened while the older infant loses the ability to accurately gain the object through reach. There is a gradual increased reliance upon vision which replaces the earlier kinaesthetic orientation. If these studies bear out with repeated testing, we may assume that the close physical contact with the mother provides the most important orientation to the external world (Spitz, 1949). This contact essentially involves the kinaesthetic sense.

Spitz (1965) regards this early period of mental organization as a "coenesthetic system." "Sensing is primarily visceral, centered in the autonomic nervous system and manifests itself in the form of emotions" (Spitz, 1949, p. 44).

The organization of stimuli into a coherent system of signals requires that they must be experienced as meaningful. Somehow the mother in this reciprocal dyad is able to provide the infant with a coherent ideational image of the world. She is the vehicle through which perception is learned, coordinated, and synthesized (Spitz, 1965, pp. 95–96).

The methodology involves a discrete series of timed actions on the part of the external object. For example, the hungry child requires feeding, but this feeding must not be experienced with excessive delay nor too immediate gratification.

Certain experiences must accrue between the onset of the discomfort and the decrease in discomfort. Flooding by inner stimuli interferes with orderly sequence of learning and disrupts the infant's ability to adequately organize the images of the external world. When the gratification permits no delay, no frustration, there is also a failure to integrate and organize the world of reality. The delay in the gratification and the frustration experienced patterns the memory traces which reflect the external world internally (Spitz, 1965, pp. 172–173).

The learning sequence is best ordered when it consists of hunger—delay—gratification. The need which is appropriately experienced is remembered both as a painful internal stimulus, and as gratified by a gradually recognized external source. This sequence leads to the recognition of the internal state. This is the source of ego development and consciousness. It leads to recognition of the external world, the mother.

The question to be addressed is: Are we observing a behavioral sequence with meaning derived from the nature of the pain, and the satisfaction then given, or is there a derivative of this experience which is vital for the development of communication? Is there some meaning that is derived from the particular manner in which the drives, i.e., anaclitic drives, are organized and bound through this early sequence in the pleasure-pain balance that is responsible for "deeper" meanings of words? It is my impression that in this early pre-stage of verbal communication, a meaning beyond the exact behavioral sequence is communicated to the infant or is interpolated by him. This interpolation stems from the primitive nature of early aroused emotions. A libidinous connection is established, a cathexis between the mother and infant not activated by words or word meanings but probably responsive to a quality of timing, a kinaesthetic sensory reception. Time as a rhythmic action (Freud, 1933; Greenacre, 1971) by the mother is undoubtedly experienced in the nature of a tactile, rhythmic motor movement. It is likely that in the kinaesthetic process some global meaning is transmitted. Erikson (1968,

p. 267) states that "sensory reality and logical conclusion are given form by kinaesthetic experience."

Since Spitz's studies on "Hospitalism," (Spitz, 1949, 1950) it has become increasingly apparent that good physical care does not necessarily result in good psychological care. The failure in good psychological care interferes with the establishment of the libidinal tie to the object. The resulting deprivation impedes the stimulation and development of the libidinal and aggressive drives. Bak (1956) regards an early deprived environment as a cause in the failure to differentiate between the libidinal and aggressive drive, thus interfering with appropriate ego structuralization. During the meaningful interaction between the mother and the infant, some element in the kinaesthetic and tactile interchange organizes visceral, coenesthetic elements into mnemic traces, the prelude of a diacritic organization.

An example by Spitz (1965, pp. 95–96) may provide some clue as to kinaesthetic communication between the mother and the infant. He cites an infant of a few days who refuses to feed at the mother's breast but instead bottle feeds from another object with milk expressed from this same mother. We must assume that the mother's disturbance is transmitted to the infant in sensory-motor movements. Perhaps this is the earliest origins of what Erikson (1968, pp. 82–83) calls "Basic Trust" and "Basic Distrust."

How are we to characterize this kinaesthetic element in early communication? Perhaps it lies in the subtle nature of the timing, both in the exactness and the flexibility of the mother's ministrations. Or is it in the holding, the taut or supple hold by the mother? Perhaps sounds that conform to musical time and rhythm (Stern, 1977)—a motherly *étude*—help to distinguish that which is pleasurable from that which is unpleasurable.

The behavior of the infant is not always a clue to early disturbance. A sleeping, quiet infant tends to be viewed as in a state of infantile bliss or euphoria when this may equally represent a withdrawal, a self-induced reduction in tension. This passive withdrawal has implications for the future course of object relations and the nature of the defense mechanisms. The feeling of unpleasure perceived via bodily sensations in the infant gives rise to definite reactions that evolve into particular meanings. What is felt as unpleasure is spit out and is experienced as outside the infant (Freud, 1925, p. 237).

Whether or not the source of the mother's displeasure stems from the infant cannot be distinguished by the child. He does not have the capacity to understand why she is troubled or the nature of her responses; only the general state of discomfort is perceived by him (Spitz, 1965, p. 239). The wish is to push away, to spit out that which is perceived as unpleasure. This naturally leads to pushing away the mother. In this early state of pushing out what is uncomfortable and keeping in what is pleasurable, we have the beginnings of judgment. Judgment "affirms or disaffirms the possession by a thing of a particular attribute; and it asserts or disputes that a presentation has an existence in reality" (Freud, 1925, p. 237). "... The attribute to be decided about may originally have been good or bad, useful or harmful" (Freud, 1925, pp. 237–238). Meaning bears a close relationship to judgment, for meaning is also derived from the early experience of what gave pleasure or what produced unpleasure. The sense of reality is determined by this early development of judgment. Meaning and the sense of reality have a similar point of origin in the earliest experiences of infancy. Reality develops from the search internally for the previously gratifying object (Freud, 1925, pp. 237–238). Meaning, therefore, derives its intent from the early relations with the mother. The positive or negative valence to meaning will depend upon the nature of the mother-child dyad. These early experiences which give interpretation to behavior influence the judgment and perceptions in adult life.

DISTORTION OF REALITY AND PSYCHOANALYTIC INTERPRETATION

The effectiveness of an interpretation is influenced by the timing (Brenner, 1976). Timing correlates with the movement between the repressive forces of the defense and the upsurge of the drives seeking discharge and gratification, with the negative and positive valence in the transference, and with the unending flux between the libidinal and aggressive drives. The interpretation is judged against the need to maintain a balance in the psychic apparatus. A too pervasive interpretation may expose the psyche to an overflow of the drives, subject the ego to a harsh attack by the superego, or present the possibility of internalized object loss. Such an interpretation therefore precipitously lowers the defense structure. A poorly-timed interpretation can also result in a solidifying of the defenses, a stiffening of the resistances, the danger being that the patient becomes more removed and less accessible to self-awareness.

In this shifting balance of forces even within rather stable ego functions (Hartmann, 1950); the shifts occur under the influence of the pleasure-unpleasure principle.

Therefore, we attribute to the role of communication in the therapeutic situation some ability to influence or mobilize these shifts in the pleasure-unpleasure series as they effect psychic structures and defense mechanisms. Meaning derives in part from the patient's experience in the pleasure-unpleasure sequence. How the analyst modulates or regulates these shifting sands in the homeostasis of the psychic apparatus relates to the theoretical premise and methodological procedure of the therapeutic intervention. The queries are posed as: What in the treatment enables the analyst to comprehend the meaning of the patient's utterances? Does what the manifest content convey really signify the meaning, or are the words adorned in a costume merely to deceive? One may compare, provided the analogy be loosely applied, the analytic session to a scene from a play. We observe the cast of characters brought into the session, their symbolic or metaphorical role, the language spoken, the tenor of the voice, the body movement, and the historical period of the event. Like Hamlet, we observe:

The play is the thing
Wherein I'll catch the conscience of the King.
[Shakespeare, *Hamlet,* Act II, ii, 545–603].

I do believe you think what now you speak,
But what we do determine oft we break.
Purpose is but slave to memory,
Of violent birth, but poor validity.
  [Act III, ii, 142–190].

The analyst is charged with understanding the patient's meaning and attempts to communicate in a manner that will effect some change in the defense system, the structural relationships between ego and id, ego and superego, ego and the external world, and in the love-hate balance. Whether it is the words the analyst uses or the transference state that conveys the necessary insight regarding the conflictual constellation[2] is beyond the scope of this paper. The issue confronting us is the mode of verbal communication that the analyst uses at a particular moment. Further, I have chosen not to examine the role of silence as a communicative act, for I wish to focus on the meaning of the verbal interchange.

---

2 Sternbach, O. Unpublished paper. Contribution to the Panel on "Psychoanalytic Technique: The Relationship of Insight to the Transference," held at the meeting of the National Psychological Association for Psychoanalysis in New York on March 31, 1978.

Case Vignette

A 25-year-old female patient relates an incident that occurred the morning of her session. Her supervisor, a younger woman, asked the patient to prepare an outline of her work in a particular way. Instead of the patient listening silently to the instruction, she repeatedly interrupted, exclaiming, "that's just what I am doing." The result of this interchange left the supervisor exasperated and the patient both frightened for her job and self-righteous in her behavior. The patient repeated the incident over and over in the session, and with each telling it became more incomprehensible to me. If I decide to point out to the patient how she exasperates people with a calm, stubborn, and impenetrable manner, she will experience what I say as an attack; she will feel criticized, and this will evoke anger toward me though she cannot consciously experience it. She will need to defend herself from this unconscious aggression.[3] The patient will now be confronted with an additional situation wherein the aggression evokes anxiety which she must also defend against. This is precisely what I decide to do, to try to shift the scene of the conflict from the external world to the analytic situation. Since the external situation is not grave, the experience in the transference will be the prominent issue. I point out her stubborn, defensive manner, her failure to listen to anyone, and how she provokes people with this behavior.

What I had anticipated occurred. She became defensive with me, repeating, explaining, and listing all the persons with whom she cooperates. I now have the opportunity to demonstrate in microcosm behavior that is governed by infantile conflicts and to effectuate the unconscious conflicts

---

3 The conflict at this moment for the patient is the degree of aggression which is provoked by ordinary relationships with people. The source of the aggression derives from oral, anal and oedipal phases. The point at issue is the rise in tension created by the aggression, the discharge patterns and the distortion of reality. Since the object ties are tenuous, the object world is constantly threatened by the increase in aggression. The purpose of my statements was to center the conflicts in the transference relationship.

in *statu nascendi*. There are several possibilities of response that must be anticipated. She will be hurt by what I had said. I also know that hurt feelings for this patient activates aggression, due to the narcissistic injury that she experiences, and this further evokes in her the primitive mechanism of identification with the aggressor. Aggression is dangerous for her because of the problem of ambivalence and the danger that the object representation can easily be lost. Her positive feelings towards me are tenuous and must be protected. If she permits herself to experience the aggression towards me, she is in danger of feeling alone and helpless. Either she will use rationalization and denial, or experience a feeling of helplessness and hopelessness about her ability to change. This aspect of the depressive response is primarily a shifting of the aggression to her own ego. I had to await the next day's session to see the unfolding of the dynamic interplay of forces.

The patient began the session by relating that she had many dreams last night but could not remember them. This patient has infrequently brought in dreams; the unconscious is too frightening. Why then does she begin this session with drawing attention to dreams and to her resistance? She wants me to know that she really cannot help the resistance. She would like to be a good analysand but cannot help herself. She then repeats the events of yesterday almost verbatim in defense of her behavior. I listen quietly to this repetition and then tell her that I dreamt of her last night.[4] It is obvious that an empathetic response was elicited in me that also referred to some aspect of my own conflicts. I dreamt that the patient and her supervisor were arguing and the supervisor yelled "you are always arguing about politics." I inform her that in the dream that I felt a "sorrow" for her in that she used

---

4 The question may well be raised, "what if the analyst had had no dream regarding the patient?" Certainly, another means to evoke the conflict would have been sought. The utilization of a countertransference response was determined not by a theoretical position that attempts to share mutual feelings or experiences with the patient in order to establish a "new object" but rather purposefully considered as the most effective means to evoke from the deep the repressions and its manifestation in the character defenses of the patient.

politics to defend herself as a means to establish her personal integrity. I also related that the dream had reference to my own conflicts in order to provide an honest therapeutic model and give some understanding of the dream work. "Oh, thank you, for caring about me," she rejoined. The compromise formation of this statement (White, 1978) pointed to the conflict and some attempt to compromise the conflicting drives. My having dreamt about her was an indication that I "cared" for her or at least had some concern for her beyond the session. This was bound to induce guilt as my expression of affection could only remind the patient of her ambivalent and contrary feelings. We may well ask why it is that ambivalence seems generally to side with the aggressive or hostile feelings rather than the libidinal cathexis.

The patient recalls a conversation with her supervisor about the patient's therapy. The supervisor is curious as to how "therapy works." "I talk, and my therapist listens, sometimes she points something out to me about my behavior." At the end of this conversation the supervisor is left frustrated and exclaims repeatedly "but how does it work?" The patient laughs and the conversation is repeated several times. Noteworthy is the patient's damning me with faint praise. Never once did the patient say that I was good, I was wonderful or understanding, or mean or tough. I was presented as an abstract mouthpiece without flesh and blood. The listener, therefore, missed the emotional element in the therapy. She could not find the emotional tone that would help her perceive the analytic process, essentially an unconscious understanding of transference elements.

I remained silent and the patient's next associations led to her father. He was her only sustained love object and his death three years ago left her feeling abandoned. The relationship with the mother has always been poor and in fact the mother's treatment of her bordered on cruelty. Her father, though he had paid for therapy sessions three times a week for three years while she was a college student, had always objected to therapy. She again tells me how her father was opposed to therapy and always said that hard work would solve all problems. She laughs as she lists his problem, the family quarrels, the brawls, and the disturbances among the siblings.

What is the patient indicating about her own analysis? She is ambivalent: analysis helps, it doesn't help. I help her, but she still has problems. She is disappointed in me but cannot completely agree with her father's disparagement of therapy. This patient is on an emotional see-saw, a constant state of tension that is unable to find release in direct discharge or sublimation. At this moment, I judge it admissible to address her ambivalence; but not directly as it may threaten her tenuous object tie to me and strengthen the resistance. I postulate that possibly her father was correct. After all the years of treatment she still has problems with working relationships, particularly the men in authority; treatment can't be considered too successful. The attempt was to relate to her disappointment and ambivalence, to permit its expression and then possibly to judge the situation more realistically. The patient responds, "but I have followed his advice" and "it hasn't got me anywhere." "Therapy will help, it has helped; you will help me, won't you, you will nudge me!"

The patient's response seemed to be a beginning triumph of the ego's capacity to master somewhat the ambivalence and judge more accurately the task of the analyst in view of her character defenses. Freud (1925, pp. 236–237) indicated that judgment requires ability to evaluate the attribute or a quality of a thing and that the function of judgment also requires that one re-find an object which was lost but once provided gratification. If the analysis can be seen in a more positive light, then the analyst can be cathected with libido; we will then see a shift in the balance between libido and aggression.

I felt that at this point I had an opportunity to respond to the emotional turmoil in this patient without eliciting an undue amount of guilt; that I could strengthen the positive transference. I commented in a tone that I hoped was neither too matter of fact nor too emotionally laden, "how painful to be governed by blind forces over which you have no control. I know you want to like people, to be friendly; instead, you are caught by your feelings of envy and jealousy that appear to dominate your relationships." "If only I could be different," responded the patient, "I do so want to like people, only I am afraid that I do not have this capacity. I really do not care about anyone, I don't love anyone, and I never have except maybe my father. What a horrible thing to recognize about myself; I have no connection to anyone. Oh, Betty and I go to the movies once a week, but we never talk. I don't want to be an old maid, a spinster."

In the next session the patient reveals that for the past year she believed that I had been in touch with her previous place of employment and recently had telephoned her boss. She prefaced this revelation with, "I know I am paranoid but I can't help it. How else can I explain things that have happened at work? Certain things happen at work which seem to follow immediately from discussions that you and I have here." "Do you want me to call your boss?" Yes, in this way you can help me to understand what I am doing wrong that antagonizes people." She hopes that I and her boss can "show her" as she has no awareness of her behavior.

Why now does this paranoid suspicion of over a year's standing emerge? Is it that the suspicion is somewhat mitigated, or the positive transference strengthened and there is less fear of object loss and retaliation?

There was not sufficient evidence in the treatment to judge that this paranoid expression represented an increase in psychotic ideation or represented a more pervasive cathectic withdrawal with an increase in aggressive drive. It was rather my estimate that the ego was better able to tolerate the ambivalence, with an increased ability to judge reality. The element of wish for good and protective oedipal parents is also inherent in the statement; notwithstanding the existence also of the powerful and destructive fused parents that basically represent the "bad mother." Reality develops from the search internally for the previously gratifying object (Freud, 1923, pp. 237–238). Meaning, therefore, derives its intent from the early relations with the mother. The positive or negative valence to meaning will depend upon the nature of the mother-child dyad. These early experiences which give interpretation to behavior influence the judgment and perceptions in adult life.

The purpose of this vignette was to demonstrate how meaning is received and interpolated by the analyst, and the modes by which the analyst attempts to address and redress these meanings. Despite this patient's correct manner, soft tones and no visible anger, her obsequious timidity and self-righteous posture betrayed a negative transference from the inception of treatment. Her difficulty in deriving positive meaning from the analyst prevented an adequate perception and judgment of reality. The degree of unpleasure experienced by the patient in the treatment relates to earlier failures in neutralization of aggressive energy. Correlated with this failure in neutralization was the development of poor object relations. The inability of the patient to have experienced the mother with sufficient positive feeling presages the dominance of unpleasurable reactions in her object contacts and creates an always threatening imbalance in the homeostasis of the pleasure-unpleasure mechanism. This reduces the efficacy of reality testing. The situation is repeated in the transference. A primary task for the analyst was to modulate the quantity of unpleasure experienced by this patient. Too great a degree of unpleasure placed a heavy burden upon her weak ego structure and activated primitive and pathological defenses. The greatest danger lay in the quantity of unmanageable aggression which threatened not only the integrity of her ego but her tenuous object ties as well. This leaves her in a lonely, helpless, and ungratified state.

The hungry infant must be fed in a particular manner; a manner that satisfies the instinct of hunger and reduces the tension which has interfered with the homeostasis. The tension reduction is dependent upon the anaclitic relationship between the instincts for survival and the libidinal and aggressive drives. To the degree that there is a drive imbalance or unpleasure created by kinaesthetic responses derived from the mother, a negative meaning will ensue in regard to the mother, to the meaning of her ministrations, and will result in a wish to spit out or push away. To the degree that a pleasurable, and therefore positive, meaning is derived from the gratification of survival needs, we may assume that a positive meaning will then derive from the experience with the mother.

In the therapeutic relationship, it is possible to follow these early patterns of global responses of pleasure-unpleasure in a more specific manner. We may observe the fluctuations of the drive balance between libido and aggression, changes in the defense mechanisms and the ego in relation to the internal psychic structures and the external world. Meaning is derived not only from what is intended but how the intention is perceived. An interpretation that shifts the balance between pleasure and unpleasure, due either to the distribution between narcissistic and object libido, structural relationships, or the nature of the transference, will be responded to accordingly. The current psychic template reflects the influence of the earliest derivates of the period of infancy when the kinaesthetic sense dominated the pleasure-unpleasure balance and from whence the precursors of defensive mechanisms developed.

The task of the analyst is to attempt, as expeditiously as possible, to influence the apperceptions of the patient through a series of studied meanings of the unconscious conflicts and their effect upon the economic principle.

REFERENCES

Bak, R.C. (1956). Aggression and Perversion. In Lorand, S. (Ed.) *Perversions, Psychodynamics and Therapy.* New York: Random House, pp. 231–240.

Bower, T.G.R. (1977). *The Perceptual World of the Child.* Cambridge: Harvard University Press.

Brenner, C. (1976). *Psychoanalytic Technique and Psychic Conflict.* New York: International Universities Press.

Erikson, E.H. (1968). *Identity, Youth and Crises.* New York: W.W. Norton.

Freud, A. (1936). *The Ego and the Mechanisms of Defense.* New York: International Universities Press. Revised Edition, 1966.

Freud, S. (1891). *On Aphasia,* London: Imago Publishing, 1953.

_____ (1925). Negation. *Standard Edition*, 19:235–239, 1961.

_____ (1933). New Introductory Lectures on Psycho-Analysis. *Standard Edition,* 22:81–111, 1964.

Glover, E. (1938). *The Psychoanalysis of Affects. On The Early Development of Mind.* New York: International Universities Press, 1956, p. 301.

Greenacre, P. (1953). *Certain Relationships Between Fetishism and the Faulty Development of the Body Language. Emotional Growth, Vol.* 1. New York: International Universities Press, 1971, p. *22.*

_____ (1958). *Early Physical Determinants in the Development of the Sense Identity. Emotional Growth, Vol. I.* New York: International Universities Press, 1971.

Hartmann, H. (1950). Psychoanalytic Comments on the Psychoanalytic Theory of the Ego. *Psychoanal. St. Child,* 5:74–96. I

MacFarlane, A. (1977). *The Psychology of Childbirth.* Cambridge: Harvard University Press.

Spitz R.A. (1949). Hospitalism: An Inquiry into the Genesis of Psychotic Conditions in Early Childhood. *Psychoanal. St. Child*, 1:53–74.

_____ (1950). Hospitalism: A Follow-Up Report. *Psychoanal. St. Child*, 2:113–117.

_____ (1965). Collaboration with W. Godfrey Cobliner. *The First Year of Life*. New York International Universities Press.

Stern, G. (1977). *The First Relationship: Infant and Mother*. Cambridge: Harvard University Press, p. 15.

Waelder, Robert. (1936). The Principle of Multiple Function: Observations on Over-Determination, *Psychoanal. Q.*, 5:45–62.

White, B. L. (1978). *The First Three Years of Life*. New York: Cenon.

CHAPTER 2

AMBIVALENCE: ITS RELATIONSHIP TO NARCISSISM AND SUPEREGO DEVELOPMENT

[(1989). *Psychoanalytic Rev*iew (76)(4):511–527.]

A discussion of ambivalence in the current annals of psychoanalytic theory has the ring of an anachronism. New theoretical concepts (new in the sense of extended meaning) dominate the intellectual climate. These have evolved from our attempts to grapple with rather pervasive and resistant character structures and character pathologies that, on the surface, seem untreatable by the old theories and methodologies. One such construct is the concept of splitting, first formulated by Breuer and Freud in *The Studies of Hysteria* (1893–1895), and further elaborated by Freud in his writings on fetishism (1927, 1940). The current thinking evolving from the writings of Klein, Fairbairn, and Kernberg places the mechanism of splitting in a central position in the structuralization of the psychic apparatus. It has become the *sine qua non* of mental activity. It is not possible within the framework of this paper to enter into a discussion or comparison of the two concepts. At best, I can only draw attention to the factor that many conditions in mental development, which formerly would have been discussed as indicative of ambivalence, now fall under the aegis of splitting mechanisms.

I propose in this paper a reconsideration of the concept of ambivalence in regard to time of onset and to show the centrality of its role in the integrative process of ego and superego structures. Further, it is my intent to show that the failure to adequately resolve ambivalence has serious implications for clinical practice. Conflicts due to ambivalence result in treatment failure on par with those we ascribe to the negative therapeutic reaction, to the persistence of the repetition compulsion and those stemming from a wide range of ego deficits. The concept of a pre-ambivalent phase, a time when ego and object world are not clearly defined, is rooted in the early history of psychoanalytic thought. Ambivalence in this framework was seen to arise from the conflicts inherent in the relationship to the object; it results from a love/ hate polarity (Abraham, 1924; Fenichel, 1945). I contend that this formulation tends to disregard Freud's energic concepts and the inherent conflict between the two drives, Eros and Thanatos, each with divergent aims. That Freud himself also postulated a pre-ambivalent phase is most interesting. For if we follow his (1915a) earlier thoughts, we observe that he regards ambivalence as an "incomplete fusion" of the drives. The concept of fusion refers to quantitative factors, an economic principle of drives interdigiting in a specific manner. For Freud to have suggested a pre-ambivalent phase does injustice to his metapsychology.

I shall also set forth the hypothesis that ambivalence as a condition reflective of the earliest narcissistic stage of development exerts a primary influence on the binding of the drives. Thus, the manner by which primary and secondary process influence the course of drive development will, in circular fashion, affect the ego's capacity to resolve ambivalence.

Further, an examination of superego development and functions points to identical sources of identification as that of the ego, that is, the superego in its evolution derives from the same object cathexes. It is the change of function that will differentiate the superego identifications from those of the ego. Ambivalence affects the structuralization of the superego by the nature of its role in the identification process and in regard to the problems of neutralization and binding of aggression.

Bleuler first coined the term ambivalence in 1910. Freud's early reference to ambivalence appears in the *Three Essays* (1905) in which, incidental to a discussion of the sadistic anal phase, he states:

This form of sexual orientation can persist throughout life and can permanently attract a large portion of sexual activity to itself.... It is further characterized by the fact that in it the opposing pairs of instincts are developed to an approximately equal extent, a state of affairs described by Bleuler's happily chosen term "ambivalence" [p. 199].

In *Instincts and Their Vicissitudes* (1915a), Freud discusses the issue of the transformation of love into hate. He states, "since it is particularly common to find both of these directed simultaneously toward the same object, their co-existence furnishes the most important example of ambivalence of feeling" (p. 133). He regarded ambivalence as a result of the incomplete fusion between love and hate, a result of the ways and manner the two classes of instincts "are fused, blended and alloyed with each other" (1923, p. 41). That is, ambivalence represents an economic outcome of the way the two kinds of instinct (the sexual and the destructive) (1923, p. 41), are interspersed in "every particle of human substance." Freud states:

Once we have admitted the idea of a fusion of the two classes of instincts with each other, the possibility of a—more or less complete —"defusion" of them forces itself upon us. The sadistic component of the sexual instinct would be a classical example of a serviceable instinctual fusion.... We perceive that for purposes of discharge the instinct of destruction is habitually brought into the service of eros; ... making a swift generalization, we might conjecture that the essence of a regression of libido (e.g., from the genital to the sadistic-anal phase) lies in a defusion of the instincts, just as, conversely, the advance from the earlier phase to the definitive genital one would be conditioned by an accession of erotic components. The question also arises whether ordinary ambivalence, which is so often unusually strong in the constitutional disposition to neurosis, should not be regarded as the project of a defusion; ambivalence, however, is such a fundamental phenomenon that it more probably represents an instinctual fusion that has not been completed, (pp. 41–42)

The concept of fusion refers to quantitative factors, an economic principle of drives interdigiting in a particular manner in which the erotic elements dominate by an "accession of erotic components." Thus, ambivalence would appear to be the result of a failure in the quantitative dominance of the erotic drive.

In 1920, Freud regarded sadism as the basic exponent of Thanatos: "Wherever the original sadism has undergone no mitigation or intermixture, we find the familiar ambivalence of love and hate in erotic life" (p. 54). In 1924, masochism superseded sadism in the theory as the original mode of the destructive drive: only in its mixtures with Eros is the force of aggression diluted. What would represent an adequate indicator of fusion? Is it a question of distribution of the energy of the drives within each component or between them? There is some question of quantitative distribution between the parts and the whole. Let us go further: How do we examine fusion of the drives in regard to the polarities or mode of function, for example in activity and passivity? Is activity equated with libido—which strives to unite, to bind—and passivity equated with Thanatos—which strives to reduce tension, to go back to its original state? Would ambivalence then be characterized not only by the inherent contradictory aim in terms of external function of the two, but more basically by quantitative distributions of the two drives that push in different directions—one to a state of union and the other to a state of dissemblance?

Having considered ambivalence from the position of economic distribution of the two drives and the problems of understanding energic displacements within the component instincts, it might be useful to examine ambivalence in regard to the regulatory principle—the pleasure-unpleasure principle. Freud indicated that:

In the theory of psychoanalysis, we have no hesitation in assuming that the course taken by mental events is automatically regulated by the pleasure principle.... In taking that course into account in our consideration ... we are introducing an "economic point of view" [p. 7].

To what degree or if at all does ambivalence influence the functions of the pleasure-unpleasure principle? After all, a regulatory mechanism does not apply to a specific form or content. It measures and regulates other processes very much like the pressure of the flow of blood in the human body. Since that which regulates is affected by a series of processes let us see if there is some interrelation between ambivalence and the pleasure principle. Is it possible that ambivalence due to doubts, stalemates, inaction, doing and undoing, or inhibition, interferes with discharge mechanisms? If so, then a build up in drive tension would be created and a sense of unpleasure would ensue. But, is it not also possible to consider that delays in discharge due to the conflicts of ambivalence may in fact support the reality principle?

The function of the pleasure principle is also dependent on other mechanisms in the psychic economy, for example, the state of the drives whether they are bound or unbound, or whether they are in a state of primary process or influenced by secondary processes. Freud stated in 1920 that, "We have decided to relate pleasure and unpleasure to the quantity of excitation that is present in the mind but is not in any way bound, and so relate them in such a manner that unpleasure corresponds to an increase in the quantity of excitation and pleasure to a diminution" (p. 8). Yet, later in this paper, he seems to contradict this statement and states that "binding of the instincts ensures the dominance of the pleasure principle." Reversing himself again, he writes, "This raises the question of whether feelings of pleasure and unpleasure can be produced equally from bound and from unbound excitatory processes, and there seems to be no doubt whatever that the unbound or primary processes give rise to far more intense feelings in both directions than the bound or secondary ones" (p. 62). The capacity to bind the drives presupposes some lessening of intensity, some diminution for direct discharge. Is it possible that a diminution in drive discharge due to the inhibitory act of ambivalence enhances the binding of the drives? It is questionable that this occurs, for clinical experience teaches us that inhibition, or even massive repression does not necessarily coincide with secondary process. Quite the contrary, repression may be hiding the most primitive of drive states. It is more plausible to consider that ambivalence may indeed be a factor in the ego's difficulty to adequately bind the drives. The failure to resolve ambivalence, the almost equal pull between the libidinal and the aggressive wishes that press for discharge without modification of aim interferes with the ego's capacity to effect neutralization. Simultaneously, the failure to bind the drives tends to interfere with the resolution or, more accurately, the modification of ambivalence, for, drives in an unbound, unneutralized state push for immediate discharge. Frustration increases the force of aggression which, unmodified by a change in aim and the reality principle, obstructs the ego's capacity to adequately resolve the ambivalence.

Quantitative factors in the energic distribution between the libidinal and aggressive drive play a pivotal role in the integrative processes within psychic structure and influence the course of ambivalence. I have attempted to show the multiplicity of areas and conditions from which ambivalence emerges and in turn effects. However, quantitative factors alone cannot sufficiently explicate the issue of ambivalence. It is in qualitative factors that we shall find the complementarity to quantity, for the former is responsible for the modification of the latter. Fenichel (1945) has indicated that to speak of ambivalence prior to the inception of object relations has no serious relevance, it is a matter only of definition. But, if ambivalence is inherent in the very nature of the two drives, then something must occur that makes possible some modification of the drives, some capacity for fusion and neutralization. Something is added to the quantity of the drive, and that is a matter of quality. But what is responsible for the qualitative change?

Freud (1914), in his paper on narcissism, states that in primary narcissism a quantity of energy that resides within the "ego" is extended to the need gratifying object. In the course of the ego's development, these cathexes are brought back from the object world in the form of internalizations by means of a redistribution of energy between the outside and the inside (Freud, 1923). That is, there is a dialectical relationship between energy, object, and internal structure. Freud (1923) indicated that initially identification and object cathexis occur simultaneously; the ego is the precipitate of abandoned objects. Freud further considered that the path for both neutralization and sublimation was through the relinquishing of the libidinal attachment to the object. In this formulation, it is clear that the nature of the object cathexes will effect quantitative aspects of the drive and, in essence, are the determinants of qualitative factors. Further, the task of reducing and modifying ambivalence will fall to the nature of the object relations and the internalized representations in the form of ego and superego structures.

I would like to consider at this juncture a factor that perhaps adds to the complexity of the process: Is it not necessary to believe that some neutralization, some binding of the drives must also occur either prior to or in unison with the identificatory process? If this does not occur, how can we conceive that the primitivism and forcefulness of the libidinal drive is moderated and internalization is effected? Similarly, in regard to both the aggressive drive that modifies the force of its discharge and the imprimatur of its powerful destructiveness on the frustrating object, some fusion, some neutralization and binding must be in progress. Of course, this is conjecture of a very hypothetical nature for there is no way to measure or to observe these processes of mental integration and internalizations. Can Freud's (1923) statement that the superego is both a "precipitate" and a repressor of the oedipus complex add some credence to the postulate that the fusion and binding of the drives (which make possible the establishment of object cathexes and internalization) are simultaneously dependent on this very process? The two functions occur simultaneously in a form of synchronization where exquisite timing can result in what Hegelian thought postulates as thesis, antithesis, and synthesis. Waelder's (1936) theory of "multiple functions" also explains this process by which psychic mechanisms can perform a number of functions simultaneously. In this context, we can understand quality as arising from sensations from the nature of the ego cathexes that result in particular internalizations. The character of the object will become metamorphosized into an internal quality in the identificatory process. The degree by which ambivalence is resolved will determine the kind and character of the internalization; and in parallel process the quality of the external object will influence the modification of ambivalence. Quality is not just derived in relation to quantitative shifts in energy, as Freud indicated, nor does it result from the mode of rhythmic intervals. Rather, it is quite dependent on the nature of the object.

Earlier, I indicated my disagreement with the conception of a pre-ambivalent phase. To speak of a phase of pre-ambivalence as was first postulated by Abraham (1924) does not do justice to our understanding of the metapsychological concepts of energic processes. Spitz (1983) has stated that the "collaboration of the aggressive drive with the libidinal drive is a prerequisite for the formation of object relations" (p. 323), yet he too holds to the theory of a pre-ambivalent stage. I believe that certain writer's tenaciousness in holding on to the idea of the pre-ambivalent stage is due to their preference for regarding ambivalence as primarily the result of frustrations from the object world. If we follow Freud's earliest thoughts (1905, 1915a) that ambivalence results from "incomplete fusion," then an energic model must carry equal weight and ambivalence thus should be regarded as deriving from a multifaceted source— sometimes from the action of the objects and sometimes from the side of quantitative energic factors.

Spitz (1983) provides us with some interesting material from infant observations that may further corroborate my thesis. He indicates that the infant in the course of development establishes the "invariable percept" of the mother's face. Once this is done the next step permits him to combine the "giving" mother's face with the "frustrating" mother's face into a unified percept of the mother. "With this is the establishment of object constancy, and it is evident that this development starts with the inception of the reality principle" (p. 278). To refer to the reality principle regardless of the crudity of its function and the ease by which pure pleasure can supersede it with the introduction of a hallucinatory wish or a "negative hallucination" (Freud, 1911) or a demand for gratification is to implicitly make a statement regarding the functioning of the two drives in some form of synchronicity. It is within this process, that of fusing and binding, and within the matrix of the object relationship that ambivalence results. There is always the constant of the quantitative factors that are responsible for the great variations and difficulties in the process of drive fusion and in the establishment of the reality principle, that is, the accession of the secondary process.

Therefore, the phase of primary narcissism is the locus of great activity on the part of the drives in the structuralization of the ego. To regard this as a phase of pre-ambivalence is, as I have indicated, a disregard for the influence of the energic principle in early mental life.

In general terms, I have indicated that the resolution or, more accurately, the modification of ambivalence is achieved by the resolution of conflicts that have their inception in the very beginnings of life. A primary role has been ascribed to the mechanism of identification. The structure of the superego, just as the structure of the ego, develops in large part by means of identification. The hypothesis put forward is that without adequate fusion and binding of the drives, diminution of ambivalence would not occur and therefore the superego as an effective structure would suffer impairment.

Ambivalence as a quantitative force that acts on objects impedes the process of identification.

Can the reverse also hold forth? That without the development of the superego, the mitigation of ambivalence would encounter major obstacles? The superego is regarded as the "seat" of judgment (Freud, 1931), as a development from the ego's first judgments, which were concerned with what is "good" and what is "bad"; it continues the determination regarding the qualities of the object, only a change now occurs, the object is now the ego. The aggression that was once directed outward—a redirection from the original masochism—is turned inward, is "introjected" (Freud, 1931, p. 123), and the authority of the object as internalized structure has taken over the task of managing or mitigating the aggressive drive.

Freud (1923) stated that the

> first identifications always behave as a special agency in the ego and stand apart from the ego in the form of a superego. . . .The superego owes its special position in the ego, or in relation to the ego, to a factor which must be considered from two sides; on the one hand, it was the first identification and one which took place while the ego was still feeble, and on the other hand, it is the heir to the Oedipus Complex and has thus introduced the most momentous objects into the ego [p. 48].

It would appear that this statement is the quintessence of a paradox, for how is it that one and the same identification, in the same time sequence even, structures both the ego and the superego? Why the duality of structure? And what, if any, is the nature of the distribution of the "first" identifications? The problem presents itself even prior to the onset and resolution of the oedipus complex. What then is the nature either in content or function of the identifications that constitute the superego prior to the oedipal phase?

A moment's reflection reveals that by "first" Freud meant early, and since he rarely presented schematics or specificities of time except in broad general outlines, we might say that "first" essentially refers to the first objects of libidinal attachment. Therefore, "first" is not meant in a time frame but refers to the emotional importance of the objects for psychic development.

Yet, a strict reading would belie this interpretation. Freud (1923), in discussing the origin of the ego ideal, states:

> For behind it there lies hidden an individual's first and most important identification, his identification with the "father" [a footnote indicates that behind the father are the parents] in his own personal prehistory. This is apparently not in the first instance the consequence or outcome of an object cathexis, it is a direct and immediate identification and takes place earlier than any object cathexes [p. 31].

In the 1924 paper on masochism, Freud also indicates that the superego comes into being through "the introduction into the ego of the first objects of the id's libidinal impulses—namely, the two parents" (p. 167). How are we to proceed with his exposition of the "first" and "direct" identification as the content of superego structure when we have presumed that the contents are precisely the constituents of the ego? Perhaps it has been the nature of our own thinking that has divided the tripartite structure of the mind with rather rigid structural boundaries.

In the *New Introductory Lectures* (1933a, 1933b), Freud warns us that in thinking about the division of the personality into id, ego, and superego,

> You will not, of course, have pictured sharp frontiers like the artificial ones drawn in political geography. We cannot do justice to the characteristics of the mind by linear outlines like those in a drawing

or in primitive painting, but rather by areas of color melting into one another as they are presented by modern artists. After making the separation we must allow what we have separated to merge together once more [p. 79].

To follow this thinking, it is possible to conceive that initially the ego and superego structures were simultaneous in development and derived from the same sources, that is, their development is not linear. Further, it seems that the ego, due to its relationship to the external world through the agency of the perceptual system, leaps while the superego's development is tandem. When Freud states that "the superego owes its special position in the ego or in relation to the ego" (1923, p. 48), I believe that this very point is at issue. For, if the superego has a position initially in the ego, the developmental lines are similar, the contents are the same, but at a point, or several points, there is a differentiation of the content into different functions. It is this dialectic that explains Freud's thoughts that the superego is both heir to the oedipus complex and simultaneously is responsible for repression of the oedipus complex. Perhaps that which is in a state of becoming has already been. Freud states that the "superego is, however, not simply a residue of the earliest object choices of the id, it also represents an energetic reaction-formation against these choices" (1923, p. 321). His thought on the phylogenetic origins of the superego, that the superego is a "resurrection" of former egos through the inheritance of the id (1923, p. 38), provides further evidence for the idea that the superego is not simply a linear descendant of the ego, nor simply the heir of the oedipus complex, but derives from sources similar to the ego in drive energy and in mental contents.

To regard the ego as the representative of the external world, or reality, and the superego as standing in "contrast" to it as the representative of the internal world of the id (1923, p. 36) is a means of pointing to a differentiation not so much of topography, but rather a differentiation of function. The function of the superego supersedes certain functions of the external object; it takes on what was early experienced in the relationship to the parents in the role of protector, and censor, for both are intimately related in their survival value. Freud indicated that "the way in which the superego comes into being explains how it is that the early conflicts of the ego with the id—cathexes of the id—can be contained in conflicts with their heir, the superego" (1923, pp. 38–39). The superego continues the object attachment of the id. In its more primitive aspects, the attempt is to regain, via the repetition compulsion, the very early libidinal gratification from the "first" objects of attachment.

Arlow (1982) has indicated that the "superego is a conglomeration of many identifications derived from experience with objects, from fantasies and imagination, and stemming from almost all levels of development, not necessarily inclusively those of the oedipal or post- oedipal period" p. 234).

If the superego is structurally seen to contain both the higher aspects of man's development—his moral sense—and at the same time is the "expression of the most powerful impulses and most important libidinal vicissitudes of the id" (Freud, 1923, p. 36), then the superego's evolution comes not only from the ego but also derives its genesis from the id. As a structure like the ego, it is a twin in time and sequence, but with a very different time frame—like the emergence of secondary characteristics. Though its effectiveness is not established until the resolution of the oedipus complex, we cannot discount earlier functions.

Freud regarded the superego as a repository for the aggressive drive, an energic displacement from the externalization of aggression to "internalization"; also, as a reaction formation, whereby the energies, as acquired internally from the id, are controlled and molded into a structure by the very act of function. Hartmann (1939) pointed out that:

we must also keep in mind the phenomenon of the "change of function," the role of which in mental life, and particularly in the development of the ego, seems to be very great and behind which, genetically, there is always a particularly interesting bit of history. An attitude which arose originally in the service of defense against an instinctual drive may in the course of time become an independent structure [p. 26].

Why the superego is fueled more by the aggressive drive than the erotic drive can best be understood by the specific character and function of internalization. The identification with the external object relates to characteristics of mastery, judgment, critical faculties, and censorship; active aims which require the force of the aggressive drive. It is interesting to note that Freud regarded the structure of the superego as an aspect of the ego's "character." He indicated that:

we have already made out a little of what it is that creates character. First and foremost, there is the incorporation of the former parental agency as a superego, which is no doubt its most important and decisive portion ... [1933b, p. 91].

My point is that a distribution of function which leads to a differentiated structure may also require a differentiation in drive energy, that the function of the superego requires by its very nature an increment of aggressive energy. What, then, is the relationship of ambivalence to the genetic root of superego development and the aggressive drive? Aggression in the course of development is modified by some restriction in aim and inhibition in discharge. In the very nature of identification with the parental authority, qualitative changes are introduced in the drive. Hartmann (1939, p. 196) hypothesized that the aggressive drive is the source of neutralization. Does the drive undergo some characteristic change due entirely to the fusion with Eros and in relationship to the object, or is there something in the very nature of the identification with the functions of the parental authority that gives a special quality to the aggression? Perhaps it is the nature of function that provides a change in the aim of aggression. Is this what Freud means when he speaks of raising the "passage of events in the id" (1940, p. 199) to a higher dynamic level?

Ambivalence creates a disruption in the identification with the parental authority; it interferes with the internalization of the objects. As a result, certain functions continue in the domain of the original object or may instead be taken over by the ego in defiance of the superego. We may observe an excessive degree of dependence on the external world for approval, excruciating doubt that pervades love relationships, work, and cognition. Perhaps most interesting is the manner in which the ego, in defiance of the parental authority, enhances the power of the id and acts for the superego, but without the past history of values and judgments that the superego encompasses. Here we might say that the pleasure principle overrules the reality principle. What occurs is a disequilibrium between the psychic structure and the mind (Hartmann, 1939).

Ambivalence has an interesting relationship to aggression, for it appears to increase the quantity of aggression not only by the failure of Eros to bind aggression but also due to increments resulting from the frustration of individual wishes. In relationship to the superego, this poses an interesting possibility. For, if the superego is heightened in aggressive cathexes, it becomes a receptacle for the discharge of the aggressive drive. We may at times be deceived in regarding the problem as an intersystemic conflict rather than a means for discharge. Freud (1933b) indicated that we are in fact in doubt whether we should suppose that all the aggressiveness that has returned from the external world is bound by the superego and accordingly turned against the ego, or that a part of it is carrying on its mute and uncanny activity as a free destructive instinct in the ego and the id. (p. 109)

It is not only the ego that provides a vehicle for the discharge of free aggression, but the superego can also "take over the dangerous aggressive impulses" (Freud, 1933b, p. 110). The superego, rather than function as a regulator of aggression, can, under the influence of ambivalence, fail in its psychic task as the guardian of civilization and act in the guise of the most powerful and destructive forces in mankind.

Case Vignette

My purpose in presenting this vignette is to show the way in which a powerful ambivalence interfered with an adequate resolution of the homosexual/heterosexual conflict and, thus, permeated every decision in this patient's life. The profusion of doubt that affects his object relations and career choice is derivative of the ambivalence.

A 40-year-old male came for treatment in a state of "high" anxiety, with difficulty in sleeping and fears that he could not complete his work according to schedule. The failure to complete was a long-standing symptom. It was evidenced 20 years previously as a student doing graduate work in a rather esteemed university. He did not complete his studies in Law and, in what seemed a rather abrupt change of interest, turned to another field. At the time of entering treatment, he was again embarking on a new career, so to speak. I say, "so to speak," for the analysis revealed that the seeds of his current interests were sown in childhood.

Mr. P was the oldest of three children: one sister two years his junior and a second sister born when he was five. The father was a successful lawyer, and the mother was a socialite and housewife. Mr. P was wracked with doubts that extended to indecision on whether to remarry; the worth of the woman;

repeated self-attacks regarding his creative ability, his intellectual acumen, and his knowledge of his field. This self-doubt was indeed striking in view of the superior intelligence of this man, his fecundity of knowledge in many fields, and rather direct evidence of his talent. He had won a number of awards and recognition for his work. Mr. P was engaged in two activities both related to the content of his field, one engaging him in theoretical discourse the other in performance.

The vacillation between the two was evident, though it was possible to continue both levels of functioning. It was clear that much of the work inhibition had to do with fears of criticism from his peers; he was preoccupied by thoughts that, like a "snake," they would attack him.

Certain obvious explanations come to mind to account for his anxiety and his symptoms; castration anxiety being primary among them. The identification with the father in the oedipal rivalry has not been adequately resolved—to be the father, to replace him in a regressive form is a powerful motif. But equally compelling is the regressive aspect of the identification (one of the components of empathy); that is, he experiences the father's feelings of rivalry and fear of being superseded by his son, and thus withdraws in favor of the father. Indeed, there is some evidence for the correctness of this perception. The issue is why the oedipal conflict did not succumb to identification and a more successful resolution, rather than resulting in a psychic structure with a punitive superego. This leads to a variety of levels of investigation; nothing new in the methodology of psychoanalysis. We observe the emergent passive wishes to the father, the masochism that gratifies both the passive sexual wishes and the aggressive drive turned against the self. We observe the modal distribution of aggression discharged by the ego and the superego; the nature of the father's rivalry, its genetic impact and etiological roots for the patient; the influence of the narcissistic wishes; fear of failure, of criticism, and so on; a particularly strong overlay of infantile omnipotency that is vulnerable to narcissistic injury.

I have pointed out these sources of conflict in serial form, not for the purpose of reducing them to a secondary position, but rather as an indication of their central importance: Without analysis of them, no steps toward resolution can occur. Yet, underlying the issue of the failure to resolve adequately castration anxiety and the destructive impact of the superego and narcissistic issues, lies an unduly strong ambivalence. Further, it is not my intent to claim that all negative therapeutic reactions and powerful superego resistance fall victim to the strength of ambivalence, but rather, to emphasize its pivotal role in mental functions.

What was basic to this man's ambivalence was the almost equivalenced homosexual and heterosexual identification and a particularly strong attachment to the mother, resulting in a specific feminine identification which, in the unconscious, worked as an antithesis against pursuing a successful career. To be successful would move him to the masculine position and thus force a relinquishment of the feminine position. To complete a major piece of work would result in another antithesis. For this man, the wish to produce a baby was powerful and when his wife could not become pregnant, he had fantasies of replacing her in the labor room. The act of creative work did not result in a sublimation of this wish, but rather, it intensified the unconscious conflicts between the masculine and feminine roles. Thus, work appeared to him as giving up the feminine wish to give birth. There were many fantasies, dreams and acts that epitomized this conflict. The patient had a dream that he was in bed with two women, his former wife and his girl friend. The wife's body was stiff; she was dressed in striped pants and a shirt; the girl friend had on a night gown. On one occasion, the patient was strolling down the street and observed two men, one youngish and rather goodlooking, the other older; they were exchanging money. He looked at them and smiled and they, catching his smile, called him "fag" and chased him with a hammer.

The attempts to resolve this conflict resulted in a repeated act of incompletion —perhaps symbolic for castration. Yet, the problem was not just the sexual ambivalence and the ensuing doubt that permeated most of the important functions of his life, but a rather powerful ambivalence to the first love object, his mother. This mother was a source of both support and over gratification. The degree of her investment, her wish to possess him, played a major role in his difficulty in both tolerating frustration and modifying the infantile wishes. She is the woman described by Freud (1914) who turns her love to the son and away from the husband. The first major trauma occurred when the patient, at the age of two, was confronted with the birth of his sister. The narcissistic injury was not simply due to feelings of loss of love or the effects of sibling rivalry, but rather, to an intense sense of bodily injury that he could not produce a baby, albeit a fecal baby, like his mother. It was this injury that intensified the oedipal conflicts and the castration dangers. The danger of narcissistic assault is genetically related to two phases of development: the anal and the genital. The incestuous wishes for the mother were amplified by the mother's prolonged seductive behavior toward the son well into his teens, exemplified by walking around in the nude, excessive caressing of almost a masturbatory quality, and family showering. The defense against the incestuous wishes strengthened the identification with the mother and this reinforced the feminine position.

One of the major problems for this patient in the structuring of his ego has been the difficulty in relinquishing the infantile objects and the imitative identification mechanism of "to be" in favor of the more abstract nature of identification, "to be like." The capacity to transfer object love to new representatives of the primary love object has been interfered with by the ambivalence that had contributed to the fixation to the primary love objects, that is, mother and father, and to the pregenital phase. I wish to emphasize that I regard the fixation as partial, relating to specific aspects of the phase.

To the degree that the patient continued to wish to be the mother, to give birth, success in a career meant a frustration of the wish; on the other hand, to act on this wish to enact the feminine role could not result in a narcissistic injury, the denial of his masculinity. What is significant in this patient is the persistent power of memories; the hypercathexis maintains the fixation to the infantile objects. Thus, we observe the failure to retreat from the incestuous objects of childhood. The adhesion to the early objects and the infantile phases of development exacerbates the ambivalence and interferes with a more adequate resolution.

What I wished to stress in this vignette was the role of ambivalence as an impediment to the synthetic functions of the ego. Ambivalence implies a dominance of primary process, problems of binding the drives and incomplete fusion. The sublimatory process also bears the imprimatur of ambivalence. The superego, though at times harsh, can become more a vehicle for the discharge of aggression under the aegis of the id than an internalized structure reflective of the identification with an authority that has been defused of its infantile nature.

REFERENCES

Abraham, K. (1924). *A Short Study of the Development of the Libido, Viewed in the Light of Mental Disorders. Selected Papers of Karl Abraham.* London: Hogarth.

Arlow, J. (1982). Problem of the Superego Concept. *Psychoanal. St. Child,* 37:229–244.

Fenichel, O. (1945). *The Psychoanalytic Theory of Neurosis.* New York: Norton.

Freud, S. (1905). Three Essays on the Theory of Infantile Sexuality. *Standard Edition,* 7:125–244

_____ 1911). Formulation on the Two Principles of Mental Functioning. Standard Edition, 12:213–226.

_____ (1913). Totem and Taboo. *Standard Edition,* 13:1–160.

_____ (1914). On Narcissism: An Introduction. *Standard Edition,* 14: 67–104.

_____ (1915a). Instincts and Their Vicissitudes. *Standard Edition,* 14:109–140.

_____ (1915b). Thoughts for the Times on War and Death. *Standard Edition,* 14: 273–300.

_____ (1920). Beyond the Pleasure Principle. *Standard Edition,* 18:1–64.

_____ (1923). The Ego and the Id. *Standard Edition,* 19:1–66.

_____ 1924). The Economic Problem of Masochism. *Standard Edition,* 19:155–172.

_____ (1927). Fetishism. *Standard Edition,* 21:147–158.

_____ (1931). Female Sexuality. *Standard Edition,* 21:221–246.

_____ (1933a). The Dissection of the Psychical Personality. *Standard Edition,* 22:57–80.

_____ (1933b). Anxiety and Instinctual Life. *Standard Edition,* 22:81–111.

_____ (1940/[1938]). An Outline of Psychoanalysis. *Standard Edition,* 23:149–208, 71–278.

Hartmann, H. (1955). Notes on the Theory of Sublimation. *Psychoanal. St. Child,* 10:9–29.

_____ (1958). *Ego Psychology and the Problem of Adaptation.* New York: International Universities, 1939.

Spitz, R. (1983). *Dialogues from Infancy: Selected Papers* (Ed. R. N. Emde). New York: International Universities.

Waelder, R. (1936). The Principle of Multiple Function. *Psychoanal. Q.,* 5:45–62.

CHAPTER 3

REGRESSION: A RECONSIDERATION OF TOPOGRAPHIC THEORY

[(1996). *Psychoanalytic Review* (83)(6):813–825].

Since the publication of Freud's seminal paper on *The Ego and the Id* (1923), structural theory has replaced topographic theory as the conceptual mode for understanding the psychic apparatus. This shift away from the topographic mode has resulted in an underestimation of the value of the unconscious as a system separate in function and different in organization from the structural organization. Further, there has been a tendency to equate the unconscious with the id. While certain parallel functions or modes of operation bear similarity, such as the quality of energy, i.e., unbound cathexis (Gill, 1963), and the mechanism of primary process, as hypotheses the difference between structure and system lead to divergent modes of clinical investigation and understanding of the data. The id as part of the structural organization refers to a complemental series of parts, a constituent of interrelated units, and this complex unit, this structure, is ordered in part by a phylogenetic inheritance (Freud, 1923) and a constitutional basis which unfolds in a sequential series of maturational processes. The unconscious is delineated as a system—a concept sometimes overlapping with the derivative meaning of structure—but as a system it is better defined by explanatory tenets or postulates (Ricoeur, 1970) which can describe phenomenological and dynamic modes within the entire structural organization.

The conceptualization of a topographic system as a mental locale with barriers between the system's conscious, preconscious, and unconscious provides a somewhat different understanding of the psychic apparatus with its progressive and retrogressive alterations and vicissitudes of perception than does the structural organization. The means by which an affective state can recall a past experience either through a mnemonic perception without a functional change in the structure, or can reproduce the phenomenological experience as a result of a cathectic shift in the associative pathways is best accounted for by the theoretical constructs of the topographic theory. Freud (1923, 1940), as we know, did not abandon this construct when he introduced the structural theory (Eissler, 1962).[1] In *The Ego and the Id* (1923), Freud stated that the "division of the psychical into what is conscious and what is unconscious is the fundamental premise of psychoanalysis" (p. 13). And somewhat further, he added that the "property of being conscious or not is in the last resort our one beacon-light in the darkness of depth psychology" (p. 13). The division of psychical phenomena between what is conscious and what is unconscious is explained in structural theory as a result of the function of repression, and more broadly by a variety of defense mechanisms. Since defenses are mechanisms within the orbit of psychic structure, a parallel theory with a similar set of functions would thus seem redundant. Yet, a topographic theory of the unconscious whose explanatory value derives not only from the role of defense, but primarily that of repression, is likewise intrinsic to the mode of unconscious mechanisms. Therefore, a topographic theory sustains itself as a necessary correlate to structural theory. I support this view despite the position of such classical theorists as Anna Freud (1963a, b) and Arlow and Brenner (1964, 1988), who have restated Freud's systemic concepts in genetic and structural terms, and who indicate that topographic theory is inconsistent with structural theory.

---

1 I do not consider Brenner's (1994) concept of a compromise formation as an adequate explanation for this process. The patient eventually reconciled with her boyfriend and six months after termination of the treatment married him.

In this paper I intend to discuss the following issues: the regressive mechanism from a topographical perspective, the manner by which unconscious memories intrude upon conscious thoughts, that is, the return of the repressed in a regressive state, much like a dream, but without the distortion, and the loss of secondary processes. I shall also consider the means by which the transference can evoke a rather sudden temporal affective state, or elicit a memory of an infantile experience. This will be examined within the context of clinical case material. Related to the evocation of a memory is the question of whether memory is reflective of a topographical or a structural regression.

The distinction between structural and topographical regression is not without blurred boundaries, and, perhaps, the acceptance of either will depend upon the logical and internal consistency of the definition, and phenomenological observations. Structural regression is best designated as the decomposing of the whole or parts of integrated structures into partial units of previous levels of development, and these earlier developmental levels are evidenced by actions behavioral in the nature or in verbal expression, denoting earlier developmental levels and affecting judgment and the perception of reality. In contradistinction, topographic regression affects changes of state while leaving the ego's relationship to the other agencies of the mind relatively unchanged. Like the dream, topographic regression sustains itself as a unitary mode without discharge.

Similar to a verbal reconstruction, it provides a schematic presentation of the past, a view of infantile wishes, either through imagery or affects related to ideation. Further, topographic regression may serve a constructive purpose as an adaptive response to a present reality, a means by which present conflicts are filtered through past events, fantasy formations, and infantile wishes. Brenner (1957) has called attention to this aspect of repression in its changing role of both "doing and undoing" of repressed drive derivatives and ideation. Similarly, topographic regression affords a discharge through symbolic thought by shifting the relationship between the unconscious and preconscious. Prohibited wishes can be expressed in a mode that eludes the superego's criticism, very much the way humor may pierce the Gordian knot of the unconscious.

Modell (1968) has suggested the need for a model that would better conceptualize the ego's relationship to the environment and would enhance our understanding of the alterations in object-relationships. He refers to the scholarly debate as to whether Freud replaced the topographic by the structural model, and he suggests: that the alterations of function and structure require two different but interrelated modes of conceptualization. For this reason, we wish to retain a topographic metaphor applied to functional alterations within the ego, while maintaining the structural metaphor to represent more or less abiding configurations within the ego that are the result of developmental (historical) processes. (p. 125)

Arlow and Brenner (1964) have called attention to the "misconception regarding the global nature of regression." Contrary to popular thought, regression is not uniform; it is often a transient state and, certainly, reversible. Observation confirms this view within a treatment hour or in everyday normal functioning. A recathexis in memory of the infantile object can affect emotional changes and mood swings that are reflective of a temporal regressive state. Ideational content that at one moment attests to man's highest educational achievement can at another moment be permeated with ideas that reflect the influence of childhood grandiosity and primitive thinking surfeit with magical wishes. It is the fluidity of pathological and normative behavior that, I believe, merits a reappraisal of topographic theory's role in the therapeutic situation.

Topographic regression can act as a medial conveyor (Eissler, 1962) between memory, thought, word, and affect. The partitive manner in which regression is expressed gives to this defense a qualitative characteristic that differs from the function of other defense mechanisms with the exception of repression. Both mechanisms, regression and undoing of repression, can provide access to the unconscious without the subsequent modification of the ego.

However, the neglect of topographic theory, aside from the introduction of structural concepts, is also a result of the increased disenchantment with economic concepts. Loewald (1960) refers to a shift in theory from an economic base to a structural one. He indicates that it is not a question of development from a narcissistic position to object relatedness, i.e., a redistribution of libido, rather, it is a "differentiation into id, ego, and object out of the primary state of unity or identity." With this formulation he has further modified structural theory by shifting from an instinct base of mental development to an interrelational mode, the dyadic interchange between mother and infant. This kind of formulation reduces the conceptual importance of the unconscious as a system of drive-derivative content and cathectic displacement.

Modell (1968) hypothesized the regressive process as indicating significant changes along a given "parameter." Topographic regression, he states, "can be defined as a shift in cathexis from the external to the internal world," and in this formulation a quantitative element is implied. In the transference neurosis the patient attempts to recreate in the outer world the contents of the inner world. The fantasies, the revival of earlier memories and identification, indicate a schema of differentiating organization within the ego in terms of function; thus the structuring of the perception of the external world has been altered in accordance with the contents of the inner world (pp. 120–129).

I have left Freud's definition and discussion of topographic regression for the summative section of this paper, for it illuminates the system unconscious as a construct in relation to the perceptual conscious and continues to provide a depth psychology to our clinical work.

Freud (1900) defined topographic regression according to the following characteristics: topographic, which relates to the first perception of stimuli, correlates to the first in time and the first of the associative links in memory traces; temporal refers to the earliest of the structures; and formal regression relates to a mode of presentation—more "primitive methods of expression and representation take the place of usual ones." All three types of regression are, "however, one at bottom and occur together as a rule, for what is older in time is more primitive in form and psychical typography lies nearer to the perceptual end." In all regression, what we find is a renewal of childhood, of the "instinctual impulses which dominated it and the methods of expression which were then available" (p. 548).

The unconscious as a system is accessible by a number of routes. Freud (1915) has pointed to the methods of undoing of repression by the analytic work and the manner by which the infantile wishes excluded from consciousness and the means of gratification operate as a constant force upon the mind. Topographic regression is stimulated by the force of repressed wishes which press for discharge and provide the unconscious with a mode of expression through experiential memories (Klein, 1966). Memory may also find expression in metaphorical and allegorical turns of speech, affects, and beliefs. Earlier modes continue to influence current experiences and give rise to opportunities for regression that offer satisfaction for primitive instincts on fairly primitive levels (Balint, 1936b). Topographic regression also affords the psychic apparatus with an economic redistribution in that anxiety which may overload the mental economy is leveraged by the defusion of the danger situation (A. Freud, 1956–1965).

As I have indicated, my focus upon topographic regression does not diminish the importance of structural regression, but rather provides a differential means of comprehending the patients associative material and ego status. I have stressed the importance of the unconscious as an arena for psychoanalytic investigation. And while to make what is unconscious conscious is no longer our primary focus, it is clearly an ultimate aim in the psychoanalytic process.

Case Vignette I

Ms. B, a 40-year-old woman, requested therapy some months after she had been abandoned by her lover of 12 years. He had suddenly announced that he was leaving her for another woman who he planned to marry. This was a repetition of an earlier trauma as her former husband had also deserted her.

She was depressed, cried uncontrollably, was unable to sleep, and experienced a loss of appetite. She developed a number of somatic symptoms and became particularly concerned when her work performance deteriorated.

Ms. B was a very attractive woman, shapely, soft spoken, her voice at times trailing off to a whisper, and in general she carried herself with the comportment of upper-class gentility. This demeanor was not consistent with her background of origin; her father was an underpaid salesman, and her mother was a housekeeper. The siblings, a grandmother, and her parents lived in a small apartment in a lower-middle-class neighborhood. She is the eldest of two siblings; she has a brother five years her junior with whom relationships are strained. Her mother was described as critical, demanding, harsh, unloving, and the dominant member of the household who was more involved with her own mother than her husband and children. Her father was experienced as a mild-mannered, loving man who was seen as basically ineffectual in the home and at work.

The initial treatment was therapeutically supportive; she required time to mourn her loss, yet, it was soon possible to begin a more exploratory process. It became clear that the patient's ambivalence in all relationships, and most noteworthy, those with men, played a significant role in her lover's leaving. She had refused to marry her lover, and in regard to her former husband had only disdain almost from the beginning of the marriage. Early in the treatment, her masochistic patterns were evidenced in her work place and in relationship to family and friends. The patient did not resist this awareness and accepted the interpretations that indicated the masochistic behavior rather readily. I would qualify this recognition as the first stage on the long road to insight. It was based upon a cognitive appraisal, and in fact, was so easily accepted by the patient by virtue of the gratification and narcissistic investment in the masochistic suffering. Issues regarding her sexual identity and latent homosexual conflicts emerged, but these were only very gradually interpreted.

The treatment was begun with twice-a-week sessions, and soon increased to three times a week. About five months into the treatment, I suggested that she increase her sessions to four times a week as psychoanalytic treatment would be very beneficial for her. She was rather surprised by this suggestion, and after discussion for several sessions, agreed to an analysis. Three months into the analysis, she decided that she wanted to reduce the sessions back to twice a week. There were reality factors that contributed to this decision as the treatment posed a very real financial hardship. The investigation of this wish soon revealed a powerful resistance; the process was "too painful and too burdensome." She did not want to think about herself all the time. She wanted to be "happier, lighter," not burdened with her problems. After some discussion, a powerful affect emerged; she did not want to become too dependent on me. All her life she strove to be independent, to free herself from her mother's control. The issue concerned separation problems and identification. From the history, it was evident that she was warding off infantile dependency wishes. Her fear that these passive, dependent wishes would emerge in the transference accounted for the major resistance to the analysis. With a twice-a-week treatment she felt in better control of her affects. She expressed her fears of loss of "control," and stated that she was afraid that I would "take control" of her, take away her "independence." In her personal relationships she became the caretaker, the altruist, and it was this very defense that was threatened by the analysis. I connected her fear of loss of control to her expectancy that, like her mother, I would take away "her power of free will"; for example, "I demand that she come four times a week." The transference implications are clear: a transference neurosis has emerged and I, like her mother, was experienced as too dangerous. It was also apparent that the need to avoid the intensity of the transference was an attempt to protect her from emergent homosexual wishes and, at the same time, to diminish the decidedly aggressive affects in the transference.

A decision regarding methodology at this point led me to avoid pursuing transference issues for I concluded that to proceed in this fashion would only increase the resistance. My apprehending her fears and understanding the vicissitudes of her wishes could result in a narcissistic injury. It seemed preferable to permit the transference experience to act as a stimulus for remembering, and that these remembrances would emerge in a more gradual fashion. I therefore chose an educative path, wherein we engaged in an intellectual discussion about psychoanalysis, the meaning of the transference, the relationship of affects to memories of childhood, and why increased sessions produce stronger feelings than less-frequent sessions. The purpose of this discussion was to mitigate her feelings of passivity that is both inherent in the analytic situation and is at the core of her unconscious fantasies. I then pointed out that "strong emotions of a positive and negative nature toward me would in all probability arise." At this juncture, she categorically dismissed this as ridiculous. "You are a neutral person, a sounding board, nothing more. I like you, but that's it; I am not supposed to feel anything towards you."

On the following day, she entered with a smile and stated that she was "incredulous" at what had just occurred in my waiting room. She felt a sudden rush of anger—fury toward me—she had the thought that I was deliberately going to keep her waiting, that maybe I "wasn't even here," though, "of course" I had buzzed her in. Needless to say, the analysis was continued four times a week.

The emergence of the regressive wish to be maltreated by the analyst is expressive of a more fundamental wish, that is, to be beaten by the analyst.

This beating fantasy emerges from a particular function of the transference which has re-created a relationship that had existed with the mother. Though the mother has been deceased for the past five years, she continues to be deeply mourned by the patient who at her mother's demise had experienced a severe depression. The fantasy that I would keep her waiting, or that I was not there, are mirror images of the many kinds of encounters with her mother. Even as an adult the patient always bore the "injustices" with patience and humiliation, and without a word of anger. What was evident at this juncture in the treatment was the emergence of the transference neurosis, an indication of a regression—structural in nature—to an earlier phase of libidinal organization. Further, if it were just a matter of lifting the repression, the patient would have brought forth memories wherein she had experienced these masochistic encounters, but instead of remembering, she produced a fantasy that I was deliberately humiliating her. It is this fantasy that points to the topographic regression, a re-emergence from the unconscious of a wish that in no way was enacted in behavior or could elicit a masochistic act. Also, the deliria (Freud, 1909), the irrational juxtaposed against the reality in that the unconscious fantasy was hypercathected and therefore modified her perception of reality for a brief moment supports the concept of a topographic regression. It is this brief alteration of external reality by wish, and the containment in fantasy that signifies the topographic regression, and is the distinguishing characteristic between the topographic and the structural mode of regression.

Case Vignette II

Mr. F., a commercial artist in his early forties, was seen in a five-times-a-week psychoanalysis. He was divorced and had an 11-year-old son who resided with his ex-wife. The patient had recently remarried. Mr. F. was planning a fishing trip with his son to the Great Lakes area. They would be in relative isolation for approximately ten days. From there, they would visit his parents who resided in Canada. This expedition was in its third season and planning should have been a relatively routine affair. Several weeks prior to the vacation, Mr. F. became overly preoccupied with food preparations. In contradistinction to other times, where food was purchased in bulk from a supply company, he began to cure and can his own supply of food. He became anxious over the amount of time that was absorbed by these preparations. But he seemed unable to stop or reduce the activity, or the mess he created. He neglected his work, and was withdrawn from his wife. He explained that this was all very necessary because of his concern over the possible contamination of canned food, and with an exclamatory statement he voiced the thought: "people die of food poisoning."

My leaving for vacation precipitated the onset of this transient phobic symptom, that is, his fear of being poisoned by an anonymous source. In previous years, the advent of my vacation or his departure resulted in a series of catastrophes: a broken leg, a cut finger requiring numerous stitches, and other more minor injuries, or specific difficulty with work that could jeopardize his position. In this earlier phase of treatment, the anxieties and ensuing injuries reflected the unconscious conflicts of the genital level organization. The symbolic self-castration was a defense against the dangerous oedipal rivals, "the pack of wolves "ready to get him. The separation from the analyst during summer vacations generally was the time that he too went on vacation with his son. Thus, two concurrent drive derivatives were aroused by this event. One, the loss of the analyst as the oedipal and protective mother left him in danger from his male rival, and without a modifying influence against his own rivalrous wishes. Therefore, to inflict self-injuries reduced the level of anticipatory anxiety. This turning around upon the subject insured a masochistic gratification, for the pain yielded a gain of pleasure, and secondarily provided just punishment for his aggression. He also achieved a secondary gain reminiscent of childhood when illness secured him the coveted attentions of his mother; the hope, therefore, being to secure the concern and sympathy of the analyst.

At this present point in the treatment there was a regressive shift in the libidinal phase organization. The compromise between the aggressive wishes to destroy his father and son, and the defense against these wishes resulted in a displacement of the conflict from the genital phase to an earlier more primitive state, the oral phase. The structure of the phobic symptom by its regressive mode erected a secondary defense. In structural terms, the regression in libidinal phase development indicated a compromised id. Moreover, his ego structure was also compromised by the regression; he spent endless hours in preparation which in the end had to be interrupted, and further, much of the food was unsatisfactory.

Inherent in all structural regressions are the components of a topographic regression while the reverse is not true, for a topographical regression can occur without a change in the structure. The multilayers of the unconscious gained currency in this patient by a sudden cathectic shift that responded to a dangerous situation from one level of development to an earlier level, but one also fraught with danger. It was the transference reaction—the separation from me that activated earlier memories of his mother—in the kitchen cooking, family scenes at dinner when his angry, sarcastic father brought his mother to tears and impotent rage. His fear of "being poisoned "was not a projection of a dangerous mother whose "milk" is poisonous, rather, the poisoner is the oedipal father, a composite of himself and his father. The danger results from the mutual rivalry between father and son. Thus, the separation from me increased the danger of his oral sadistic wishes to devour his oedipal father and his son. Mr. F. gave expression to obsessional fears that his son might drown, overturn the canoe in the rapids, or that some disaster may befall him. In approaching the structure of Mr. F.'s phobia, it was possible to observe the expression of cannibalistic wishes which Shengold (1980) has pointed to as a variant in the relationship between poisoning of one's ambivalently loved enemy and cannibalism. The destruction in an oral mode of the object by poison is given expression in colloquial language which describes the course of poison "as eating up the body." The aim is an incorporative one: to eat one's enemy is to introject their characteristics. By this method, the patient also incorporates me, the separated object who abandoned him, and thus by a symbolic act undoes the separation.

Symbolic language enables the most primitive of psychic structures to enter consciousness in a temporal form, and simulates the stimuli that first acted upon these structures. A correlative exchange between psychic locale and content provides the current that leads us back in time through idea and metaphor. This, I believe, is the essential of topographic theory. In the patient, we observe the defensive coalescence of two phases of libidinal development—the genital and the oral phase. Through the lens of topographic regression, it is possible to decipher the components of the symptom formation—the phobic structure and the regression by which he defends against castration anxiety and gratifies an oral sadistic wish.

Biblical tale and mythology support this formulation of an oedipal wish expressed in an oral mode. The Greek god Zeus is protected by his mother, Rhea, from the cannibalism of his father Kronos. Jacob, one of the four father figures in biblical lore, steals his brother Esau's birthright. It is not a far leap to recognize that Esau is a displacement from Isaac his father, and that Rebecca, the oedipal mother, not only plans the betrayal but executes the symbolic cannibalistic act. By preparing the food which Jacob brings to his father as ritual to receiving the birthright of succession, Rebecca protects the son against the castration dangers of the father. In the biblical tale, the eating of the son is sublimated by a shift in aim: the father eats food and not the son.

These myths are refracted through topographic theory.

CONCLUSION

My intent in this paper was to provide the clinician with an opportunity to reconsider the value of topographic concepts in the regressive process, and to focus upon the mode by which the unconscious as a storehouse of infantile wishes and conflicts is made more accessible to preconscious thought. By means of symbolic process and cathectic shifts, the inner world alters the perception of the external world. The apprehension of reality occurs essentially through the mediation of symbolic form (Cassirer, 1946). The retrieval of memory without remembering is an example of the metaphoric role of topographical regression. Affects and moods can reflect temporal shifts without structural change, and, like the dream, topographic regression sustains itself as a unitary mode without discharge. Topographic regression is ubiquitous and provides the clinical work with a lyric quality that by means of surprise (Reik, 1948) may often bypass the censorship of the superego and the defenses. Though structural theory is monumental to our understanding of psychic organization, Freud never disclaimed the topographic approach. It has remained as a parallelism with structural theory.

REFERENCES

Arlow, J. & Brenner, C. (1964) *Psychoanalytic concepts and the structural theory.* New York: International Universities Press.

_____. & _____ (1988). The future of psychoanalysis. *Psychoanal. Q.,* 57:1–14.

Balint, M. (1936a). The regressed patient and his analyst. *Psychiatry* 23:231–243.

_____. (1936b). *Thrills and Regression.* London: International Universities Press.

Brenner, C. (1957). The nature and development of the concept of repression in Freud's writings. *Psychoanal. St. Child*, 12: 19–46.

_____. (1966). The mechanism of repression. In Loewenstein, R., Newman, L., Schur, M., & Solnit, A. eds. *Psychoanalysis—A General Psychology.* New York: International Universities Press.

Cassirer, E. (1946). *Language and Myth.* London: Dover Publications.

Eissler, K. (1962). On the metapsychology of the preconscious: A tentative contribution to psychoanalytic morphology. *Psychoanal. St. Child*, 17:19–41.

Freud, A. (1956–1965). Research of the Hampstead child-therapy clinic and other papers. In *The Writings of Anna Freud, vol. 5.* New York: International Universities Press.

_____. (1963a). The role of regression in mental development. In *The Writings of Anna Freud, vol. 5.* New York: International Universities Press.

_____. (1963b). Regression as a principle in mental development. *Bull. Mennin. Clinic.*, 23(3):*126–139.*

Freud, S. (1900). The interpretation of dreams. In J. Strachey, ed. *Standard Edition,* 4 & 5:548.

_____ (1909). Notes upon a case of obsessional neurosis. *Standard Edition,* 10:153.

_____. (1915). The unconscious. *Standard Edition,* 14:161.

_____ (1923). The ego and the id. *Standard Edition,* 19:13.

_____ (1940). An outline of psychoanalysis. *Standard Edition,* 23:141.

Gill, M. (1963). *Topography and Systems in Psychic Theory.* New York: International Universities Press.

Klein, G. (1966). The several grades of memory. In Loewenstein, R., Newman, L., Schur, M., & Solnit, A. eds. *Psychoanalysis—A General Psychology.* New York: International Universities Press.

Loewald, H. (1981). Regression: Some general considerations. *Psychoanal. Q.*, 50(1):22–43.

Modell, A. (1968). *Object love and reality.* New York: International Universities Press.

Reik, T. (1948). *Listening with the third ear. New* York: Grove Press.

Ricoeur, P. (1970). *Freud, Philosophy: An Essay on Interpretation.* New Haven: Yale University Press.

Shengold, L. (1980). More on rats and rat people. In M. Kanzer & J. Glenn, eds. *Freud and His Patients.* New York: Jason Aronson.

CHAPTER 4

A BRIEF DISCOURSE ON PSYCHOTHERAPY AND PSYCHOANALYSIS: HISTORICAL PERSPECTIVE

[(2003). *Psychoanalytic Review* (90)(2):153–177].

The relationship between psychoanalysis and psychotherapy has been a heated, unresolved issue for over 50 years. "There has been intense controversy, indicating how complex the issues are. The history of the attitudes towards the relationship between psychotherapy and psychoanalysis has been determined by increased explication of, and changes in the dynamic process as well as the impact of economic, social and political influences" (Schwartz, 2000, p. 1). In a historical context, psychotherapy was initially the term applied to all treatment of mental disorders. Psychoanalysis as formulated by Freud was a specific specialty or subcategory of psychotherapy. As psychoanalytic theory developed and extended its conceptual base, a hierarchical reversal emerged, and psychotherapy seemed subsumed under the aegis of psychoanalysis in both theory and practice. Tarachow (1963) stated that "psychoanalysis represents a basic model and is the theoretical baseline for various psychotherapeutic departures." (p. 8) He indicated that the "technique of psychotherapy is not the technique of psychoanalysis," but that the theory involves an understanding of the same factors derived from psychoanalytic concepts.

The decision to write on the essential difference between psychoanalysis and psychotherapy was stimulated by the results of a survey conducted by the National Psychological Association for Psychoanalysis (NPAP, 1995–1996, *Psychoanalytic Review*).

New insights may not be gained from reopening this old dialogue, yet the fact that the majority of respondents indicated that their preferred mode of practice was psychoanalysis rather than psychotherapy despite the fact that the reality of their practice was primarily psychotherapy presented an interesting quandary. Of further interest was the difficulty in distinguishing between psychotherapy and psychoanalysis in their modes of practice. Why was psychoanalysis the preferred mode and what interfered with the analysts' ability to function in this mode? It was obvious that there was a distinct difference between the two modes in both methodology and aim in the minds of the respondents. Unfortunately, the survey was somewhat limited in that qualitative factors about how the respondents viewed the differences either in technique or goals were not discernable. Since the respondents did indicate that they considered that there was a distinct difference between psychotherapy and psychoanalysis, one must assume that they used specific criteria to distinguish the theoretical differences. Furthermore, there was no attempt to investigate why psychoanalysis was the preferred mode of treatment. Was psychoanalytic practice more gratifying for the analyst? Did the analyst deem psychoanalysis more challenging than psychotherapy? Was psychoanalysis considered the most efficacious method of treatment? Or was there some unconscious status conferred upon the practice of psychoanalysis over psychotherapy?

In spite of the limitations of the survey regarding these issues, a discussion from both a historical perspective and a focus on current thinking may provide some clarity in what appears to be obfuscation and overlap in thinking regarding the practice of psychoanalysis and psychotherapy. Furthermore, a broader discussion may change the attitude that psychoanalytic institutes have regarding the teaching and practice of psychoanalysis. Though this is already beginning to change (Margolis, 2001), the question remains as to whether psychotherapy will retain its second-class citizenship.

HISTORICAL BACKGROUND

We credit the Greeks with developing the first scientific approach to treating the mentally ill (Chessick, 1974). They introduced two forms of therapy that continue to be used as part of a therapeutic treatment, sleep therapy and the interpretation of dreams. Herbs and drugs were also used therapeutically. It was not until the sixteenth century that we witness the systematic study of psychology and the development of psychiatric treatment for the mentally ill. In the eighteenth century Anton Mesmer (1778) proclaimed a method of treating people by the use of "influence," initially referred to as "mesmerizing." Unfortunately, Mesmer was considered a fraud and his work vanished until it was rediscovered by James Braid (1841), who introduced it under the term "hypnotism." Though Braid felt that the psychological cures did not last, hypnotism had additional usage for surgery and dentistry. Despite Braid's negative findings regarding efficacy for psychological treatment, the French School of Nancy under Liebault (1823–1904) and Bernheim (1837–1919) reported success with the method.

Charcot (1825–1893), with whom Freud studied in Paris (October 1885 to February 1886), also utilized hypnosis but became increasingly skeptical of its efficacy.

Freud had already evidenced the use of hypnosis in his observation of Breuer's treatment of Anna O (1880–1882), prior to his study in Paris. Breuer had worked with both hypnosis and talking, that is, he attempted to have Anna O review the events of the day and correlate them with past events that had succumbed to repression. It was this "talking" cure' that probably influenced Freud more than hypnosis, though Freud first began to treat patients with the hypnotic method. Furthermore, Freud was a product of his century: The primary authorship that we attribute to Freud regarding sexuality was a known factor. Sexology as a specialized field was well established under the aegis of such physicians and psychologists as Krafft-

Ebing (1874–1904), Havelock Ellis (1890–1939). Albert Moll (1889–1936) Paul Nacke (1883–1906), and William James (1842–1910).

The concepts of libido, erotogenic zones, autoerotism, narcissism, and component instincts were part of the nomenclature, and research concerning normal and aberrant sexual behaviors was well established. Theories regarding homosexuality, the perversions, their etiology, the sequential unfolding of sexual development, and infantile sexuality had already been *pari passu* of the scientific discourse. By the time that Freud had written his "Three Essays on Infantile Sexuality" (1905), he had been preceded by Moll, who had published extensively on childhood sexuality, homosexuality, and the role of jealousy and rivalry of children toward their parents (Sulloway, 1979).

What, then, can we attribute to Freud as the originator of psychoanalysis, since sexuality and its impact on psychic development was subject to study and investigation from a variety of perspectives and hypnosis as a psychological method of treatment had already been established? Freud established an "extensive synthesis" of existing ideas on psychosexual development and at the same time "contributed distinct psychoanalytic innovations and conceptual transformations" (Sulloway, 1979, p. 38). He provided an in-depth understanding of the origins and the role of pathogenic fantasy in the formation of symptoms and removed psychotherapeutic treatment from the aegis of neurology and even from psychiatry as it was then practiced. Freud produced a totally new method of psychological practice. The systematic application of a comprehensive theoretical base for a methodological procedure led to the development of psychoanalysis as a new field of science. Freud further separated psychology from biology to investigate the psychological factors that influence mental disturbance but, this separation is in form only, for Freud (1895, 1905) never negated the role of biology or constitution in the development of mental structures.

As we indicated, Freud first began his practice treating mental disorders by using what was common to the times—hypnosis, electrical stimulation, spas, and hydrotherapy. Hypnosis was the more important therapeutic tool that provided him with a systematic approach to explore the unconscious. As a technique, it was possible to bring to consciousness traumatic events from the past, and, by abreaction, catharsis, and suggestion, symptomatic relief was achieved. But Freud soon found this method inadequate and only a temporary palliative. Furthermore, Freud did not regard himself as a very successful hypnotist. Yet, it is to be remembered that the hypnotic method is considered the origin of psychotherapeutic technique. The second and most significant step in the development of a psychotherapeutic technique resulted from Freud's recognition of the role of free association.

This was a fortuitous discovery aided by one of his patients, who castigated him for interrupting her. Clearly, Freud became increasingly aware that some barrier existed to the patients' recovery of repressed memories, which no amount of suggestion or cajoling could elicit. The most efficacious mode of dealing with what Freud viewed as resistance was to allow the patient to speak freely, and by quietly listening, both patient and analyst could better understand and break the barriers to the unconscious. The introduction of free association as a basic treatment tool shifted the emphasis from the analyst as an active interpreter of psychic events to the more passive role of listener and recorder.

As psychoanalytic theory developed as a theory of the mind, Freud regarded his findings within the purview of science, a science of human development with particular psychological functions that are developmentally replicable. Closely paralleling his theories of mental development and psychic structure was the theory of technique. In fact, technique frequently preceded theory and, historically, the two function in such close proximity that there has been an almost inseparable connection between them. Vassalli

(2001), in a discussion on the development of Freud's technique, quotes from a letter written by Freud (1930) on problems in science:

> When I recollect isolated cases from the history of my work, I find that my working hypothesis invariably came about as a direct result of a great number of impressions based on experience. Later on, whenever I had the opportunity of recognizing an hypothesis of this kind to be erroneous, it was always replaced—and I hope improved— by another idea which occurred to me (based on the former as well as new experiences) and to which I then submitted the material, [pp. 395–396].

In no other profession has there been such an intimate connection between theory and technique, except for certain aspects of biological research. Freud's metapsychology derives from inductive constructs. His theories of the unconscious, the meaning of dreams, repressed memories, and the role of infantile sexuality evolved in the course of psychotherapeutic treatment. Rangell, in his 1954 presentation to the meetings of the American Psychoanalytic Association also indicated that in the historical sequence of events,

> First came the origin and the development of psychoanalysis as a therapy and simultaneously as a mode of investigation, [and] from this the gradual accumulation of the psychoanalytic body of facts, and from the latter the evolution of other rational dynamic psychotherapies [pp. 735–736].

Whether we shall call Freud's early treatment methods psychoanalysis or psychotherapy depends on one's historical perspective. For Freud, at the early inception of psychoanalytic theory, the terms were interchangeable.

Anticipation of the repressed material played a very minor role in this new treatment, for what emerged was certainly new to Freud. In one sense, the history of psychoanalysis can be viewed as a fusion between theory and technique, and a continuous struggle to undo both and to maintain this fusion. Unfortunately, this interpolation between theory and technique has led to a rigidity in the methodology of psychoanalysis and has deepened the gulf between psychotherapy and psychoanalysis more on the basis of technique than on a more basic theoretical construct.

Freud, interestingly, escapes this charge of rigidity. He had been attacked for supposedly breaking his own ground rules. Gill (1979) accused him of contaminating the transference, and Kanzer and Glenn (1980) felt that he exceeded the bounds of friendliness and the use of suggestion. Though Freud established certain guidelines for technique, neither in his writings nor in his practice did he adhere to them with the inflexibility that subsequent generations of analysts proposed. Freud advised against the use of suggestion (1911–1915) yet, in the An Outline of Psychoanalysis (1940) he pointed to "suggestion" as one of the analytic tools. He recommended that it was advisable to interpret material when the patient could almost make the interpretation, that is, when the material is at the preconscious level, yet from his case studies we observe that this was not always the rule (Dora, 1905; The Rat Man, 1909). Can we accuse Freud of blind or contradictory behavior in his methodological approaches? I think not. Rather, his suggested guidelines were outlines of technique and not dicta that were immutable. Remember, Freud (1912) stated that the task of analysis was to resolve transference and resistance, and within that framework there was a good deal of technical latitude.

The struggle to define the techniques of psychoanalysis as different from the techniques of psychotherapy has frequently resulted in the failure to separate theory from specific practice, as though any change in technique was inviolate and would undermine the analytic process. Even Ferenczi, who certainly deviated from classical technique by engaging in physical contact with his patients, and in mutual analysis, displayed a rather inflexible stance when he warned against the use of suggestion in psychoanalysis. For him, suggestion belonged to the aegis of psychotherapy and was regarded as an interference in resolving transference. Clearly, he too was concerned that the divide between psychoanalysis and psychotherapy remain fixed. Interestingly, suggestion has remained as the hallmark of psychotherapy and until recently (Wallerstein, 1995) was considered as taboo in any psychoanalytic treatment. Freud's early warnings against the use of suggestion were probably stimulated by its closeness to hypnosis. Since Freud viewed hypnosis as antithetical to the analysis of transference due to the hypnotist's active suggestions and authoritative coercion, suggestion was viewed as anti-analytical. But this was only within the historical context of treatment as practiced during the early beginnings of psychoanalysis. As we have indicated, in "Outline" (1940), Freud includes suggestion as one of the tools of psychoanalysis.

Historically, the sharp divide between psychotherapy and psychoanalysis is heralded by the theories of Alexander and French (1946). They considered that the distinction between psychoanalysis and psychotherapy was an artifact of a rigid methodology applied hegemonically by a status-conscious profession and did not reflect a fundamental difference between the two procedures. The differences, according to French, "lie merely in the extent to which the various therapeutic principles and techniques are utilized" (p. vii). Alexander argued against the ideas that the depth of therapy is necessarily related to the length of treatment and to frequency, and disclaimed the charge that shorter therapy resulted in a more superficial and temporary outcome. Both asserted that we are working with the same "kit of tools," that is, applying psychoanalytic concepts, and that the work is necessarily psychoanalytic. Alexander expressed the belief that the theory of psychoanalysis has been connected to methodology beyond its clinical usefulness, and that a more flexible approach was necessary. Thus, flexibility in time and supportive or uncovering types of treatment were best left to the diagnostic assessment of the analyst, and whatever method was decided upon should be considered psychoanalytic. Alexander and French did distinguish between supportive and uncovering or expressive analysis. These concepts initially gained a good deal of popularity, that then gave rise to concern among the more classical members of the American Psychoanalytic Association (the "American," henceforth). As a result, a series of meetings were organized to clarify the issues and to define psychoanalysis and psychotherapy. The primary concern that led to these discussions was the fear that the parameters that defined psychoanalysis as a theory and treatment methodology would be undermined by Alexander and French.

The meetings held by the American and associated societies between the years 1952 and 1954 became known as the "Great Debate." The publication of these debates in the *Journal of the American Psychoanalytic Association* in 1954 finally crystallized the major issues that distinguished psychoanalytic theory from psychotherapy. It was believed that a definitive distinction between psychoanalytic theory and dynamic psychotherapy had been established and that the majority of psychoanalysts in the United States rejected the theoretical positions of Alexander and French. Alexander and Weigert represented the untraditional view and Frieda Fromm-Reichman joined them but essentially presented a somewhat different conception in her work with psychotic patients. Stone, Gill, Rangell, Bibring, and Anna Freud were the exponents of the classical position. The primary source of contention between the two groups was the centrality of transference and the mode by which the transference was conceptualized and worked through psychoanalytically. All other issues such as frequency and free association emerged as derivative concepts of the primary theoretical position of the transference. Alexander regarded transference as a means of providing a "corrective emotional experience." The analyst's task was to undo the pathological effects of trauma resulting from early relationships with the parents. By behaving in a particular manner in the transference, the analyst would be able to undo these negative effects through the creation of a new object relationship. It was not necessary for the patient to understand or gain insight into the old or new configuration. The analyst's job was to figure out what the patient needed and to enact these needs by changes in his or her behavior. Transference was to be manipulated to provide a "corrective emotional experience" for the patient. The length of treatment and the frequency of sessions were changed according to the analyst's prescription. The methodology utilized supportive techniques, direct suggestion, exploratory uncovering, and direction. Sessions of one time a week and treatment lasting from one week to several weeks were considered to be psychoanalysis. It is evident that some of the early theories of Ferenczi regarding "active therapy" and Rank's theories of limited time were echoed in Alexander and French's' theories with one essential difference, that of the analysis of the transference. Ferenczi (1919) indicated that all wishes and behavior by the patient and the therapist had to be understood in the context of transference and, ultimately, must be subjected to analysis.

Rangel (1954) countered Alexander's and Frieda Fromm-Reichman's assertions in his statement that not only is there a basic difference in technique but, more significantly, that the technique stems from a different conceptualization of theory. He claimed that there were differences in their concept of repression, of the primary unconscious and preconscious. Their emphasis on the interpersonal relationship in early childhood development was opposed to the theories that viewed normal and pathological conditions as derivative of intrapsychic structures. The etiology of these mental structures derived from psychosexual development based on libido theory, and these differences in etiology and in basic theoretical constructs of mental structure must necessarily, according to Rangel, result in a very different treatment methodology. Rangel defined psychoanalysis as a method of therapy whereby conditions are brought about favorable for the development of a transference neurosis, in which the past is restored in the present, in order that, through a systematic interpretive attack on the resistance which opposes it, there occurs a resolution of that neurosis (transference and infantile) to the end of bringing about structural changes in the mental apparatus of the patient to make the latter capable of optimum adaptation to life [pp. 739–740].

Gill (1954) defined psychoanalysis as that "technique which, employed by a neutral analyst, results in the development of a regressive transference neurosis and the ultimate resolution of this neurosis by techniques of interpretation alone" (p. 775). Regarding psychoanalytic technique, he felt that it was "foolish" to try to define "the technique by such quantitative matters of how often the patient comes, or by such matters of physical arrangement, such as the recumbent position and inability to see the analyst" (p. 774). For Gill, though these features are important, he considered them to be auxiliary devices that enabled the application of certain technical principles, and that by elevating them to the position of technique, analysts ran the risk of losing the usefulness of the word "technique." He went on to state that some analysts can see a patient three times a week and that what occurs is closer to the psychoanalytic ideal than other analysts who see their patients five times a week. He raised concern that some "so-called" classical analysts have been bridled by a rigidity of "ritualistic details" when these are merely the "outward trappings of really crucial technical matters" (p. 775).

In regard to psychotherapy, Gill clearly stated that psychotherapy cannot do what psychoanalysis can achieve. Yet intensive psychotherapy may result not merely in shifting defenses but may also achieve certain structural changes. He addressed these changes in the light of increased autonomy of derivative conflicts. Though the basic conflicts have not been altered, the derivative conflicts can develop a degree of autonomy that is subject to change and can maintain independent conflict-free functions. Gill conceptualized this as an intrasystemic change within the ego. He asserted that the polarization between psychoanalysis and intensive psychotherapy as discrete opposites is a false dichotomy, and that the newer formulations in ego psychology regarding intrasystemic alterations and methods of adaptation will clarify this position. Gill himself stated that, on one hand, he had made a definitive distinction between psychoanalysis and intensive psychotherapy and, on the other hand, he had indicated that these differences could not be firmly established.

Despite Gill's empathic statements and apparent clarity, he was basically unable to resolve these differences to his own satisfaction.

Stone (1954) presented a position similar to Gill's regarding the modification of derivatives of the basic conflict that are capable of maintaining autonomous ego functions. He indicated that in psychoanalysis

> we dissolve or minimize resistance, and make the ego aware of its defensive operations, ultimately of id and superego contents and operations. Through this accurate awareness, implemented by the process of 'working through,' we expect the effect of abolition or reduction of id and superego qualitative distortions and pathological intensities, the resolution or reduction or at least the awareness of intrapsychic conflict in general, and finally the extension of the ego's positive sovereignty over instinctual life, with the freeing of facilitation of its synthetic, adaptive, and other affirmative capacities [p. 26].

He further indicated that the mobilization of the "transference neurosis holds a central place" (p. 26) in psychoanalytic treatment. In regard to intensive psychotherapy, he indicated that, in some instances, it was possible to use some aspects of the pathological transference that separates the reality of the "physician-patient" relationship from the transference relationship and that can be used to "great and genuine interpretive advantage by a skilled therapist" (p. 30). He did not support the position of Knight (1945, 1949) and others, which disclaimed the role of interpretation in intensive psychotherapy. Stone (1951) had already addressed the widening scope of psychoanalysis, and though he supported those who include, nosologies other than the transference psychoneurosis and character disorders of an equivalent degree of psychopathology, he warned against an overoptimistic view. He indicated that success decreased as one approached the "nosological periphery." Though Stone argued that it was not always easy to make a clear-cut distinction in practice between intensive psychotherapy along with what he referred to as "modified psychoanalysis," and psychoanalysis proper, it was necessary to delineate a reasonably clear distinction for understanding and investigation. In the end, after all our discussions that the "distinction between psychoanalysis and psychotherapy will never be adequate, aside from linguistic consideration, for psychotherapy is or should be a large and complicated field" (p. 27).

Bibring (1954) outlined five basic principles that were capable of explicating all psychoanalytic principles in their various "differential selection and combinations." These therapeutic principles—suggestion, abreaction, manipulation, insight through clarification, and insight through interpretation—are used in various combinations and appear in "differences in spread, frequency and saliency" (Wallerstein, 1995, p. 83). They form a hierarchical structure in that "insight through interpretation is the principal agent and all others are—theoretically and practically subordinate to it" (p. 762).

Psychoanalysis uses all therapeutic principles in varying degrees, but insight through interpretation is the primary agent. Psychotherapy by contrast shifts the goal from insight through interpretation to "experiential" manipulation, that is, learning from experience.

Anna Freud's position was in agreement with Stone, Rangell, Bibring, and Gill. She took exception to only one factor, and that was the degree by which the current discussions focused on the more extensive inclusion of so many different nosologies within the orbit of psychoanalytic treatment. She felt that if a more concerted effort were made to study the neurosis we would have developed a greater understanding of the neurosis and treatment possibilities.

During this period, the Menninger Psychotherapy Research Project (PRP) organized in the early 1950s and covering a thirty-year span (1952–1982) was concerned with developing an evaluative tool to test the success of each perspective treatment modality. They established a series of treatment categories: psychotherapeutic counseling, supportive psychotherapy, expressive psychotherapy, and psychoanalysis. We will refer only to their differentiation between expressive psychotherapy and psychoanalysis, as it is in this area that the major theoretical conflict and obfuscation has occurred. The PRP defined expressive psychotherapy as effecting significant change without having to uncover the "infantile genetic root," and as useful with those patients whose conflicts were relatively circumscribed. Psychoanalysis, to the contrary, evoked through the transference neurosis a re-creation creation in consciousness of the repressed infantile neurosis. The goals were elastic and nonspecific, for the principal aim was extensive ego modification.

The theories presented in the 1954 debates appeared to crystallize the positions, and to establish a consensus within the American Psychoanalytic Association that finally laid to rest the specific demarcation between intensive psychotherapy and psychoanalysis (Wallerstein, 1995). The concepts were not essentially new ideas, for they had been part of the intellectual and political discourse through the 1940s and well into the 1950s. Kubie (1943), who had been president of the New York Psychoanalytic Society, had been concerned with the status of psychoanalysis within the medical establishment and in preserving Freud's metapsychology within psychoanalysis. He was concerned that psychoanalysis maintain its independence from the medical establishment, especially in the light of its anti-psychoanalytic bias. Knight (1945, 1949), who had been at Menninger and then became Medical Director of Austen Riggs, was primarily interested in uniting psychoanalysis with psychiatry and establishing the principles of psychoanalytic theory as the basic theoretical model. Knight's model of differentiating the two modalities provided the dominant theoretical core throughout these discourses.

Kubie had elaborated on three main areas as the domain of psychotherapy: (1) supportive techniques such as advice, guidance, and management in living and dealing with the environment; (2) emotional support—sympathy, empathy, exhortation, humor; and (3) reorienting education, consisting of attempts to modify guilt, fear, hate, and depression by educating the patient to tolerate his or her preconscious and unconscious conflicts and feelings. He referred to the first two methods as "palliative psychotherapy," and the third method as "scientific psychotherapy" (Wallerstein, 1995, p. 35).

Knight (1945, 1949) was able to bring to psychiatry a dynamic conception of psychology and to influence the psychiatric hospitals throughout the country. He articulated "a basic science of dynamic psychology ... on which all psychotherapy must rest ... [and] the chief contributions to which have been made by psychoanalysis" (1949, quoted by Wallerstein, 1995, pp. 36–37).

He classified the various gradations of psychotherapy: supportive therapy which relies on suggestion, inspiration, education, reassurance, and guidance. This method was considered "superficial psychotherapy." The second category was termed expressive psychotherapy and considered major psychotherapy. Here, the goal was investigative and uncovering. The methods utilized dreams, catharsis, abreaction, insight, and interpretation. Yet Knight took great pains to distinguish very clearly between psychoanalysis and psychotherapy, despite overlapping methods. In expressive psychotherapy, there is no aim to alter ego structures, nor to widen the scope of the analysis beyond the immediate conflict situation or explore infantile roots of conflict.

The polemics between psychoanalysis and psychotherapy regarding the roles of the transference neurosis and of interpretation had its forerunners in another set of conflicts during the 1940s that seared the integrity of the psychoanalytic movement, and eventually led to a rupture within the American Psychoanalytic Association and the International Psychoanalytic Association. The struggle went to the basic core of psychoanalytic theory, that is, the metapsychology, and centered on the place of drives versus object relations in the etiology of neurosis. By extension, these fundamental differences were reflected in the conflicts regarding treatment methodology. Horney and Rado were expelled from the New York Society. Horney set up a new training institute and a new psychoanalytic association—the American Academy of Psychoanalysis—and Rado founded The Columbia Psychoanalytic Institute, which remained within the aegis of the American and International societies. These debates and splits had their counterpart in England between the Freudians and the Kleinians, and the various offshoots of the British object relation school. Though maintaining the conceptual framework of psychoanalysis and techniques such as free association, the use of the couch, and frequency of sessions, the theoretical differences gave rise to different methodology that was reflected essentially in the manner by which transference was handled (Wallerstein, 1995)

Unfortunately, the theoretical battles in the late 1940s and 1950s had serious consequences for "lay analysts," and despite Freud's tome on lay analysis and support for the practice and training of nonmedical analysts, the psychoanalytic profession succumbed to the dictates of the medical establishment. Alexander, as president of the Chicago Society, had strong ties with the medical profession, and one of his major goals was to achieve a coalescence of psychoanalysis with the medical establishment. His innovations and abbreviated therapies had a greater appeal to the medical profession than Freud's metapsychology and lengthy treatment procedures, and it is conceivable that many of Alexander's theoretical positions grew out of his desire to gain the support of the medical schools and the psychiatric establishment. (Bergman, personal communication; Eisold, 1998; Wallerstein, 1995). Certainly, the concern of many of the medical psychoanalysts in the United States reflected a desire to gain recognition from the medical establishment, and in pursuing this wish they capitulated to the medical hierarchy by repudiating lay analysis. They saw their primary task as preserving psychoanalysis as an independent discipline in concert with Freud's metapsychology, even if it meant forgoing his stated opinions about lay analysis (Freud, 1938). Despite the fact that Alexander's theories finally lost their appeal, he did succeed in tying psychoanalysis and psychotherapy to the dominion of the medical establishment. Psychotherapy gained in prestige by this amalgam with medicine, and was raised to a new theoretical level with a rationale and theoretical base that had not been previously achieved; psychoanalysis also increased its popularity and recognition.

Unfortunately, the divide between psychotherapy and psychoanalysis, rather than creating a cooperative atmosphere for investigation and research, served to establish a hegemonic power structure where psychoanalysis assumed the superior role (Wallerstein, 1995). Most analytic institutes did not deign to teach or include psychotherapy in their curriculum, and psychotherapy did not benefit from the rigor, the supervision, and the cohesive training that the analytic institutes could have provided. This negation of the value of psychotherapy left the field unwieldy and unlicensed, to the detriment of the public. As Wallerstein noted in his seminal book, *The Talking Cures* (1995), the failure of the psychoanalytic institutes to recognize the value and legitimacy of psychotherapy as a significant treatment modality and to engage in a continuous discourse within the institutes created a polemical atmosphere that served only to cloud the issues between the two methods and to isolate the fields. Stone (1951) was critical of psychoanalysis for neglecting psychotherapy both clinically and theoretically as a major complement to psychoanalytic work within the life "of the community."

Despite the relative calm that the "Great Debates" of the 1950s appeared to establish by crystallizing the theoretical distinctions between the two modalities and by setting the course of psychoanalysis as the dominant treatment mode, this was short-lived. The dissension continued to percolate, and the distinctions succumbed to doubts. Furthermore, it was not possible to ignore the growing popularity of psychotherapy as a treatment mode, nor its increased body of theory. Expressive or insight psychotherapy was the treatment mode in a large number of psychiatric hospitals, together with supportive and environmental methods. The blurring of distinctions continued to disturb the profession. In this context, a number of analysts addressed these issues: Robert Knight, Medical Director at Austen Riggs, whose concepts we have already discussed.

Sidney Tarachow and Paul Dewald Tarachow (1963), a training analyst and the Medical Director of Hillside Hospital, a psychiatric and teaching hospital, outlined a number of significant distinctions between the two modes. He indicated that "psychotherapy is an elective, limited treatment in which a rearrangement of certain conflictual elements is aimed at" (p. 41). Transference, repression, and resistance are dealt with so that their stability is maintained, while the analyst tries to effect certain therapeutic goals. If the relationship between the patient and the therapist is taken as real, then the unconscious conflicts, fantasies, and anxieties are not analyzed. Within the therapeutic context, he believed that the "state of the transference which exists in psychotherapy cannot be differentiated from an ordinary relationship" (p 10). For Tarachow, the uninterpreted relationship is a reality. He suggested three principles as inherent in a psychotherapy process: (1) We supply the infantile object in reality, and the transference is unanalyzed; (2) we help supply displacements, new symptoms, and/or new resistance; and (3) we supply stability for the ego and the superego by building on education and reality events (p. 43) Tarachow's main stress was on the transference and the difference between the handling of the transference in psychoanalysis and psychotherapy. In psychoanalysis the transference remains an "as if transference"; in psychotherapy the transference is perceived as real.

Dewald (1969), who had also been at the Menninger Clinic, made a significant contribution to the theoretical distinctions between psychotherapy and psychoanalysis. He elaborated on the nature of the transference neurosis as the most pertinent distinguishing factor between the two. Transference that does not grow into a full-blown regressive neurotic transference cannot be considered psychoanalysis. To work through the regressive neurotic transference, referents to the early period of childhood, the unconscious, and primary process material become the goals of the analytic treatment. In comparison, the goals of psychotherapy are less ambitious, focusing more on the period of latency and adolescence and dealing more with preconscious ideation. Techniques and methods are also distinguishing features. In psychoanalysis, the patient uses the couch, sessions occur four to five times a week, the analyst is generally more silent, and the treatment is longer. In psychotherapy, conflict resolution is contained within the "here and now," and transference is used as a positive medium to effect change mainly through identification and cognitive processes operating in tandem.

By 1979 we observe a reopening of the old debate within the American with a cast of similar characters—Stone, Rangel, and Gill. Alexander and French no longer played a significant role in this discussion and by then had lost much of their influence. Gill, who had addressed the dichotomies between psychoanalysis and psychotherapy in the 1954 debates, appeared to have taken a radical turn. He narrowed the distinctions both in theory and in method between the two methods of treatment. The claims for frequency of sessions, use of the couch, and free association, while not previously viewed as de rigueur in psychoanalysis, are still considered important tactical methods but no longer of real essence. The major shift for Gill was in the nature of the transference. He shifted his view of transference from a replay of the infantile conflicts to an expression of the interplay between the therapist and the patient. The genetic implications or interpretations of the past drive states or object relationships paled before the current interaction between the patient and the analyst. It was "the here and now" of the transference that Gill conceptualized as the main therapeutic agent. The infantile predecessor, the need for reconstruction of early constellations of wish and defense were not as significant as the focus upon the derivative of these conflicts as they emerge in the interplay in the present analytic discourse. Though this may have appeared startling considering Gill's earlier theories, seeds of this evolution can be gleaned from a 1954 statement:

> I would still like to hold open the question that even though the basic [i.e., infantile] conflict is unsolved and under sufficient stress can once again reactivate the derivative conflicts, the derivative conflicts develop a relative degree of autonomy, and exist in a form which allows a relatively firm resolution even under psychotherapeutic techniques, of the more intensive and less directed form I have described [p. 793].

What is most startling in Gill's new position is his divorce of psychoanalytic methodology from psychoanalytic theory. Because frequency of session, use of the couch, and free association were considered the fundamental underpinnings of a method by which it was possible to reach back to the past, to loosen the defenses, and to gain greater access to the unconscious, what he introduced was not only the severance of these tools from psychoanalytic technique but a totally different approach. There was nothing revolutionary about Gill's approach, for much of what he advocated had already been proposed by Alexander and French (1954). The primary difference between Gill and Alexander and French was Gill's focus on the analysis and interpretation of transference as a current enactment, whereas the latter used transference either by manipulation or suggestion to achieve change.

Stone (1979) remained fairly consistent, and though he agreed that an attempt to clearly distinguish the methods of psychoanalysis from psychotherapy was an admirable task, it was not always possible to make such clear distinctions nor specifically to work with such rarefied borders. Support, which was the hallmark of supportive psychotherapy, also played an important role in psychoanalysis and, on the inverse side, interpretation played a role in psychotherapy.

> The effort is to provide a sense of friendly and reliable alliance in the therapeutic situation, involving the ordinary modalities of sympathetic listening, rational encouragement, sometimes simple advice and guidance. To varying degrees, there may be added whatever modicum of broad understanding of himself and his environment that may seem to contribute to the patient's comfort and effectiveness, or to be required by the emergence of confronting conflict.... Interpretation always remains distinctively and often critically useful even in essentially noninterpretive contexts [p. 93].

He posited a dialectical relationship between the various modes of support and interpretation. Stone, certainly, cast a shadow of doubt over the rather rigid proscriptions of psychoanalytic practice and particularly on Eissler's (1954) theory of "parameters." He continued to maintain his belief that psychoanalysis works most effectively with the transference neurosis and "the reasonably severe character neurosis."

Rangell (1979) modified his earlier position but still maintained conceptual clarity around their differences (Wallerstein, 1995):

... just as analysts apply analytic principles freely and copiously to their practice of dynamic psychotherapy, reciprocally and empirically, with ever increasing complexity and length of psychoanalysis, the opposite also holds. There is no analysis without its share of the technical maneuvers noted by Bibring (1954) [i.e., suggestion, abreaction, manipulation, and clarification, along with interpretation] ....There is no analytic case treated by interpretation alone .... If this were a prerequisite, no treatment would qualify as analytic [pp. 670–671].

Rangell further noted that in psychoanalytic psychotherapy he could reach the infantile roots of the patient's current conflicts and to treat them with interpretation. Though Rangell recognized the overlapping areas between the two modes, he continued to make a distinction between psychotherapy and psychoanalysis. He noted the differences in quantitative and qualitative terms "in consistency and goals, in the uniformity and relentlessness of approach" (p. 682).

The consensus achieved in the early 1950s could not be sustained, and the 1979 discussions gave evidence of the theoretical fragmentation (Wallerstein, 1995). The consensus foundered over the fundamental issues of the transference, that is, the nature and mode of working through, interpretation, clarification, manipulation and insight, the real object, the "as if object," the transference neurosis, and genetic construction versus the "here and now." Auxiliary tools such as the couch, frequency of sessions, gratification versus frustration, suggestion, expanding parameters, and neutrality all became either inviolate or relegated to an open-ended position without careful clinical or theoretical study and examination. We observe some attempt to frame previous divisions between supportive psychotherapy and psychoanalytic psychotherapy or dynamic psychotherapy and psychoanalysis in an interactive mode, and within this schema, a new vocabulary is introduced.

Thus, Oremland (1991) refers to supportive psychotherapy as interactive psychotherapy and psychoanalytic psychotherapy as psychoanalytically oriented psychoanalysis. The nomenclature for psychoanalysis remains constant but is framed within the dialogue of the interactive mode. There is value to indicating that every relationship between patient and analyst has an interactive element, that interpretation itself is interactive, and that a false dichotomy had arisen that equated neutrality and abstinence with lack of interaction. Oremland attempted to clarify- the distinctions and simultaneously bridge the gap between the classical model and the interactive model. He (1991) indicated that psychoanalytically oriented psychotherapy focuses on the internal soliloquy more integrally as part of the external dialogue, whereas in psychoanalysis the interpretations reveal the internal soliloquy within the external dialogue. It is possible to reach the transferences with greater depth within the "actualities of the interplay." Differences between the two are complicated by the fact that the past is reconstructed by both approaches within the "dyad" as a past that is "but one of many pasts." (p. 119) Oremland's attempts to frame the discourse in an interactive mode and to distinguish the three approaches to treatment adds little to clarify the differences between dynamic or psychoanalytic psychotherapy and psychoanalysis.

The era faced not only obfuscation between psychoanalysis and psychotherapy but, perhaps, a more significant challenge in the development of a series of different theoretical constructs that questioned the basic Freudian constructs of psychic structure.

No longer was the drive/conflict, ego psychological model the pivotal idea behind psychic development; the object relational schools derived from Kleinian theory, self psychology, and, in more recent times, the interpersonal and intersubjective approach have achieved prominence. The shift from a drive conflict model to an object relational theory inevitably changed the theoretical understanding of the nature of the transference and the method of working with transference. Though the interpersonal school as best represented by Greenberg, Mitchel, and Stolorow and Atwood continued to view the transference as the exemplar of past object relations, the very prominence given to the object in psychic structure, with the concomitant undermining of drive, conflict, defense, and resistance, made the transition to intersubjective theory a logical outcome. By the late 1990s, the intersubjective school achieved a dominant position within the mainstream of psychoanalytic thought. The influence of Harry Stack Sullivan, Clara Thompson, and Eric Fromm are reflected in the intersubjective positions, but with a somewhat different emphasis in the manner by which transference and countertransference are used in the treatment. The movement from an objective evaluative position to a subjective hermeneutic place created a new dialectic in the treatment mode. This process also had its forerunners in Gill and Hoffman in the early 1980s and was carried further by Hoffman, who is regarded as the theoretical "father" of the intersubjective school. Clearly, the influence of Alexander and French is also reflected in the mode by which the transference is conceptualized and worked with, but without the authoritarian approach that was inherent in their style.

Essentially, the introduction of new concepts regarding the mode of psychic change and the intensification of focus on enactments in the analytic dyad mitigate any real need to distinguish between psychoanalysis and psychotherapy. The adjunct tools of psychoanalytic practice, such as frequency of sessions, use of the couch, interpretation, analytic neutrality (a concept that has been distorted by both its adherents and antagonists), and free association are no longer part of the theoretical dialogue, except as a negative discourse. Within the parameters of intersubjectivity, the transference as we have historically understood

its meaning is radically changed and is viewed as ever evolving into a new experience, intertwining between the patient and the analyst, and therefore, it is no longer framed by the conflict model as a repetition from the past. Bromberg (1993) argues that the narrative told by the patient "cannot be edited simply by more accurate verbal input. Psychoanalysis must provide an experience that is perceivably (not just conceptually) different from the patient's narrative memory" (p. 391). The central aspect of this process is that the patient-analyst relationship is inevitably drawn into the process and both experience the narrative as it is relived in the analytic interchange. The core of this process is that the meaning of the narrative is continually "renegotiated" within the dyadic interchange. According to Bromberg, "enactment is the primary perceptual medium that allows narrative change to take place" [p. 391].

Validated narratives and other constructions formerly excluded begin to be reconstructed. These events are not symbolized by words but by the new "narrative constructs that words represent." The essential feature in this construction as different from the construction of the drive/ conflict model and ego/conflict is the idea of a narrative that is continually rewritten by ever evolving subjective factors. The concepts of defense mechanisms, character structures, drive/ conflict, and the tripartite division between id, ego, and superego are relegated to minor focus in the treatment. Transference, as stressed by Gill as a vehicle for interpretation, is vastly overshadowed by the intersubjective mode by which narrative is constructed and deconstructed in the active interaction between therapist and patient.

In this brief historical review, I have tried to demonstrate that the consensus regarding the differences between psychoanalysis and psychotherapy was riddled with inconsistencies, overlapping concepts, and doubts from the beginning. Gray (1994) put the issue succinctly when he stated that in the realm of intensive exploratory therapies, we really cannot expect any general agreement about which schools are practicing psychotherapy and which are practicing something else. The title has become so valued that it virtually sticks to any or all of the variations. Be that as it may, I argue that we need some kind of designation as to the kind of psychoanalysis being practiced, in order to keep alive the issue that qualitative issues are involved, a merely quantitative continuum obscures much that is clinically crucial [p. 148].

By dividing the field between psychotherapy and psychoanalysis, psychoanalytic institutes foreclosed the ability to supervise and control the educational development of psychotherapists and to integrate the various methods of psychotherapy within the theoretical constructs of psychoanalysis. Psychoanalysis was also deprived of the richness and technical assets of psychotherapy, which only an interplay between the two modes could have offered. The rigidity of technique that plagued psychoanalysis and often overrode more fundamental theoretical issues prevented a careful clinical examination of the different approaches. Given the degree of isolation between the two modalities, a comprehensive research methodology into the nature of psychic change and curative aspects of either treatment could not be established. Unfortunately, Freud's seemingly pejorative[1] reference to psychotherapy as the "copper" and psychoanalysis as the "gold" remained an *idée fixe,* within the American psychoanalytic movement. Furthermore, in the current climate, which appears to be increasingly dominated by the intersubjective school, a distinction between the two modes is not only impossible, given the theoretical constructs, but appears an unnecessary

---

1 I believe that this statement is taken out of context, for in reading the full paragraph the indication is to difference based on reality factors rather than a hierarchical status. Freud was advocating the extension and a wider application of psychoanalytic treatment for the population at large, (1919 [1918], p. 168).

task. How such issues of frequency, use of the couch, and free association are treated are left to the analyst and the patient to work out without a solid theoretical structure. Questions as to the depth or scope of treatment and the use of any of these tools seem irrelevant in the context of intersubjectivity. It appears that finally this old argument can be put to rest. Nevertheless, the intersubjective school has simply added a new conundrum to the field. The issues of defense and resistance, psychic structure, object relations, and drive derivatives have not faded from the clinical experience.

REFERENCES

Alexander, F. (1954). Psychoanalysis and psychotherapy. *J. Amer. Psychoanal. Assn.*, 2:722–733.

_____ & French, T.M. (1946). *Psychoanalytic therapy: Principles and application.* New York: Ronald Press.

Bibring, E. (1954). Psychoanalysis and the dynamic psychotherapies. *J. Amer. Psychoanal. Assn* 2:745–770.

Bromberg, P. M. (1993). Shadow and substance: A relational perspective on clinical process. In S.A. Mitchell & L. Aron, eds., *Relational Psychoanalysis: The Emergence of a Tradition.* Hillsdale, NJ: The Analytic Press, 1999.

Chessick, M. (1974). *Technique and practice of intensive psychotherapy.* New York: Jason Aronson.

Dewald, P. (1964, 1969). *Psychotherapy: A dynamic approach.* New York: Basic Books.

Eissler, R.K. (1953). The effect of the structure of the ego on psychoanalytic technique. *J. Amer. Psychoanal. Assn.*, 1:104–143.

Eisold, K. (1998). The splitting of the New York Psychoanalytic Society and the construction of psychoanalytic authority. *Int. J. Psycho-Anal.* 79: 871–886.

Ferenczi, S. (1919). On die technique of psycho-analysis. In Further contributions to the theory and technique of psycho-analysis (pp. 177–189). London: Hogarth Press, 1926.

_____ (1920). The further development of an active therapy in psychoanalysis. In *Further Contributions to the Theory and Technique of Psychoanalysis* (pp. 198–217). London: Hogarth Press.

_____ (1954). The widening scope of indications for psychoanalysis: Discussion. *J. Amer. Psychoanal. Assn.* 2:607–620.

_____ (1893–1895). Studies on hysteria, Joseph Breuer and Sigmund Freud. In J. Strachey, ed. and trans., *Standard Edition* 2:1–309.

_____ (1905a) [1901]). Fragment of an analysis of a case of hysteria. *Standard Edition* 7:1–122.

_____ (1905b). Three essays on the theory of infantile sexuality. *Standard Edition* 7:123–243.

_____ (1909). Notes upon a case of obsessional neurosis. *Standard Edition* 10:151–318.

_____ (1919 [1918]). Lines of advance in psycho-analytic therapy. *Standard Edition* 17:157–168.

_____ (1911–1915 [1914]). Papers on technique. *Standard Edition* 12: 89–170.

_____ (1926). The question of lay analysis. *Standard Edition* 20:177–250.

_____ (1940 [1938]). An outline of psycho-analysis. *Standard Edition,* 23:139–208.

Gill, M. (1954). Psychoanalysis and exploratory psychotherapy. *J. Amer. Psychoanal. Assn.* 2:771–797.

_____ (1979). The analysis of the transference. *J. Amer. Psychoanal. Assn.,* 27(Suppl.):263–288.

Gray, P. (1994). *The Ego and Analysis of Defense*. Northvale, NJ & London: Jason Aronson.

Hoffman, I. Z. (1983). The patient as interpreter of the analyst's experience. In S.A. Mitchell & L. Aron, eds., *Relational Psychoanalysis: The Emergence of a Tradition*. Hillsdale, NJ: The Analytic Press, 1999.

Kanzer, M. (1980). The transference neurosis of the rat man. In M.M. Kanzer & J. Glenn, eds., *Freud and His Patients*. New York and London: Jason Aronson.

Knight, R. (1945). The relationship of psychoanalysis to psychiatry. *Am. J. Psychiatry* 101:777–782. Reprinted in S.C. Miller, ed., *Clinician and Therapist: Selected Papers of Robert Knight* (pp. 121–130). New York: Basic Books.

——— (1949). A critique of the present status of the psychotherapies. *Bull. NY Acad. Med.* Reprinted in S.C. Miller, ed., *Clinician and Therapist: Selected Papers of Robert Knight* (pp. 177–192). New York: Basic Books.

Kubie, L. (1943). The nature of psychotherapy. *New York Acad. Med.* 199:183–194.

Margolis, M. (2001). The American Psychoanalytic Association: a decade of change. *J. Amer. Psychoanal. Assn.* 1:11–26.

Oremland, J.D. (1991). *Interpretation and Interaction: Psychoanalysis or Psychotherapy?* Hillsdale, NJ: The Analytic Press.

Psychotherapy Research Project (PRP). Menninger Foundation, 1952–1982.

Rangell, L. (1954). Similarities and differences between psychoanalysis and dynamic psychotherapy. *J. Amer. Psychoanal. Assn.* 2:734–744.

——— (1979). Unpublished paper presented at die Atlanta, GA Symposium.

——— (1981). Similarities and differences between psychoanalysis and dynamic psychotherapy. *Psychoanal. Q.* 50:665–693.

Schwartz, E. (2000). Unpublished paper.

Stone, L. (1951). Psychoanalysis and brief psychotherapy. *Psychoanal. Q.*, 20:215–236.

_____ (1954). The widening scope of indications for psychoanalysis. *J. Amer. Psychoanal. Assn.*, 2:567–594.

_____ (1979). Unpublished paper presented at the Atlanta, GA Symposium.

Sulloway, F.J. (1979). *Freud, Biologist of the Mind.* New York: Basic Books.

Tarachow, S. (1963). *An Introduction to Psychotherapy.* New York: International Universities Press.

Vassali, G. (2001). The birth of psychoanalysis from the spirit of technique. *Int. J. Psycho-Anal.* 82:3–26.

Wallerstein, I. (1995). *The Talking Cures.* New Haven and London: Yale University Press.

CHAPTER 5

FREUD, THE PROGENITOR OF OBJECT RELATIONS THEORY: A REVIEW

To re-evaluate theories and hypotheses is a necessary correlate for any scientific endeavor, and I would suggest that psychoanalytic reviews also serve that purpose. They either reaffirm hypotheses and postulates that had been established or refute assumptions and theories no longer valid considering new information and new theoretical constructs. Science progresses by a refraction of past and present constructs, and by repeated efforts at validation of old and new theories.

My review of Freud's concepts of the object and object relations is an attempt to assess his contribution to the theoretical and clinical understanding of these concepts, and to show that Freud's hypotheses regarding the bio-psychological force of drives and their impact on object relationships remains the corner stone of psychoanalytic theory. I say this with due respect for subsequent theories that emphasize the role of the object in psychic development, even though they have either de-emphasized the role of drives or dismissed their importance. Nonetheless, the "Object Theorists" have advanced our understanding and significance of the object in psychic development and in psychic structure. Freud's conceptualizations regarding object, object representation, sexual object, and object relations were fundamental factors in his postulates regarding mental structure and psychological development. His concepts on internalization, introjection, and identification could only result from an intrinsic awareness of the infant's relationship to the primary objects in his/her life, and the continuous importance of object relationships throughout the life span.

I will review Freud's theories from a thematic and chronological perspective with particular emphasis on his posthumous work "The Project", (1950[1895]) which antedates drive theory, and indicated Freud's recognition of the role of the object in psychological development. Though Freud never wrote a central paper on the object or object relations, a review of his oeuvre from 1895 through 1940 reveals the centricity of objects in his thinking. The role of the object, the place it assumes in psychic structure and in unconscious conflict, and its pivotal role in ego and superego structure are clear in Freud's major papers, (1915, 1917a, b., 1920 a, b, 1923, 1926, 1930, 1937, 1940) in other writings (1910,1913), and in his case studies (1905,1909a, b,1919). His major writings on identification and internalization of the object, and the nature of the transference (1950 [1895], 1912,1913,1914a,b, 1917a,b, 1923, 1930) signify the importance of the object from early infancy, oedipal, and post oedipal phases, and in adult life.

Freud's postulates on drive theory bore a direct impact on his theoretical position on the nature of internalization; the dynamic and energic force of the drives, composites to his metapsychology, helped define the quality of object relations by the ebb and flow of libido from ego/self to object. While I will not deal with the psychoneurosis in this paper, it is necessary to indicate that Freud considered that the "psychoneurosis are based on sexual instinctual forces."

Further, my primary purpose in reexamining Freud's concepts regarding the significance of the "Object" is not only to correct the current misunderstanding regarding his theories, but also to elucidate the significant role that the object played in the ontogenetic development of the drives. Freud even hypothesized that the ego and the superego, a construct of internalized objects, became part of man's phylogenetic inheritance. I am aware that I probably have fallen victim to my desire to present a unified picture of Freud's theories on the "Object," and I may interpolate his various theoretical positions as more cohesive than contradictory. This is particularly relevant regarding Freud's numerous claims of an objectless phase (1905b, 1914b) while in other writings he stated that the object and object choice existed almost from the beginning of infancy (1905,1916,1923). I hope that I will present sufficient evidence to prove my assertion, despite many contradictory statements by Freud, that his fundamental hypotheses regarding the development of psychic structure reflected a binary perspective, that of, drives and objects.

FREUD AND HISTORY

Freud did not invent neurosis or psychosis nor was he the first to proclaim that unknown regions of the mind, referred to as the subconscious, influenced human behavior. He had his mentors in Warner-Jauregg, Charcot, Janet, somewhat older contemporaries, and even Messmer, one century prior to his findings. Breuer, his foremost mentor, called his attention to the 'talking cure' and thus paved the way for Freud's early theories on psychoanalytic treatment. Furthermore, Freud was not the first to focus on sexuality as an important component in psychological development nor was he the first to recognize the impact of sex in psychic conflict, see Kraft-Ebing, Havelock Ellis, and Moll. Yet, Freud succeeded his contemporaries by not only integrating sexuality within the context of the individual's total psychic life, but by formulating a theory of drives resembling the instincts of animal life that were the subject of study of the natural sciences. Freud positioned the instincts on the border between biology and psychology, a meshing of soma and mind. Soma and mind were united in a dual function affecting both mental organization and drive discharge.

The idea of "lust," well known to 19th century psychology was metamorphosed into the postulate 'Libido' (1950 [1895]), a mode of psychic energy, as a driving force in the mental economy. He viewed Libido as a basic motivating force for individual relationships and social organization (1905b, 1910, 1930) [1929]). Psychic structure developed from a dynamic confluence of biological imperatives and internalization of objects. Freud, to my mind, was a revolutionary thinker, his formulation of instincts as motivating, object, and aim directed in psychological development provided an understanding of human behavior that had been compartmentalized by his predecessors and contemporaries.

FREUD'S INSTINCT THEORIES

In this section I will briefly define Freud's instinct theories, and in the next section will show the relationship of instincts to objects and the interconnection between them.

Freud's early instinct theories anticipated his later evolving concepts of instincts. He initially regarded instincts within the larger corpus of theories that included hunger, mastery, play, and sexuality. The posthumous Project written in 1895 has only one reference to instinct, that is, 'Trieb,' where in, he indicated that 'we know it by the power of the will as a derivative of the instincts.' (p.317). He made no great claim for the role of sexuality except as it became increasingly evident that repression of sexual desires underpinned much of the neurotic symptomatology. The early papers on Hysteria (1893–1895) concerned the mechanism of repression of unacceptable ideas and its impact on mental functions. Concepts of discharge as a means of dealing with repression and psychic damming predominated in his writings and were influenced by the dominant theorists of his age, Fechner, Meynert, and

Darwin. Freud's main theses focused on the organism's need for homeostatic equilibrium, a concept that evolved into the pleasure-unpleasure principle.

By 1905b in The Three Essays, Freud developed a more specific and unified instinct theory that conflated mental and biologic processes. He formulated a two-instinct theory, the ego instincts and the sexual instincts that largely determined the organization and character of psychological development and psychic conflict. The ego instincts were defined by their self- preservative quality while the sexual instincts strove for both procreation of the species and individual gratification. It is regarding the sexual instincts that Freud referred to the 'sexual object', the object that is the source of procreative value, survival of the species, and personal pleasure. In a subsequent section, I will elaborate on Freud's concept of the "sexual object" and the seeming contradiction between the nature of the 'sexual-object' and the object. The question remains whether this contradiction is more apparent than actual?

The second instinct theory emerged in the 1920a paper "Beyond The Pleasure Principle." Here Freud unified the ego instincts with the sexual instincts under one rubric, Eros, and proposed the second drive theory as the Death Instinct, Thanatos. Psychic conflict developed from the conflicting motives of Eros, which is the life force, a binding drive, and Thanatos, a drive to death, to undue life, to reduce life to its former inorganic state, a state of nirvana. Aggression as a derivative of Thanatos stands independently of libidinal frustration, and henceforth is on equal footing with the sexual drives as a component in molding psychic development. Fusion and binding of the two drives are processes in developing defense mechanisms and control of discharge.

FREUD'S OBJECT THEORIES

Freud's concepts of the "object," object relationships, the internalization of the object and identification permeate all his principal writings. I hope to make explicit that Freud conceived of psychic development as a confluence of drives and objects, each meriting importance at various developmental stages. Yet, the question as to why he did not write even one monograph on the "Object" as an independent focus has no answer. The assumption could be made, ala his critics, that he regarded object relations as almost irrelevant or minor causative factors in psychic development and in mental conflict. Yet, as I have indicated his major writings have repeated references to the centricity of the object in psychic structure and psychic conflict. As a conjecture, it is possible to posit that the role of the object for Freud was a self-evident truism, and that a libido theory without an inherent relationship to the object could serve only as a partial or heuristic explanation of psychic development. Therefore, the role of the object was an implicit assumption, and did not require a more detailed explication. Freud (1916) indicated that we do not deny the existence or importance of the ego instincts—psychoanalysis concerns itself with the sexual instincts because "it has simply been its fate to begin concerning itself with the sexual instincts because the transference neurosis made them the most easily accessible to examination and because it was incumbent on it to study what other people neglected." (p.351) It is to be recalled that the ego instincts were embodiments of ego/self, drive motivated to insure survival of the species and individual pleasure (the pleasure-unpleasure principle).

As early as the "Project" (1950 [1895]), Freud had evolved a theory of the object's role in his attempts to find a psycho-neurological basis for mental functioning and psychic structure. Freud indicated that the object in its role as satisfier of the instincts, such as, hunger, becomes immediately connected to drive discharge and is therefore, an integral component of the quality and the aim of discharge. The object representation is first preceded by a 'thing' presentation that results in the establishment of an mnemic image of the object. The libidinal investment in the 'thing' presentation derives from the infant relationship to the nurturing object, which established a permanent mnemic image of the object. These early object relationships define drive states not, simply, by quantitative factors but, importantly, determine qualitative aspects of the object relationship. Thus, following Freud's thinking (1950 [1895]), discharge of drive states from early infancy cannot be treated as objectless drive states, but are interwoven with the nature of object satisfaction. Freud (1950 [1895]) further, indicated that "qualities are linked with perception," and desire for the object as well as desire for satisfaction could, therefore, be viewed as the Janus-faced aim of the instincts. He stated that

> Thus, as a result of the experience of satisfaction, a facilitation comes about between two mnemic images and the nuclear neurons which are cathected in the state of urgency. No doubt, along with the discharge of satisfaction the Qn flows out of the mnemic images as well. Now, when the state of urgency or wishing re-appears, the cathexis will also pass over on to the two memories and will activate them. Probably the mnemic image of the object will be the first to be affected by the wishful activation [p. 319].

Though Freud was focusing on the development of wish, perception, thought, and cognition, underlying these concepts was the mode by which the object was established as a mnemic image, as a presentation, and was internalized as a stable object representation. The moment the role of the object was established, discharge had little independent meaning outside its relationship to the object. Therefore, the aim whose goal was initially gratification through release of tension i.e., discharge, was itself modified in connection with the object of gratification. Though aim and object exists as two separate entities, the former in reference to function and the latter as part of psychic structure, it is equally valid to assume that object and aim are the two interconnecting forces operative in the mode of discharge and gratification.

Further, Freud stated that regarding objects, "an object like this was simultaneously the (subject's) first satisfying object, and further his first hostile object as well as his sole helping power...." The object (the libidinal object) functioning as the primary agent for gratification becomes the means by which the subject becomes a "human being." (p.331).

He also indicated that

> ...the human organism is incapable of bringing about specific actions. It takes place by extraneous help, when attention of an experienced person is drawn to the child's state by discharge along the path of internal change. In this way this path of discharge acquires a secondary function of the highest importance, that of communication, and the initial helplessness of human beings is the primal source of all moral motives [p.318].

This concept of the mode by which the object is established in psychic structure, almost from birth, was again referred to in "Symptoms, Inhibition and Anxiety" (1926) some 31 years later. In Freud's discussion of the early precipitates of anxiety: the birth trauma, he stated, "We cannot possibly suppose that the fetus has any sort of knowledge of its life being destroyed. It can only be aware of some vast disturbance in the economy of its narcissistic libido. Large sums of excitation crowd in upon it, giving rise to new kinds of feelings of unpleasure, and some organs acquire an increased cathexis, thus foreshadowing the object-cathexis which will soon set in." (p.135).

FREUD'S SEXUAL OBJECT

Freud's reference to the object as a 'sexual object or a 'drive-driven object has led to much controversy even for the classically oriented analysts. Compton, an exponent of drive theory, (1983a,1985a, b, 1986) indicated that Freud's "drive directed object," or "sexual object" appears to undermine or at least diminish the importance that he gave to the object and object choice prior to the oedipal phase.

Though, Freud repeatedly interchanged the terms 'sexual object and the "object," we must question what his frame of reference was. Was the reference to different, isolated object representations or did these terms i.e., "sexual object" and object, refer to qualitatively different aspects of the same object regarding a variety of functions and aims? The same object may simultaneously be the subject of various unconscious fantasies and mnemic representations at different developmental phases and in various disguises. Thus, are we dealing with totally different object representations isolated by affect, need, and quality of object relationship? Furthermore, the developmental sequence in object relationships and representation, and the maturation of libidinal phases result in differentiated qualities of the same object representation. Different drive investment in the object, i.e., aggression and libido, determine the specific subjective affect to the object at a particular moment. Therefore, I would suggest that Freud regarded "sexual object" and "object" as initially identical. The sexual object assumes a qualitatively different characteristic in puberty and in adult life in the search for a different, non-incestuous object.

The term "sexual object" first appeared in the Project (1950 [1895]). I will try to elaborate on Freud's ideas as he addressed the "object" and the "sexual object" from various perspectives; at times both terms overlap in meaning and at other points have a somewhat different reference.

I will show that Freud's concept of the "sexual object" and the "object" is best understood from a contextual reading. The usage tends to reflect a particular meaning defined by the relationship between subject and object. Freud at various times referred to the object that provided "nourishment" as a "sexual object." He made this statement initially in the "Project" (1950 [1895]), and it was as surprising, as it was prescient for his later theories, for at this stage his theories on infantile sexuality and the sexual instincts had not been formulated. Strachey, in his Introduction to the Project (1950 [1895]) points out that in his (Freud's) early work there is a major difference from his later theories, "all emphasis in the picture here is upon the environment's impact upon the organism and the organism's reaction to it." The main interest is upon the defensive operations and their mechanisms. Further, he indicated that it is in the Project that we can find a "foretaste" of the structural ego that formally emerges in the Ego and the Id; "Internal forces are scarcely more than secondary reactions to external ones." The ego instincts and sexual instincts have not yet evolved in his thinking and the Id, in fact, is still to be postulated (pp. 291–292).

In the Three Essays on Sexuality (1905b), Freud again uses the term "sexual object," and this has been interpreted to mean an object that serves the sexual drive in the most concrete sense of the word. To be a sexual object seems to connote a meaning close to orgiastic functions or physical discharge, and therefore, appears to predicate an object devoid of emotional attachment. Freud did not regard the sexual drive as a simple action of discharge but, also, as I have indicated, as a mode for establishing object relationships. It serves the purpose of survival of the species and simultaneously provides the emotional basis for human relationships. Libido was viewed as a force that functioned as a unifier of individual and group processes (Freud, 1921).

The relationship between the instincts and the object, and the so-called "sexual object" was essential to his meta psychological premise to the genetic factor. True, Freud is quite categorical in his thinking that through the internalized object underlies the basic fabric of psychic structure, the compelling and motivating force in psychic development derives from the clamor of the instincts for satisfaction. It is in this sense that Freud spoke of a "sexual object," i.e., an object whose purpose is to gratify the instincts.[1] Satisfaction, in the context of Freud's usage, arises from biological needs that demand relief. Eventually, psychological needs take precedence over biology or at least are equal in demand for satisfaction, and therefore, the mode of discharge is further defined by the specific response from the object. In a teleological manner cause and effect is established. The central nervous system, the neurological base of emotional response and cognition, is functionally dependent on the drives and the object for its development as an organic structure i.e., the development of the mind. Though Freud considered the aim of the sexual drive as that of discharge, and the "sexual object" as the source of satisfaction, it is clear from his writings that this same sexual object is transformed into an object of both love and hate through the process of identification, internalization, sublimation, and frustration. Furthermore, this process occurs at every developmental stage. Sexual phases influence the character of the internalized object that in turn modifies the force of the drives

I believe that another misconception has centered on Freud's statement regarding the variability of the "sexual object." This has provided the opponents of drive theory with the ammunition to assert that the role of the object in psychic development was of minor importance (Greenberg and Mitchel, 1983). Granted, evidence for this criticism can be found in Group Psychology and the Analysis of The Ego (1921) and in The Ego and the Id (1923). For example, Freud indicated that "it is found in erotic cathexis

---

1 Compton's (1983a) distinction between an object and a sexual object in Freud's writings appears to create an artificial distinction. The object will evidence qualitative changes during psychosexual development. (Freud, 1926) Further, the concept of sublimation indicated Freud's belief in the qualitative change in drive states regarding aim and object.

where a peculiar indifference in regard to the object displays itself; and it is especially evident in the transferences arising in analysis that develop inevitably irrespective of the persons who are their object." (1923, 1924). Freud regarded this capacity to displace objects as a product of sublimation (1923), a means of loosening the erotic cathexis from the preoedipal object and the incestuous object of the oedipal phase. He indicated there could be a loosening of object ties when the object was an erotic object, and as a sexual object, is displaceable. Yet, there can be no question that Freud considered that a primary object is established and maintained throughout life in a rather fixed position. Freud repeatedly stated that during our search for an object we are always looking to re-find an old object, the object of our earliest infancy (1923).

What then, can we conclude regarding Freud's ad hoc usage of "sexual object" and "object"? Is it liking his usage of ego and self, each term employing a similar referent and used interchangeably? Since Freud regarded the first object as a libidinal object and the relationship to the object as libidinal, is it fair to assume that he regarded the quality of the libidinal investment in the primary object as subject to change and modification through the processes of sublimation, narcissism, identification, defense, and aim? Therefore, Freud saw no contradiction in his intermittent use of both the "sexual object" and the "object."

In "Inhibitions Symptoms, and Anxiety," Freud (1926 [1925]), no longer made the distinction between the "sexual object" and the "object." Freud established a hierarchy of danger situations, each of which reflected the centricity of the object and the danger from loss of the object. The first of these dangers arose from the threat of loss of the need-gratifying object, an object that is closest to the evolution of ego differentiation from the id; and that this phase would appear to be the least likely one to reflect a "sexual object." Yet, it is precisely, to this phase (1950 [1895], 1905b) that Freud gave the nomenclature, a "sexual object," an object that is cathected with libido. The most likely stage to recognize a "sexual object" would occur at the oedipal phase, a phase in which we encounter castration anxiety in the male and loss of love for the female. These dangers reflect, aside from the role of direct sexual desires for the object, qualitatively different affective relationships to the object. The derivatives of sexuality refer to affects such as friendship, affection, kindness, sympathy, and empathy. My point is that Freud considered all objects as invested with libido, regardless of the vicissitudes that the object has undergone in aim and function. In his paper on "Transference" (1912), Freud distinguished between the erotic desires toward the analyst and an affectionate current, both which stem from sexual libido. "Originally," he stated," we knew only sexual objects: and psychoanalysis shows us that people who in our real life are merely admired or respected may still be sexual objects for our unconscious" (p.105).

Thus, the complexity of meaning regarding the "sexual object" lies in the multitude of meanings that have accrued during psychic development. Eroticism, love, sex are the many aspects of the human emotion; they require a contextual understanding in relation to real life, the nature of object relationships, the character traits of the individual, specific needs, dependency, internalizations, and sublimation. The list is in all probability longer as to what differentiates love from sex and sexual love. Therefore, Freud's apparent division between a "sexual object" and a "love object" would appear to be a matter of emphasis at a particular point in his thinking and a less than exact precision in his writings. I would suggest that our reading regarding the 'object and the "sexual object" should reflect the complexity of differentiated functions of the internalized object, and the libidinous needs and desires of the subject in relation to the object.

OBJECT CHOICE

The concept of the "Drive Object" (Compton, 1985), or the "Sexual-object," as I have already discussed in the above paragraph, has created a good deal of misunderstanding regarding Freud's ideas on the "object," and object choice. In "The Three Essays" (1905b) Freud made several statements that on the surface would seem to corroborate perceptions that Freud conceived of an early objectless phase and that object choice was established only at the oedipal phase (Compton, 1985). For example, Freud stated that "the sexual instinct is not unified and is at first without an object, and the early efflorescence of infantile sexual life gives rise to the "choice of an object," that occurred around the at ages of "2–5" (p. 234). Yet, Freud's postulates from his early writings, "The Project" (1950 [1895]), and even in "The Three Essays" (1905b), "Narcissism" (1914b), and "Instincts and their Vicissitudes" (1915) indicate that it is a mistake to say that he viewed object choice as only originating in the phallic-oedipal phase. A closer reading, of those statements that referred to the idea that object choice was established in the phallic-oedipal phase are contradicted by Freud's frequent references to the choice of the object and the attachment to the object (1915) in early infancy. His ideas on love for the mother in the oral phase and subsequent statements (1905b) that the finding of an object is in essence a re-finding of the object is a clear indication that object choice began in early infancy. In "Civilization and Its Discontents" (1930 [1929]), he indicated that object choice and identification were parallel processes yet, he also, equivocated as to which process was the earlier, again referring to the infant phase. In his discussion of the prototype of the pubertal object he indicated that it is the mother who succors the infant at her breast, and the "preparations for finding the object at puberty were made from the earliest childhood" (1905b, 222).

Freud's views on the nature or inherent qualities that motivated selection of a love object, also, indicated his belief that object choice was rooted in earliest infancy indeed, almost from the beginning of life. He referred to two methods that influence the quality of the object choice: one was determined by the anaclitic or attachment relationship of infancy, and the second one, reflected a narcissistic object choice.

Again, we are met with another group of contradictions when we examine various aspects of Freud's theories on autoerotism and narcissism regarding timing of object representation and object choice. Autoerotism and narcissism (1914b) functionally, have similar relationships to the object or more precisely, lack of relationship. Freud indicated that initially the primary narcissistic state is objectless as is the autoerotic phase, and in these states the ego has no need of the external world. This statement is indeed bewildering for Freud had previously claimed that the object is invested with libido from the very beginning of life and is set down in the mind as an mnemic presentation. Further, as I have indicated in the preceding paragraph Freud (1905b, 1930) stated that object choice and identification are almost concurrent processes that begin at the onset of infant life. The conundrum may be best explained by means of the relative investment of libido in the object and the self. The narcissistic state is never a pure state of objectless. Narcissism from an energic concept implies distribution of libido, but libido that has been transformed from a direct sexual gratification to sublimated sexuality, i.e., love. It is a question of a psychological state reflecting an affective relationship to self and object. These are issues of both a quantitative distribution of libido and a qualitative factor. To conceive of love as a static affective state is contrary to empirical evidence. Love is subject to development, parallel with psychosexual development; it implies the qualities of empathy and identification, and the nature of the object relationship. Thus, within this conceptual framework, narcissism, though presented in energic terms, is primarily defined by the quality of libidinal investment in the self and in the object (Freud, 1914b, 1923). Freud's ideas regarding qualitative and quantitative considerations had been outlined in his distinction between primary and secondary narcissism (1914b), and in previous references to qualitative and quantitative factors in the Project (1950 [1895]).

Regarding autoeroticism, we are faced with the same issue of a phase of development that Freud (1914b) indicated was objectless. Since our textual readings of Freud have shown that he considered that object relations and object choice occur very early in psychic development, how are we to understand this meaning of autoerotism? I can only assume that from the perspective of a direct sexual gratification, the infant due to his/her motoric and cognitive development developed the capacity to self-gratify. This was thus, the origin of the first masturbatory acts that became fully integrated in the later genital phase. Masturbatory acts or self-gratification do not, ipso facto, require an external object; the internal object representation remains in a quiescent, minimally cathected, libidinal state.

In my attempt to unify Freud's theories, it is not possible, as I have previously indicated, to absolve him from leaving an inheritance of contradictions. Freud did state that it was at the oedipal phase that object choice was established. I propose that Freud was focusing on the various qualities of the internalized object according to different drive states i.e., oral, anal, and phallic/genital, that also, reflected successive maturational phases. I further suggest that he was concerned with the characteristics of specific periods imprinted by zonal phases that give definition to the nature and character of the ego and the internalized object representation. Thus, when he was discussing object choice at the oedipal phase, he was essentially referring to the gender of the oedipal object and not the qualitative, emotional connection to the object. Given the history of his writings on love and identification, it is my contention that he was attempting to establish a developmental and hierarchical sequence involved in object choice. Thus, object choice at the oedipal phase was concerned with the specific gender of the object, and the sexual identification of the subject.

From the full canon of Freud's writings, the evidence does not substantiate the claim that object choice was established only at the oedipal phase. And yet, it is not possible to avoid the many contradictory statements regarding the development and timing of internalization, objects relationships, and object choice in Freud's writings. Perhaps, we can conclude that various concepts were approached in isolation from other concepts, and only by a reading of the total oeuvre can we ascertain Freud's fundamental beliefs. Laplanche (1970) has stated the nature of Freud's contradictory concepts as part of a dialectic process ". . . entailing an evolution through reversals and crises, mediated by contradictions whose status will not be immediately apparent in any attempt to situate them. Even if, in an interpretive stage, all the contradictions in Freud's thought are perhaps not amenable to the same treatment, not attributable to the same "mechanism" or "agency," they are all initially deserving of the same "free floating" attention. No doubt, in practice, certain contradictions may prove to be relatively "extrinsic" or adventitious, the results of polemic or of hasty formulation: but even in such cases, they cannot be discarded without a certain loss. . . . But it is above all certain large contradictions, traversing Freud's work from one end to the other, which must be interpreted dialectically, either as contradictions of thought—consequently referable to a certain "unspoken" dimension—or as contradictions of the object itself. . . . " (p. 1) Thus, it is apparent that the contradictions in Freud's writings belong to an ongoing process of hypothesizes, reevaluation, interpolated through clinical phenomena, each interacting in an evolutionary exegesis.

FREUD'S CASE STUDIES

Freud's case studies present clear evidence that human relationships were crucial to understanding the neurosis. Beginning with the last of his comprehensive case studies, the "Wolf Man" (1918 [1914]), we observe that the treatment dealt with the Wolf Man's problematic relationships with his nursemaid Nanya, his father, and sister Katherine. Freud noted the specific consequences of maturational development and object conflicts, which resulted in the Wolf Man's infantile phobia, and the later obsessive neurosis. He indicated that the "infantile experiences are by themselves in a position to produce a neurosis." (p. 54) In this study, we again encounter several of Freud's concepts that leave us questioning how he understood his various usages of object, and his time sequencing of object presentation, object choice, identificatory object, and sexual object. For example, Freud stated that in the Wolf Man's disappointment by the nursemaid Nanya, "his libidinal expectation detached itself from her and began to contemplate another person as a sexual object. This person was his father; ..." and he was "in this way able to renew his first and most primitive object-choice which, in conformity with a small child's narcissism, had taken place along the path of identification." Further, Freud indicated that "His father was now his object once more; in conformity with his higher stage of development, identification was replaced by object-choice...." (p. 27)

We can observe from the above statements that Freud regarded object choice as intrinsic to conditions between object relations and drive interaction at each developmental stage, beginning with the earliest and most primitive phase, the oral, then anal, and later at the oedipal phase. Further, identification that occurs through libidinal interaction with the object would appear to precede object-choice. Yet, Freud (1918 [1914],1930 [1929]) also, indicated that identification takes place along the path laid down by object-choice. These statements would appear to show that the "object" and the "sexual object" are interchangeable in meaning, and are only differentiated by specific aims, functions, and referent, at various developmental phases. Since object-choice, as I have indicated, is another concept that created some conceptual confusion, we can also, observe from the pithy quotation above, that the same object- choice is modified by need and purpose at various maturational stages, and that qualitative factors, influenced by drive motivation (Rapaport, 1951), define and differentiate the earlier from the later object–choice.

In the case of Dora, (1905 [1901]), Freud indicated that:

It follows from the nature of facts, which form the material of psychoanalysis that we are obliged to pay as much attention in our case histories to the purely human and social circumstances of our patients as to the somatic data and the symptoms of the disorder. Above all, our interest will be directed towards their family circumstances—and not only, as will be seen later, for the purpose of inquiring into their heredity [p.18].

In "Little Hans" (1909a) and the "Rat Man" (1909b [1907]) the central conflict involved a decidedly ambivalent relationship to the parental objects. Little Hans was torn between passion of love for both parents, and the conflict of ambivalence inherent in the identification with his rival, the oedipal father. Freud also attributed to the "Rat Man's" emotional paralysis his inability to resolve his love-hate relationship with his father and his "lady".

Again, focusing on causative factors in a dyadic relationship in a paper on the "Psychogenesis of a Cause of Homosexuality in a Woman" (1920b), Freud commented on the nature of the narcissism in the patient's mother and its destructive influence on the patient's development. He referred to the mother's rejection of the patient, her rivalry and her preference for her sons. Freud noted the father's failure to protect the patient from the mother's willful behavior. Perhaps, in no other case has Freud so decidedly pointed to the behavior of the mother as a causative factor in the etiology of neurosis.

GENERAL WRITINGS: REFERENCE TO EGO/ SELF, IDENTIFICATION AND INTERNALIZATION

Freud's major sociological treatises, *Totem and Taboo* (1913–1913), "Group Psychology" (1921), "The Future of an Illusion" (1927), and "Civilization and Its Discontents" (1930 [1929]), are replete with references to the role of the object as central to man's emotional and social development. His concepts regarding identification, internalization, and incorporation derive from drive investment in objects, a process that has its inception from birth. The nature of empathy, a factor derived from identification, is indicative of the mutual relation between the object and the ego (1921, p. 110). In *Totem And Taboo* (1913), Freud stated that the "root of religion is the longing for the father (p. 148), and he viewed "neurosis" as asocial structures. He further commented that "to turn away from reality is to turn away from the community of man" (p. 148). In "Group Psychology" (1921), Freud indicated that "identification is known to psychoanalysis as the earliest expression of an emotional tie with another person" (p. 105), and he stressed that in the individual's mental life "someone else is invariably involved, as a model, as an object, as a helper, and as an opponent; and so from the very first, individual psychology is, at the same time, social psychology" (p. 69).

The papers on "Narcissism" (1914b), "Instincts and their Vicissitudes" (1915), and "Mourning and Melancholia" (1917a [1915]) were more directly focused on the specific role of object, self, and ego-ideal than was evidenced in his previous writings. The interdependence of love and identification, and the nature of ambivalence to the object led Freud to consider a more detailed concept of the self and the object relationship. We observe in these papers an increased concern with the development of the self-structure and the role of internalization. Where formerly, these concepts were stated in rather broad outline, Freud increasingly refined the dynamic process whereby libido invested in self and in object resulted in psychic structure. Identification as both a process and a defense mechanism (1905a [1901]), 1917 [1915]) foreshadowed his seminal paper on "The Ego and the Id" (1923). Freud gave equal weight to the qualitative relationship of self and object as he did to the role of instinctual vicissitudes as the basis of psychic structure, see "Introductory Lectures on Psychoanalysis" (1916–1917 [1915–1917]).

The ego as a specific agency of the mind had been for Freud a self-evident postulate (1895,1900). But, increasingly in his writings, the gradations in ego functions led to the structural theory. Freud (1915) stated that as objects present themselves as sources of pleasure, they are taken into the ego— they are "introjected," but when they become sources of unpleasure they are "expelled". Further, he stated, "in so far as the ego is auto-erotic, it has no need of the external world, but, as a consequence of experience undergone by the instinct of self-preservation, it acquires objects from the world" (p.135). The object is acquired in the stage of "primary narcissism," and the object cathexis is established from the experiences of satisfaction in the dyadic relationship.

The paper on "Mourning and Melancholia" (1912a [1915]) elaborated on the mechanism of introjection, albeit the focus was on the pathological aspects. Yet, of the three meta psychological papers (1914b,1915,1917a) this was the most central to his development of the structural theory, and it is in this paper that the concept of the ego as a precipitate of abandoned object cathexes was most clearly formulated. I believe that in this paper, Freud began to recognize that the entire process of internalization required further exploration and defining. In his earlier paper "On Narcissism" (1914b), Freud had also been interested in the interaction between the ego or self (these were used interchangeably) and object, but the focus was on the energic distributions of libido between the ego and the object. The specific quality of the object, the relationship between identification and object love, and the differentiation between the two were not dealt with until "Group Psychology and the Analysis of the Ego" (1921) and "The Ego and the Id" (1923). Even here, as I shall discuss later, this was left somewhat ambiguous. Yet, as I previously indicated, in "Mourning and Melancholia", (1917a [1915]) he had already begun consideration of the relationship between the ego and the object, and the role of identification as "a preliminary stage of object choice" (p. 249). He then proceeded to elaborate on pathological states where the object either for external reasons or compelling internal conflicts was abandoned. He noted that the "shadow of the object" falls upon the ego and "if the love for the object cannot be relinquished though the object itself is given up then this love takes refuge in "narcissistic identification" (p. 251). He also indicated that the Melancholic's erotic cathexis regarding his object has undergone a double vicissitude; part of it has regressed to identification, but, the other part, under the influence of the conflict due to ambivalence, has been carried back to the stage of sadism that is nearer to the conflict (pp. 251–252).

The concept of identification as a defense appears as a new thought, though there is historical precedence in the Dora case (1905a [1901]). Perhaps, the most crucial element in this paper was the recognition of how a hated object is internalized and incorporated into the patient's ego. Freud emphasized the dominance of the object in human development, and the ego's inability to flourish without objects, even a hated one. The self-attacks in melancholia are essentially attacks against the hated object. The character of the incorporated object and the self-subject are further defined by psychosexual developmental stages. This interpolation of drive and object qualifies and deepens the nature of the object in psychic life.

This paper represented a major theoretical advance in Freud's writings, for attention was now shifted to the specific processes of internalization within the ego and a somewhat different structural relationship to the ego ideal. Prior to this, the ego and the ego instincts were not the primary focus of Freud's work. Freud regarded the duality of the instincts, that is, the conflict between the ego instincts and the sexual instinct and the resultant defense mechanisms as the essential component for the development of the "nervous system, the mental structure, and even social organization."

It was inevitable that in the evolution of Freud's theories, based as they were on clinical data, that he would be confronted with the evolving role of the object in the formation of ego structure. As Freud developed his theories on psychic structure, the role of the object based on clinical findings became more integrated into his structural conceptualization.

The evolution of Freud's theoretical data on the ego, the ego ideal, and structural consideration culminated in "The Ego and the Id" (1923). The first object cathexes that form the ego are the very same objects that also structure the superego. Freud (1923) posited that both agencies are constructed on the basis of the identifications "made in the earliest childhood" (p. 31), and from the abandoned object cathexis. He further added, "this is not in the first instance the consequence or outcome of an object cathexis; it is a direct and immediate identification and takes place earlier than the object cathexis" (p. 31). Future object choices particularly those belonging to the "first sexual period" and those early relationships to the "father and the mother seem normally to find their outcome in an identification of this kind and reinforce the primary one" (p. 31). Clearly, the superego has a very early inception for it derives from the "first choices of the id" (p. 46). Indeed, Freud indicated that it is the superego that lends its hand to the suppression of the oedipus complex. The superego is not only structured by the first objects of identification but is later modified by the identificatory object of the oedipus complex. Unfortunately, Freud did not elaborate on the quality of the introjected object, and the effect that disparate, contradictory object identifications have on the quality of psychic structure, nor did he sufficiently differentiate the object of identification from current object cathexes that do not involve internalization. Nevertheless, there can be no question that he clearly recognized the implication of varying identifications and object cathexes in symptom formation and pathological development. Further, the structure of the psychic apparatus was not simply a direct derivative of the internalized objects. In discussion on the superego formation, he indicated that the superego was not only a "residue of the earliest object choices of the id, it represented an energetic reaction formation against these choices" (p. 39). According to my understanding from these readings, the external object is always to some degree, modified, contaminated, or restructured by some internal force, and that force is a derivative of drives. The internalized object is an object that does not simply replicate the external object but that the object representation undergoes some qualitative change in the internalized representation.

In the above discussion, I have attempted to follow the theoretical process by which Freud was led to his concepts of the tripartite structure of the mind. Internalization of objects was primary to the creation of psychic structure; a discrete body of mental functions comprised of self and assimilated object representations. The self is a composite of internalizations interfused with drive demands evolving in accordance with psychosexual phases—a substrate of biology and psychology. Freud's meta psychological schema reflected an uncompromising recognition of the nature and role of the object in mental development. The idea of "abandoned object cathexis," while suggestive of relinquishment of the object refers only to that process by which the object is internalized and assimilated within the ego, i.e., self and object representations. Even the Id, the "water shed of the drives," is considered by Freud as a phylogenetic repository of man's personal and social history, the values, idealizations, and characteristics of civilization. It is not possible to address issues of ego and superego pathology or normality without understanding the way in which object relations have affected these structures, in particular the demands and requirements of the family—the parental objects, the libidinal and aggressive desire toward these objects, and the reaction formations against those objects of identifications (1923). The interaction between drive and object—between object and structure and drive is evidenced in all of Freud's thinking.

CONCLUSION

I have tried to present in this review of Freud's thinking an accurate picture of the role of the object, and to refute the idea that he relegated the object to the realm of lesser importance. The object from his initial work was unquestionably the primary source of internalization, identification, and representation. By hypothesizing a phylogenetic origin to the id and superego, Freud further acknowledged the object's role as a historical antecedent of psychological structure. The concepts of incorporation, internalization, introjections, and identification derive from his theoretical postulates and clinical pursuits. Though the vicissitudes of the internalized object representations were not a central focus in his writings, Freud certainly pioneered this study. That Freud regarded the instincts as the primary motivating force in mental development in no way lessens the role of the object as a concurrent force. The interdependent role of both drive and object is at the essence of Freud's metapsychology.

The failure of the early object theorists (Fairbairn, 1952c [1944] 1952d, [1946]), Balint, 1952 [1937], and Guntrip, 1961) to recognize Freud as their most significant predecessor, or in so-minimizing his contribution to theories of object relations and the primacy of the object in psychic structure, has provided a baseline for the extinction of drive theory in clinical work. Therefore, the elimination of the interaction between drive and object has resulted in a restructured theory of psychic development. The emphasis has shifted to the manifest experience with the object and undervalues the impact of drives, defense, ego structure, and most importantly, the dynamic unconscious (Glover, 1929, Shapiro, 1990) as the major source of both psychic development and psychic conflict.

REFERENCES

Balint, M. (1952 [1937]). "Early Developmental States of the Ego: Primary Object-Love." In *Primary Love and Psycho-Analytic Technique*, 90–108. London: Tavistock Publications.

Breuer, J & Freud, S. (1893–1895) "Studies On Hysteria." *Standard Edition,* 2.

Compton, A. (1983b). "The Current State of the Psychoanalytic Theory of Instinctual drives, I: Drive concept, clarification, and development." *Psychoanalytic Quarterly*, 52:64–401.

_____ (1985). "The Development of the Drive Concept in Freud's Work:1905–1915." *Journal of American Psychoanalytic Association*, 33:93–115.

_____ (1986.) "Freud: Objects and Structure." *Journal of American Psychoanalytic Association*, 34:561–590.

Fairbairn, W.R. (1952c (1944]). "Endopsychic Structure Considered in Terms of Object-Relationships." In *Psychoanalytic Studies of the Personality*, 82–136. London: Henley, and Boston Routledge & Kegan Paul.

_____ (1952d [1946]). "Object-Relationships and Dynamic Structure." In *Psychoanalytic Studies of the Personality,*137–151. London: Henley and Boston: Routledge & Kegan Paul.

Freud, S. (1895). "A Reply To Criticisms of my Paper on Anxiety Neurosis." *Standard Edition,* 3.

_____ (1905a. [1901]). "Fragment of an Analysis of a Case of Hysteria." *Standard Edition,* 7.

_____ (1905b). "Three Essays On The Theory Of Sexuality." *Standard Edition*, 7.

_____ (1909a). "Analysis of a Phobia in a Five-Year-Old Boy". Postscript (1922). *Standard Edition*, 10.

_____. (1909b). "Notes Upon a Case of Obsessional Neurosis." *Standard Edition*, 10.

_____. (1910). "A Special Type of Choice of Object made by Men (Contributions to the Psychology of Love, I)." *Standard Edition*, 11.

_____. (1912a). "The Dynamics of Transference." *Standard Edition*, 12.

_____ (1913). "Totem and Taboo." [1912–13]. *Standard Edition*, 13.

_____ (1914a). "Remembering, Repeating and Working-Through (Further Recommendations on the Technique of Psycho-Analysis, II)." *Standard Edition*, 12.

_____ (1914b). "On Narcissism: An Introduction." *Standard Edition*, 14.

_____ (1915). "Instincts and their Vicissitudes *Standard Edition*, 14.

_____ (1916). "Some Thoughts on Development and Regression-Aetiology." *Standard Edition*, 16.

_____ (1917a [1915]). "Mourning and Melancholia." *Standard Edition*, 15.

_____ (1917b [1916]). "Introductory Lectures On Psychoanalysis." *Standard Edition*, 16.

_____ (1918 [1914]). "From the History of an Infantile Neurosis." *Standard Edition*, 17.

_____ (1920a). "Beyond The Pleasure Principle." *Standard Edition*, 18.

_____ (1920b). "The Psychogenesis of a Case of Homosexuality in a Woman." *Standard Edition*, 18.

_____ (1921). "Group Psychology And The Analysis Of The Ego." *Standard Edition*, 18.

_____ (1923). "The Ego And The Id." *Standard Edition*, 19.

_____ (1926 [1925]). "Inhibitions, Symptoms And Anxiety." *Standard Edition*, 20.

_____ (1930 [1929]). "Civilization And Its Discontent." *Standard Edition,* 21.

_____ (1937). "Analysis Terminable and Interminable." *Standard Edition,* 23.

_____ (1940 [1938]). "Splitting of the Ego in the Process of Defense." *Standard Edition,* 23.

_____ (1950 [1895]). Project for a Scientific Psychology. *Standard Edition,* 1.

Glover, E. (1930). "Grades of Ego-Differentiation." *IJP* 11:1–11.

Green, A. (1999). *Chains of Eros: The Sexual in Psychoanalysis.* London: Unknown.

Greenberg, J.R. & Mitchell, S.A. (1983). *Object Relations in Psychoanalytic Theory.* Cambridge, MA/London, England: Harvard University Press.

Guntrip, H. (1961). "The Later Freudian Structural Theory and Analysis of the Ego." In *Personality Structure and Human Interaction,* 89–100. New York: International Universities Press, Inc.

Laplanche, J. (1976). *Life and Death in Psychoanalysis.* (J. Mehlman, Transl.) Baltimore, MD: John J Hopkins University Press. (Original French, 1970).

Rapaport, D. (1951). "The Conceptual Model of Psychoanalysis." In *The Collected Writings of David Rapaport,* edited by M. Gill. New York: Basic Books, Inc.

Shapiro, T. (1990). "Unconscious Fantasy: Introduction." *Journal of the American Psychoanalytic Association.* 38:36–46.

CHAPTER 6

BEYOND THE PLEASURE PRINCIPLE: A DILEMMA FOR PSYCHOANALYSIS

Freud's introduction of the Death Instinct in "Beyond The Pleasure Principle" (1920) presented a conundrum for psychoanalytic theory.[1] The Death Instinct and the Sexual Instinct—Eros and Thanatos—now stood as the two primary instincts in mental life. Further, Freud postulated that the death drive was the dominant instinctual force and that all instincts ultimately strive for death. Aggression that had been considered as a component of the self-preservative or sexual drive was now considered a component of the death drive, and was viewed as a force to undue life, to lead life back to its inorganic state, a state of constancy or Nirvana. It is only by turning the death drive outward that destruction of the object occurs, thus viewed as the aggressive drive.

Ackerman in a panel discussion on "Thanatos: Is Freud's Concept Still Relevant?" (2023) asks the question of

why Freud didn't pair Eros with pure, outward aggression. He will tell us that we never see the death instinct in its pure form and we mostly catch sight of it as it has been projected outward into aggression, so why did he need to dream up this instinct in this particular way in

---

1 Drive and Instinct have been used interchangeably in this paper. This is following Strachey's translation of Freud's use of Trieb.

which we have to rest on his assertion, because it is not outwardly observable? [p. 673].

That by reassigning aggression from a component of the self-preservative drive to a new drive state—a component of the Death Drive, Freud did not really clarify the nature of the Death Drive or aggression. In many ways, it made it easier for those who saw drives simply as complementary to mental functions and not inherent genetic-psychic processes, to eliminate drives from their theoretical constructs. Rizutto, et .al (1993, Anna Maria Rizutto, Jerome I Sashin, Dan H. Buie, W.W. Meissner) indicated that aggression is less

> of a biological force and becomes more of a psychological construct related to and reactive to specifiable stimulus conditions including the relationship with objects. The emphasis shifts from the biological determinants to the motivational, meaning-impregnated, and object-related context of aggressive action [p. 30].

Since the inception of psychoanalysis as a treatment methodology and a theoretical construct, the issue of drives has presented controversy. Freud (1910 [1909]), in his 1908 Clark lectures, was totally cognizant of this resistance to the concept of drives especially the sexual drive, and to psychoanalysis as a treatment methodology. Unfortunately, these issues continue to plague the field. In *Civilization and its Discontents* (1930), Freud indicated that "Of all the slowly developed parts of analytic theory, the theory of instincts is the one that has felt its way the most painfully forward." (p. 117). Kernberg (2009) pointed to the fact that general culture has always reacted negatively to Freud's drive theories especially his sexual drive. That "These perennial cultural reactions toward Freud's theories are mirrored within the psychoanalytic community proper.... Additionally, Freud's concept of the death drive has been questioned within American ego psychology, and the debate about whether aggression is a primary or a secondary response to trauma and frustration permeates the psychological field…" (p. 2). Kernberg, himself, raised questions about the existence of an independent death drive yet, he concluded that ". . . clinical experience accumulated, throughout time, on the basis of psychoanalytic practice has added new evidence in support of the prevalence of severely self-destructive psychopathological constellations, indirectly supporting the theory of a death drive." (p. 6). Though, in his book on *Borderline Conditions and Pathological Narcissism* (1975), he discussed the role of the "excessive nature of primary aggression or aggression secondary to frustration, to which certain deficiencies in the development of primary ego apparatuses and lack of tolerance of anxiety probably contribute." (p. 34). He further referred to "pregenital aggressive needs" (p. 35) therefore, focusing on the primacy of an aggressive instinct. We, thus, observe that an independent aggressive instinct would seem to be a dominant feature in his theoretical constructs.

Anthony Storr (2003) disagreed with Freud's conceptualization of a death drive. He indicated that it "runs counter to biological common sense to suppose that there is an inbuilt drive to bring life to an end. It is true that every living creature dies but this seems consequent upon wear and tear rather than any drive toward death." (p. 20). Aggression in his conceptualization is closer to Freud's first drive theories in that "it is closely linked with self-preservation, self-assertion, and self-affirmation and becomes converted into hatred when self-preservation is threatened or self-affirmation is denied." (p. 21).

Zurak & Klain (Psychomedia-home-page-Seminari,1998–1999), while giving credence to Freuds' death drive, raise some significant objections that could almost invalidate the theory. They laud Freud for his early connections between the biological and the psychological in human development, and indicated that:

Although the expectations and interpretation of Freud's idea pursued a psychological direction, emphasizing the clinical-psychological experience in the concept of genesis, the biological level was directly implicated by Freud himself, and that "with the discovery of the existence of programmed death at the cellular level, current molecular biology has provided strong evidence of support Freud's theory of Thanatos. Historically, it could be stated that the concept of Thanatos at the cellular level is the initial theoretical hypothesis anticipating the existence of programmed cell death. In molecular biology, cell death as a biological program has been recognized as a genetically encoded process which is both physiologic and active [p. 2].

Yet, as much as they have tried to show the connection between the death of cells and the ultimate biologic death of the individual with a similar psychological process in Thanatos, their discussion of sadism and masochism indicate a significant difference from Freud's concepts of masochism. They state that "There is a surprising readiness for masochistic behavior of the ego, seeking suffering and pain without any tactical purpose. The question is whether such behavioral patterns necessarily imply the existence of the death instinct?" Freud in his new theoretical construct, specifically indicated that the bedrock of the Death Drive was the complement of masochism. Thus masochism, in his 1920 paper *"Beyond the Pleasure Principle"* supplanted sadism as the primary derivative and expository of this drive. Therefore, to speak of masochism as a behavior pattern rather than a derivative instinct with a very distinct impulsive force contradicts Freud's very premise of the Death Drive.

In reviewing Freud's initial formal construction of instinct theory in the *Three Essays On Sexuality* (1905), we observe that no mention is made or even alluded to of a death instinct. He formulated his conceptualization of instincts as fundamentally consisting of two basic instincts: the Sexual and the Ego or Self-Preservative Instincts. Each contained a number of component instincts. Aggression, as stated in early Freud, was considered a component of the ego or self-preservative drive (1905,1910, 1915), and, also, a component of the sexual, or, as what he referred to as the libidinal drive. Aggression, especially in males, was noted as the desire to subjugate, to overcome "...the resistance of the sexual object by means other than the process of wooing. Thus, sadism would correspond to an aggressive component of the sexual instinct." (1905, pp.157–158). While masochism, according to Freud at this period in his theorizing, appeared further removed from the sexual aim than its "counterpart". He even doubted whether "...it can ever occur as a primary phenomenon or whether, on the contrary, it may not invariably arise from the transformation of sadism" (p. 158). Freud even considered that the aggressive element of the sexual instinct is "a relic of cannibalistic desires," thus, the aim is to achieve pleasure (1905, p. 159).

As I indicated that by1920 in *Beyond the Pleasure Principle*, Freud had radically changed drive theory. In introducing the Death Drive, a drive that he claimed had historical origins dating to prehistoric times, and expressing itself in the compulsion to repeat (p. 36). He stated:

It seems, then, that an instinct is an urge inherent in organic life to restore an earlier state of things which the living entity has been obliged to abandon under the pressure of external disturbing forces... or to put it another way, the expression of the inertia inherent in organic life [p. 36].

Instincts are now viewed as conservative—"tending to the restoration of an earlier state of things," (p. 37) rather than actively pushing upward to new experiences and new objects. Freud further indicated that while the "instincts of self-preservation, of self-assertion and mastery" appear to contradict this assertion of the Death Drive, these component instincts whose primary function is "to assure that the organism shall follow its own path to death, and to ward off any possible ways of returning to inorganic existence other than those which are immanent in the organism itself (p. 39). In essence "the aim of all life is death." (p. 38).

In consolidating ego libido and sexual libido into one theoretical concept, the Sexual Instinct was now viewed in opposition to the Death Instinct. In the1924 paper on "The Economic Problem of Masochism," he reversed the order of development of the component Instincts, masochism and sadism. Previously, sadism appeared as the primary component instinct; now masochism was viewed as primary and fundamental to the functioning of the organism and genetic structure. Masochism functioned often silently within the organism, while sadism resulted concomitantly (1914,1917 [1915], 1930 [1929]) from the force of the life or sexual drive, a means to divert destructive forces outward towards the object. A fusion of the two— masochism and sadism—indicated their mutual interaction. Aggression that had originally been considered as resulting from frustrations of the sexual drive, now assumed the attributes of the death drive, that is, turned outward to an extraneous object rather than destroying the subject. It is to be noted that in this paper, Freud frequently refers to aggression, sadism, and masochism as instincts, thus creating a sense of unclarity as to the primary instinct and the component instinct.

In *Civilization And Its Discontents* (1930), he again refers to aggression as an instinct in his statement that "Civilization has to use its utmost efforts in order to set limits to man's aggressive instincts and to hold the manifestations of them in check by psychical reaction formation." (p. 112).

He refers to aggression as the "indestructible feature of human nature…" (p. 114), and suggests that the "…inclination to aggression is an original self-subsisting instinctual disposition in man." (p. 122). And yet, Freud is not ready to declare aggression as a separate instinct removed from the

Death Instinct. He will state that aggression represents an aspect of the death instinct that when turned toward the outside world ". . . comes to light as an instinct of aggressiveness and destructiveness" (p. 119). Further, he gives recognition to the facts that ". . . in sadism and masochism we have always seen before us manifestations of the destructive instinct (directed outwards or inwards), strongly alloyed with erotism; but I can no longer understand how we can have overlooked the ubiquity of non-erotic aggressivity and destructiveness and have failed to give it its due place in our interpretation of life." But recall while he views aggression as ". . . an original self-subsisting instinctual disposition in man," it is fundamentally "the derivative and main representative of the death instinct." (pp. 119–120).

Melanie Klein (1946, 1948, 1963) integrated the death instinct in her theoretical postulates, and this permeated much of her later conceptualizations. The paranoid position, the aggression to the mother and projective identification (an important contribution to defense mechanisms) all derive from the death drive. In many ways her emphases on the Death Drive exceeded Freud. Though, interestingly, she does not deal with the Nirvana principle that underlies Freud's concerns with homeostasis.

It is noteworthy that Anna Freud (1939–1945), in her notes on child development and behavior at Hampstead Clinic, does not refer to the Death Instinct in her discussion of the children but rather refers to the instincts as the sexual and the aggressive instincts. In relation to self-destructive behavior such as head-knocking, "the child enacts on his own body his own aggressive and destructive tendencies." (p. 611). In other writings (1922–1935, 1936) she does not mention Freud's Death Drive, and primarily suggests aggression as an instinct in the child. "The child destroys objects because the actual value of such things is negligible compared with the joy he experiences in their destruction." (Vol. 1, p. 100), and the sense of pleasure that the child experiences in torturing animals is paramount in his behavior. In most of her writings she refers to the sexual and aggressive wishes (more literally defined as instincts). Thus, aggression appears as a primary instinct and not a component of the Death Drive, and death wishes to self and object reflect aggression against the object or self, due to frustration, anger, and/or guilt.

Fenichel (1953) found the Death Drive difficult to incorporate into analytic theory, therefore preferring the concept of an aggressive drive or a one-drive model that modulates and evolves into different behaviors depending on external and internal forces. He stated, "There are many possible objections to this new theory. . . . The instinctual aim of destruction is the opposite of the sexual search for an object to be loved . . . Questionable, however, is this antithesis. Are we dealing with basically different instinctual qualities or is this contrast again a matter of differentiation of an originally common root? The latter seems more probable. One could group all the phenomena collected under the heading of the death instinct not as a special type of instinct but expressions of a *principle*, valid for all instincts; in the course of development this principle might have been modified for certain instincts by external influence." (p. 59).

Though Fenichel (1953) gives due consideration to the existence and importance of aggressive drives, he indicated that

> There is no proof that they always and necessarily came into being by a turning outward of more primary self-destructive drives. It seems rather as if aggressiveness has originally no instinctual aim of its own, characterizing one category of instincts in contradistinction to others, but rather a mode in which instinctual aims are sometimes striven for, in response to frustrations or even spontaneously. [p. 59].

He further indicated, "aims are more destructive the more primitive the organism due to the insufficiently developed tolerance toward tensions. The archaic instinctual aim toward objects is incorporation—an attempt to achieve closeness as well as to destroy the object." (p. 59–60). Thus, he viewed

Freud's Nirvana and constancy principles equally applicable to the function of both modes of instincts. He saw neither a theoretical nor clinical reason for the development of a separate death instinct.

Fenichel's proposal to view the death drive as a principle of mental function similar to the functions of the pleasure-unpleasure, and constancy principles is an interesting theoretical concept. Viewing the death drive as a principle rather than an instinct would best describe the functions of somatic forces—that of, living and dying—as a mode by which biological or basically genetic structures thrive and decline rather than as a force of instinct with more specific inherent functional qualities. I raise the question as a conundrum for psychoanalytic theory as the death drive would appear closer to organic principles regulating genetic and organ functions rather than an interaction of two drive states with rather specific purposeful quantitative and qualitative properties interacting in the psyche (the mental and the soma).

Ricoeur (1970), in *Freud, Philosophy: An Essay on Interpretation*, has also provided a poignant and clarifying exegeses on Freud's postulate of his second drive theory, the death instinct. Ricoeur raised the issue that "The new instinct theory questions the initial Freudian hypotheses and especially the conception of a psychical apparatus subject to the constancy principle." Ricoeur felt that the "principle of constancy, conceived as the self-regulation of a psychical system, will outlast its expression in terms of neurons: for a long time; the reality principle will be looked upon as a complication and a detour; in the face of death, life will present itself as Eros." (p. 86). What now is the relationship or polarity between the pleasure principle and the reality principle? (p. 255). Does the new principle, i.e., the death instinct, thus, displace the reality principle? Further, if according to Freud "every instinct is in every instance satisfaction, which can only be attained by removing the stimulus at the source of the instinct," how does the pleasure principle, the reality principle and the principle of constancy equate with both the life and death instinct? Essentially, according to Ricoeur, the death instinct has invaded and superseded the life instinct. If the ultimate aim of the death instinct is to reduce all instincts to its basic inorganic state. In Freud's view, according to Ricoeur, "…death is the aim of life, all life's organic developments are but detours toward death, and the so-called conservative instincts are but the organism's attempt to defend its own fashion of dying its particular path to death." (p. 290). Thus, "Freud does not look for the drive for life in some will to live inscribed in each living substance by itself; he finds only death." (p. 291).

At this juncture in our discussion of the death drive, it would be useful to introduce certain concepts from the field of neuroscience regarding a death drive, or perhaps more applicable the concept of a death principle. The neuroscientist Rabeyron (2021) has attempted to show the role of neurological functions in psychic structures, and has pointed to similar developmental concepts between the cellular and the psychic mind. He references the body "as first and foremost an inorganic composite from which living cells emerge." (p. 879). This is followed by the question regarding the origins of psychic life— "is the psychical apparatus influenced by certain principles arising from the elementary properties of matter?" Can the knowledge of the two basic principles of human life, free energy and entropy—in particular, the knowledge of free energy—prove useful for describing psychic functioning? He claims that the notion of free energy enables us to describe "certain elementary principles that organize psychic life" and that a "knowledge of these energetic logics of the psychical apparatus further the intelligibility of certain psychopathological manifestations, even the analytic process itself." Free energy is delineated as an "aspect of thermodynamics—energy that is available to preform thermodynamic work." (p. 879). It is this underlying energy that generates into organized models of ideation. The failure to adequately structure free energy into sufficient generative models results in entropy. Thus, entropy physically results in bodily and genetic disorganization and decline that may be viewed as physical death. Psychically, a similar pattern is observed in that mental structures become disordered by an excessive amount of free energy. Internal chaos, randomness, lack of predictability, disorganization and a gradual decline into disorder are usual systemic results of the failure of free energy to develop a "generative model in a predominant way". (p. 880).

These concepts of free energy and entropy bear a close resemblance to Freud's theoretical postulates of bound and unbound energy, and his conceptualization of a Death Drive. (Vol.1, 2, 14, 20, 21, 22, 23). The death drive for Freud represents the degeneration of the psychic system, a return to its original homeostatic state, that of inertia and thus death—a similar process for the physical process in entropic disorganization. Psychic binding of the drives parallels the physical organization of binding in free energy processes. What is most interesting is that in discussing the parallel development between psychoanalytic theory of the drives and the neuroscience energic system, Rabeyron (2021) questioned whether we should consider entropy—the death drive—as an instinct, or, more appropriately, as a principle (of genetic or mental functions)? In referring to the writings of Bernfield and Feitelberg (1931) he quotes them as indicating that "the death instinct is something 'other' than the instinct of destruction," and explains quite rightly "that we should be wise not to employ the term 'instinct' to describe this general behavior of systems. Thus, what Freud describes with the death instinct (or drive) is in fact the expression of a principle situated prior to the dynamics of the instinctual drive" (p. 885).

That the question of a death drive is raised regarding whether to regard it as a principle or an instinct is relevant for psychoanalytic theory. Increasingly, I feel that an Aggressive Instinct (drive) rather than a Death Instinct is both clinically more descriptive and theoretically more correct in describing the destructive aspects of psychic functioning. An Aggressive Instinct paralleled with a Libidinal Instinct would provide psychoanalysis with a more coherent theoretical and clinical structure.

To continue the investigation regarding the validity of a death instinct, despite valid doubts, we may contemplate a fundamental issue as to how the death drive as formulated by Freud may be dealt with and verbally formulated in the treatment? In what manner can the death drive be modified in the treatment situation? What form would our interpretations take? Can psychoanalysis reduce the impact of the death drive so that it does not result in internal self-destruction or object destruction? Freud applied the concept of sublimation to the sexual drive—a defense mechanism—but is this defense mechanism also applicable to the destructive—the death-drive? Can we assume that some fusion between the life and death drive will contain the force of the destructive components in the death drive?

Freud had indicated in his early papers on Technique (1911–1915, [1914]) that the aim of treatment is to resolve the transference neurosis and the resistance, and posited that neurotic conflict (1912a, 1912b) resulted essentially from a basic inhibition and regression of libido. He outlined four different though related causes that give rise to neurotic conflict. The first and "most obvious" (1912b, p. 231) resulted from frustration in the external world, the failure to be satisfied, to receive the love desired from the "real object." This frustration has a "pathogenic effect" and it leads to a damming up of libido that increases psychic tension. The second factor that can result in neurosis is the person's inability to secure satisfaction in the external world due to internal issues, the incapacity to find the gratifications that exists in the external world, the failure to adapt to reality. The third factor that is very similar to the second, results from "an inhibition in development—falling ill from the demands of reality." Essentially, the individual's libido has remained fixated to infantile developmental stages. The fourth factor relates to quantity of libido that is not sublimated or encounters external frustrations that cannot be adapted to. The unsatisfied and dammed-up libido "can open paths to regression and kindle the same conflicts" that were encountered in the case of "absolute external frustration." (1912b, p. 236). We observe that the sexual drive was primarily the culprit in the neurotic constellation. In the 1920 paper, he indicated, that though the conflict between the "ego instincts and sexual instincts continued, they basically melded into one instinct" and "emerged in some *qualitative* manner that must now be characterized differently, namely as being *topographical*." Differences lay in the individual's ability to master the demands of libido, i.e., the ego's capacity to deal with reality, to both gratify the sexual drive and to also adhere to the exigencies of the external world. Further, the role of the reality principle that Freud indicated as a necessary development from the self-preservative or life instincts becomes an imperative for psychic maturity and ego integration.

Thus, in reexamining the Death Drive as a separate drive state, numerous questions may arise. How, one may ask, does the Death Drive impact on psychic conflicts and psychic functions? Does the Death Drive interfere with the resolution of the transference and the resistance? In *Beyond The Pleasure Principle* (1920) Freud suggested that the introduction of the Death Drive posed a conundrum for our treatment methodology. In *Analysis Terminal and Interminable* (1937), he presented several obstacles to psychoanalytic cure or significant improvement. He indicated that the strength of the drives, their resistance "to the taming of the ego," led to difficulties and even failure in the treatment. An unfavorable alteration in the ego acquired in its defensive struggle in the sense of its being dislocated and restricted (p. 220–221) also impacted upon the success of the treatment. These factors are major issues in the interminability of the treatment and to its failure. Do these factors reflect the silent operation of the Death Drive? Do they impact the resolution of the transference and the resistance? Further, how to psychically interpolate in the treatment the desire to achieve a state of Nirvana and to reestablish the basic inorganic state?

And yet, perhaps, would a more accurate explanation as to one of the primary bases for psychic conflict, and the failure of treatment reflect the role of aggression as a drive whose quantitative and qualitative factors interfere with the development of the reality principle, and a more stable based ego structure. Further, difficulties in the failure to fuse aggression sufficiently with libido could also account for neurotic conflict and behavior. Thus, aggression toward the object would increase guilt, superego attacks, and fear of object loss.

To raise the issue of an aggressive drive also, receives some reinforced from the work of the geneticist, Dawkins (1976) who in his book *The Selfish Gene* posited a genetic principle that appears to support the role of the aggressive instincts. The selfish gene fights for survival with all other genes indicating that the winner, the survivor, must utilize aggression as a means of furthering the life force, its inherent sexuality, in order to survive and defeat the other genes. This would perhaps provide an explanation with greater clarity for destructive behavior expressed either externally or internally, that is psychical and biologic. Therefore, to place aggression as a component of the death drive increasingly appears contradictory to the constructs of neuroscience and clinical psychoanalytic theory. The death drive is more reflective of the principles of an entropic disorder and the breaking down of biological systems than the function and behavior of an "aggressive instinct."

A THEORETICAL CASE DISCOURSE REGARDING THE DEATH DRIVE

The patient, now in her sixties, entered treatment over twenty-five years ago. An attempt at psychoanalytic treatment was made but soon collapsed after the third session when she got up from the couch and indicated that she needed to see me. It became evident that essentially a supportive approach was the most efficacious treatment method. Though psychoanalytic concepts were given, these played primarily an intellectual role that strengthened sublimated thought processes but did not sufficiently modify her id, ego, and superego structures nor the intensity of her drive states, particularly the aggressive drive. Her sessions were essentially emotive, a means of discharge for both conscious and unconscious affects that represented displacements and conscious negation of wishes and drives. This mode of speech and representation continues though it is somewhat easier to touch upon the underlying conflicts and desires.

In this case discussion, I will discuss, along with the primary conflictual wishes, the force of her instincts, and the nature of her infantile psychic structure, a possible role played by a Death Drive that led to a "negative therapeutic reaction," and the failure of psychoanalytic psychodynamic therapy.

There was a marked failure developmentally in this patient to establish the consistency of the reality principle in her object relationships, and to resist the excessive demands of the pleasure principle. The inconsistent hold on reality, despite a superficial surface picture that could approximate sound judgment indicated the underlying organization of a powerful narcissistic self-investment. That there also existed a sense of reality does not mitigate the strength of the pleasure principle but points to what Freud (1923) referred to as a primary recognition of the external object, a need-gratifying object. For this patient the internal object's proclaimed role, aside from recognizing the objective world, was to essentially gratify—to ensure the dominance of the pleasure principle. Fear of loss of the object and superego attacks for her rage reactions led to withdrawal, and the defenses of displacement and projection.

Further, the patient's primary and secondary narcissism parallels Freud's (1914) conceptualization of the early relationship between the id and the ego ideal—a pre-oedipal constellation. This fixated and regressive constellation lessened the operative functions of a more mature ego and benign superego development. Thus, the establishment of her ego ideal as closer to id functions, the early incorporative mode of oral identifications and omnipotence continues to characterize her ego and defensive organization.

Roussillon (2010), who was influenced by Winnicott's theories, added an important concept to the theories on narcissism and the first years of life. He indicated that when the infant first sees the mother, he sees not only her face but her entire body and behavior, thus an early imprimatur is made. A mirror reflection of the mother is made, that is her face, is established when she is "sufficiently malleable and sensitive towards the infant's needs." This has the effect of producing a "narcissistic double to the self—and also 'an other.'" (p. 830). Yet, since a double, according to Roussillon (2010), can never be simply the same, the mother must also become a different object. The double is, therefore, the same and simultaneously somewhat separate. This concept of the double is an important addition to psychoanalytic theory for it adds to our comprehension of narcissistic states, and patients' needs to see their reflection in the object. It is quite evident that my patient is constantly searching for her double. This emerges frequently in the transference as she echoes my exact words or requires me to echo her words or her affects.

The patient's identifications further reflected a pre-oedipal self-organization in that there was an equal valence between the feminine and the masculine. Consciously, she evidenced almost no conflict over her hetero and homosexual desires, and her homosexual fantasies did not appear to arouse unconscious conflicts, though currently there appears to be a lessening of homosexual desires. Freud in his *Introductory Lectures on Psychoanalysis* (1916–1917 [1916–17]) indicated that pre-oedipal sexual desires are not concerned with the "contrast between 'masculine' and 'feminine,' rather the polarity existed between active and passive aims." Perhaps, it is possible to consider that "passive aims" reflect the functioning of Freud's Death drive, the wish to reduce all tension, to achieve the state of Nirvana and homeostasis. This patient continually struggles with the wish to withdraw and not deal with the world. She is constantly searching for love and acceptance in order to ward off the danger of loss of the object. The seclusion from the world of objects represents a source of peace, an escape from her guilt and internal attacks by her ego ideal that create both a fear and wish for death. The repetition compulsion is evident in her psychic structure, and she continues to repeat similar patterns of relationship—intense love, over-giving and then rage at disappointments.

Though there is intellectual recognition that she feels guilty for her anger, her sense of neediness, and internal judgement that she is not a good enough mother, she is unable to access these feelings prior to an anxiety attack or some self-destructive behavior. The capacity for turning an emotion into a feeling state that reflects ideas or visual images (Demassio, 1989) is limited and meets with a good deal of resistance. Her speech in sessions is primarily a canopy of discharge, a recitation of every interaction and word that distresses her. Thus, we can observe the power of her need for discharge, repetition compulsion, homeostasis and the Nirvana principle. There is a great deal of resistance to understanding or abstracting the underlying ideations.

While there are many causes that prevent cure in this treatment, or more improvement, we will consider one aspect that emerges rather distinctly, i.e., the negative therapeutic reaction. There is a persistence in her rage reactions and in self-destructive behavior. Fighting with her children and siblings can easily occur, particularly when she feels uncared for, unloved, not respected, and neglected. It appears that when the external reality makes too many demands "the need for illness" gets the "upper hand" (Freud,1923). Freud felt that the negative therapeutic reaction was more powerful than "the familiar ones of narcissistic inaccessibility, a negative attitude toward the physician and clinging to a gain from illness" (p. 49).

While negative feelings toward the analyst exist, they are minor in comparison with the rage of her superego against her own ego, and the external objects that frustrate her. Her conflict between active and passive wishes and between the pleasure principle and the reality principle continues unabated. To be active is to be masculine; to wrest pleasure from the external world, while obeying the laws of the reality principle runs counter to her guiding pleasure principle that is passivity. Passivity is to be feminine and to be taken care of, to hold onto the need-gratifying object, the infantile mother; these are her dominant motifs. While she can intellectually comprehend the strength of her passive wishes and fears of object loss, the fixation to this infantile level of object relationship and ego organization appears almost unshakable.

I think it is important at this point to raise the issue of what is supportive treatment. Educative and supportive treatment were the primary methodologies utilized with this patient. Secondly, why has it not been more successful? Especially, in that currently, there is evidence of an exacerbation of her underlying disturbance due to increased conflicts with her siblings and her children. By supportive treatment, I refer to support of the ego against the id's demands for excessive gratification, and to help the ego develop more of an object relationship mode of relating rather than primarily an incorporative mode of object relationship. Support of a realistic superego that can help lessen the demands of an idealized superego and thus, reduce or change the structure of a primary narcissistic self, is an important goal. The analyst permits an incorporative mode in the therapeutic relationship by not challenging by even gentle questions or analyzing her mode of relating. There is a good deal of humor, some personal sharing, and exchange of opinions.

The question arises as to why now is this supportive and educational method not adequately succeeding? I will suggest that primarily, the quantitative factors of her aggression have not been sufficiently bound by the libidinal drive despite an essentially gratifying relationship with the analyst. Further, her narcissism while modified in some areas has increased in others by ingesting the idealized analyst. Yet, is it possible to conceive that we observe a subtle emergence of the Death Drive as a result of the pressures of external factors—realistic conflict with siblings over inheritance, and separation of her children, their marriage and children. That these current conflicts arouse her infantile conflicts and anxieties, the libidinal and aggressive wishes not sufficiently modified by a more mature ego suggest the wish to undo life and return to a state of Nirvana.

That I raise Freud's Death Drive as possibly operative in the failure to achieve success or even sufficient psychic change in the treatment is driven by the need to re-evaluate this theoretical precept within our theoretical and clinical constructs. Increasingly, I am convinced that the Death Drive is more of a biological principle than a mental construct or instinct that influences human mental functioning. Masochism, sadism, repetition compulsion, etc., are either drive derivatives, components or defenses that are inherent in psychic structures, and represent the internal organization of drives and character development.

Failure in this treatment may be best ascribed to the structure of the patient's character defenses, the failure to achieve meaningful separation from the infantile object, the strength of the aggressive drive turned inward and outward, the repetition compulsion, and the dominance of the pleasure principle. Further, as I evaluate all the factors, particularly the role of aggression and its relationship to self-preservation, I am more inclined to regard aggression as an independent drive, and to view death as a biological principle not an instinct.

I should further add that to address failure in the treatment is to view failure from the lens of a particular developmental schema. I am referring to the development of an independent ego, a capacity to maintain separation from the object, and simultaneously the capacity for mature object love: what I indicate as a bound libidinal organization. I am stressing the difference between supportive treatment that can last a multitude of years from a more defined psychoanalytic oriented treatment that maintains an object-subject separation between the patient and the analyst.

REFERENCES

Ackerman, S.& (Zavin, L., Hook. D., Lichtenstein, D.,& Goldblatt, M.) (2023). . Thanatos: Is Freud's Concept Still Relevant? *Journal of the American Psychoanalytic Association.* 71:669–702.

Bernfeld, S. & Feitelberg, S. (1931). The Principle of Entropy and the Death Instinct. *International Journal of Psychoanalysis* 12:61–81.

Damasio, A. (1994). *Decartes' Error: Emotion, Reason, and the Human Brain.* New York: Putnam

Dawkins, S. (2016). *The Selfish Gene.* Oxford: Oxford University Press.

Fenichel, O. (1953). *Collected Papers of Otto Fenichel. New York:* Norton.

Freud, A. (1976). *The Writings of Anna Freud. Volume 3, 1939–1945. Infants without Families; Reports on the Hampstead Nurseries.* International Universities Press, Inc. New York.

Freud, S. (1905). Three Essays on The theory of Sexuality. *Standard Edition* 7.

_____ (1910 [1909]). Five Lectures on Psychoanalysis. *Standard Edition* 11.

_____ (1911–1915 [1914]). Papers on Technique. *Standard Edition* 12.

_____ (1911). Formulations on the Two Principles of Mental Functioning. *Standard Edition* 12.

_____ (1914). On Narcissism: An Introduction. *Standard Edition* 14.

_____ (1917 [1915]). Mourning and Melancholia. *Standard Edition* 14.

_____ (1915). Instincts and their Vicissitudes. *Standard Edition* 14.

_____ (1920). Beyond the Pleasure Principle. *Standard Edition* 18.

_____ (1923). The Ego and the Id. *Standard Edition* 19.

_____ (1924). The Economic Problem of Masochism. *Standard Edition* 19.

_____ (1930 [1929]). Civilization and Its Discontents. *Standard Edition* 21.

_____ (1937). Analysis Terminable and Interminable. *Standard Edition* 23. London: Hogarth Press.

Kernberg, O. (2009). B*orderline Conditions and Pathological Narcissism.* Lanham, MD: Jason Aronson.

Klein, M. (1975 [1946–1963]). *Envy and Gratitude and Other Works.* New York: The Free Press, A Division of Macmillan, Inc.

Ricoeur, P. (1970). *Freud & Philosophy: An Essay on Interpretation.* New Haven & London: Yale University Press.

Rabeyron, T. (2021). Beyond the Death Drive: Entropy and Free Energy. *The International Journal of Psychoanalysis* 102:5.

Rizutto, A.M., Sashin, J. Buie, D.H., Meissner, W.W., (1998). A Revised Theory of Aggression. *Psychoanalytic Review* 80(1): 29–54.

Roussillon, R. (2010 [1991]). Working Through and Its Various Models. *International Journal of Psychoanalysis* 91:1405–1417.

Storr, A. (2003). *Human Destructiveness.* New York: Grove Weidenfeld.

Zurak, N. & Klain, E. (1999). The Concept of Programed Cell Death and Freud's Theory of Thanatos. *Neurologia Erotica Official Journal of Yugoslav Neurological Associat*ion 48(2):105–117.

PRACTICE

THE APPLICATION OF PSYCHOANALYTIC THEORY TO THE TREATMENT OF THE MENTALLY RETARDED CHILD

[(1979). Psychoanalytic Review (66)(1):133–141.]

The majority opinion within the psychoanalytic community has tended to be that an analytic approach to the mentally retarded is futile. It is generally felt that the problems in communication, the limitations in insight, and problems with ego synthesis mitigate against the use of this tool. Under the aegis of intellectual deficits, the retarded child has been shunted aside and offered only the most concrete of interventions. Moore, in a review of changing concepts of the infantile neurosis, suggested that "children with ego and libidinal defects, the intellectually retarded or those with organic defect do not respond to the usual analytic technique that has been devised for the infantile neurosis." Leland and Smith claimed that the methods and theories of play therapy used with emotionally disturbed children of normal intelligence had been applied to retarded children, and that this application was ineffective. They ascribed the failure to essentially two basic problems: first, retarded children had inherent problems with communication which limited their ability to gain insight "through the usual methods," and "their daily life experiences [did] not usually contain sufficient elements to permit them to utilize the play material traditionally available for the expression of their emotional problems;" second, the clinicians were at fault because "they expected verbal communications and all of the other trappings of play therapy which occur with the emotionally disturbed children who have normal intelligence."

The French existential analyst Mannoni is one of the few who have made an eloquent appeal for the psychoanalytic treatment of the "feebleminded" child. Mannoni views the mother-child relationship as the central source of conflict for the child. The feeble-minded child experiences himself as the object of the mother, never as a subject in his own right; therefore, he can never resolve symbolically the castration complex, as he is webbed to the mother's unconscious. Further, there is always a suspicion in Mannoni's work that the "feebleminded" is only a pseudo-retardate, and that the origin of the disorder lies in deep psychogenic sources. Whatever the theoretical difference, she has applied psychoanalytic theories, i.e., an approach to understanding conflict and the unconscious, to the retarded child.

The general consensus that the usual psychoanalytic methods are inapplicable to retarded children is due more, I suspect, to speculation than to experience. It may well be that in a society where psychotherapeutic treatment resources are indeed limited; the retarded child is the last recipient of these coveted and highly specialized skills. The subtle priorities of the society have indeed operated to limit the number of analytically trained personnel in the treatment of the retarded. But beyond the social pressures of service application, underlying attitudes exist that have deterred the development of necessary skills and interest in an analytic approach to the retarded.

Countertransferential responses are induced by the extreme incapacity of the retarded child and his lifelong dependency on parents and society. Feelings of helplessness, unconscious fears of being damaged, and an uneasy sense of his own ambivalence regarding dependency are evoked in the therapist. The damaged, the depressed, and the hopeless always invoke countertransferential fears in the therapist so that he prefers to avoid these problems or make concrete interventions rather than deal with the underlying emotional issues. Even the severely neurotic and schizophrenic appear to pose a more optimistic challenge and present the therapist with the possibility, if not the reality, of ultimate satisfaction. Here we observe the unconscious wishes transferred altruistically to the patient. The treatment of older retarded adolescents and adults arouse added feelings of frustration and even annoyance, for indeed the limitations of the intellectual deficits present themselves. The ingenuousness of the younger retarded child, his capacity for rich play and fantasy, for humor and direct aggression, can overcome countertransferential reactions, but not so for the older retardate. The concreteness of intellectual responses, the proscribed thinking, and the repetitiveness of ideas combined with frequent shallowness of affect are indeed trying. The clinician experiences boredom and constriction of his own intellectual and emphatic responses.

Before proceeding, the role of intelligence in the analytic process must be considered. What is the quality or nature of intelligence required for this procedure? The treatment requires that the patient be able to abstract, to communicate unconscious content symbolically, and to recall mnemic residues of experience. Further, intelligence plays a basic role in the structuring of the personality. Freud ascribed to the ego the task of

> laying down an accurate picture of the external world in the memory
> traces of its perception, and by its exercise of the function of reality
> testing must put aside whatever of this picture of the external world
> is an addition derived from internal sources of excitation.

The ego, then, is structured partly by its perceptions of the external world and partly by primary identifications, initially through imitation of the primary objects that required the exercise of perception. Primary process ideations arising from the id likewise bear the imprint of intelligence in the scope and richness of fantasy, the range of condensations and displacements.

That intelligence is a necessary ingredient in the ordering of the personality structure does not imply the reverse: that the personality structure will achieve a higher degree of integration or successful mediation with the social environment in direct proportion to the intelligence quotient.

It has been commonly accepted that the retarded child lacks attributes of intelligence that are necessary for psychotherapeutic work. However, he has the capacity in varying degrees to communicate in symbols, to abstract, to call upon the past, and to test reality. Further, he has the emotional and intellectual resources to identify with objects, to shift the economics of the libidinal and aggressive distribution, and to revise the structural relationships between the ego, the superego and the id. We really do not know the amount of intelligence required to effect psychic structure or psychic change. At best, we know only that the severe and profoundly retarded who have almost no higher cortex functioning are poor candidates for psychotherapy. For the moderate, mild, and borderline retardate, clinical experience indicates that psychoanalytic psychotherapy can be successfully applied.

CLINICAL EXAMPLES

The clinical examples that follow are taken from the case records of retarded children treated with psychoanalytic therapy. The discussion will demonstrate the viability of psychoanalytic principles in the management and treatment of such children.

Case 1

Rodney, a seven-year-old boy with chocolate-colored skin and big brown eyes, had a face of such rounded handsomeness that the therapist wished that this youngster who tested in the mild range of retardation should not only be of normal intelligence but of superior cast. He stood emotionally clinging to his mother, a woman garbed in a plainness inappropriate to her years and with a face that expressed both fear and anger. She "had no problems" but agreed to therapy for Rodney, who would soon be transferred to an educable C.R.M.D. class. Rodney had suffered from a failure to keep up with the children in a regular class. He was extraordinarily shy, fearful of contact with adults and peers. He was submissive to his younger sister, a "sissy" in the eyes of his father. A change to a class wherein he could intellectually compete would strengthen his self-esteem, yet he had to deal with the recognition that he was intellectually slower than most children, especially his sister and the street children, who were mean, not out of malice but out of fear. The intensity of his fear, his unresponsiveness to adults aside from his mother, and his distance from his father indicated that more than environmental change was required.

At the beginning of treatment, Rodney made no contact with the male therapist. He went quietly to the play therapy room, played, stopped exactly on time, and put the toys away in an orderly fashion. This procedure was repeated week after week. He came obediently without a word, only a bare nod, and played repeatedly with the toy soldiers, lining them up and knocking them down. He rarely spoke in play, and when he did he was so inaudible that the therapist could not hear. What was the purpose of this? Certainly, the child could play at home in the same manner, and if this was curative, he could be cured at home. If we recall that the aggressive drives, like the libidinal drives, require an object, then the therapist's presence was vital. This child required a therapeutic audience for his play, the acceptance of his fantasies. If the mothering object was too intrusive, the therapist had to be silently active. Rodney had the run of the therapy room. Occasionally the therapist would ask what was happening—"Nothing" was the reply. Then quietly they put the toys away. This continued for three months with little variation until one session, when Rodney turned to the therapist and asked in a half-questioning voice, "Can we play ball?" With the emergence of the transference wish to contact the therapist, the feared aggression toward the father began to emerge. Until this time, the aggressive wishes had to be guarded.

Freed from these restrictive repressions, increased aggressive and libidinal wishes emerged toward the therapist, in both play and words. At one point, when the aggression directed toward the therapist was too intense, Rodney turned it upon himself, stating, "I am dead."

The unfolding of the drives freed to develop—i.e., the unfolding of the maturational stages—brought with it improvement in school functioning and improved relationships with peers and adults. For the first time this boy made attempts to reach his father and began the necessary separation process from his mother. Not only did improvement in intellectual achievement result from a change in class placement, but the freeing of the drives made the ego more accessible for cognitive activity as less energy was required for the repressive defense. Further, direct gratification of the drives permitted sublimatory activity to develop in the sphere of learning.

Case 2

Martha, a thirteen-year-old girl of Spanish background, tested in the moderately retarded intellectual range. Her appearance belied the intellectual deficit. She was an attractive, well-developed pubertal girl. Her parents had separated some five years before. Her father had remarried, and her mother had a succession of boyfriends and possibly homosexual relations.

Martha was a terror in school; she was physically abusive toward the teachers and fought with boys and girls alike. She was undaunted by suspensions. Would anyone guess that this seemingly fearless girl slept under her bed on the floor for fear of witches and voodoo dolls? She had frequent nightmares and was preoccupied with thoughts of violent death.

The therapist made the initial error of holding the first session in the playroom. Martha fought for months to go back "to play." She would run from the office, roll on the floor, put out the lights, and quack like a duck. When the therapist repeatedly explained that playing was not good for her, that it was more helpful to talk out her problems, Martha promptly replied that she couldn't talk, she wished she didn't have a mouth, "I am a baby." When the therapist disclaimed that she was a baby although she knew she would like to be one, and reminded her she was thirteen years old, Martha promptly rejoined "I am a baby", "I am nine—seven—five years old." It took eleven sessions to gain some control over this girl, to get her to spend most of each session in her seat talking. It was apparent that a radical internal change had occurred when in subsequent sessions she began to relate her fear of being pursued by voodoo magic. She expressed a desire to learn to read and told the therapist two stories—Hansel and Gretel and Peter Pan. The symbolic art form represented her capacity to abstract, to transfer the meaning of her unconscious conflicts to universal wishes and fears. It represented a beginning willingness to deal with these conflicts and to relinquish infantile wishes. She achieved what early man accomplished by the creation of myths. He relinquished his infantile wishes by putting them into story form.

Case 3

Jaime, a big, husky, seven-year-old boy, attended a preschool program because he could not manage the Head Start program or public kindergarten. His behavior was bizarre. On the bus or in the park he would suddenly burst into animal behavior, crawling on all fours. This behavior mortified his mother, who had already shrunk from human contact and whose reclusiveness suggested paranoid features. She felt the world was full of devils and even resented the visits by her children's father. Her ambivalence to this boy was evident. Her fear for his health led her to dress him in double sets of underwear, a flannel shirt, and sweaters to protect him from the cold, but at the same time the overheating and perspiration caused him colds.

Jaime's psychological tests revealed a child of borderline intelligence with a borderline personality. He immediately involved his therapist in his play. She was to do exactly as he instructed—crash trucks, fight with the monster machine, tie the puppets to the railroad tracks and run them over gleefully. Every race with cars or trains he was to win. In every monster fight he was victorious. She was to speak exactly as instructed by him, imitating his voice in a high, squeaky pitch.

In the development of the child, it is the infant who mimics the parent. Here we observe a reverse situation. The therapist mimics the child. The purpose, though, is essentially the same: learning through imitation. The therapist's imitation reflected this boy's primary narcissistic need: to have a dyad with a mother, a sharing and exchange of the emotional climate of mother and child. By the therapist's acceptance and understanding of Jaime's drives and affects, the preliminary stage of identification was set into motion. Secondly, this boy was able to turn what he had felt as a passive experience into an active one. This capacity for active mastery of events and relationships is a necessary requisite for ego development.

Almost no interpretations were given during this period. It was only necessary that the therapist interpret the meaning of his behavior for herself in order to respond with the correct therapeutic technique. When Jaime dropped "poo poos" from his truck and laughingly shouted, "Look at the poo poos," she smilingly said, "How nice, what lovely poo poos."

The "poo poos" gradually changed into "boo boos" coming out of people. He asked, "Do real people make boo-boo? Do you make it?" Phallic interests soon followed and presented the greatest source of anxiety for this boy. He jokingly told the therapist that she was the beautiful girl in a scanty bikini he had just seen on a magazine cover. Did she "pee-pee" standing up, he asked, after drawing a big tree and instructed her to draw a small flower. He then wanted to leave the session early.

In the next session, as a surprise to the therapist, he asked her to close her eyes and while she was doing so, he began to draw a large shark with big teeth. His anxiety became overwhelming and he asked to call his mother.

The therapist was now faced with certain structural problems which blocked the free unfolding of psychosexual stages. His ego was too weak in relation to the drives and the force of castration danger.

Economically, the admixture of aggressive with libidinal wishes, due to serious problems with the mothering relationship, overtaxed his ego. His defense against the danger was flight. It was necessary to more actively verbalize and to use interpretations in order to reduce the anxiety, to study with him the source of the conflicts and dangers. Words provide the ego with a lever in the control of both the id and the superego. Thoughts are an experimental way of dealing with anxiety. The ability to anticipate danger may either reduce it or eliminate it entirely. Further thoughts provide some discharge for the drives and can be a source of direct gratification by keeping some balance with the pleasure-unpleasure principle.

The retarded child, like other children in treatment, responds essentially to a variety of techniques used within the transference. What the transference must elicit are new identifications essentially through the influence of love. This does not imply that the technique is one of giving love or gratification. On the contrary, it is often necessary to prohibit impulsive behavior and deny gratifications. Some interpretations may even be experienced as a criticism. What is necessary is sufficient resolution of negative and aggressive feelings which may result either from a frustration of wishes or from a regression due to anxiety which arouses more primitive aggressive feelings.

The ability to identify with the therapist is the end result. It is this which moves the child to abandon the impulse gratification and accede to the demands of reality. In the first stage the child fights very hard to maintain the status quo, to realize the gratification of either libidinal or aggressive wishes. This search for gratification is only slowly transformed into an acceptance of understanding, i.e., from the therapist, and then from himself. Understanding is synonymous with love. It can also be synonymous with knowledge, and knowledge provides the ego with tools of mastery over the internal and external world. There is power to be gained from knowledge of oneself and the world. Mastery not only affords strength to the ego but is a source of narcissistic gratification. It implies the ego's capacity to invest in itself libidinal satisfactions which were formerly sought from other objects. Structurally this is accomplished through the formation of ego ideals. The identification with the therapist must proceed from "I want what you have" or "I want you" to "I want to be like you." This internalization of the object provides an internalized mediator more amenable to socialization, better able to control impulses and find substitute gratification. The gratification of ego ideals is a narcissistic gratification which leads to increased independence and self-control.

In summary, it was my intention to show that psychoanalytic theory and psychoanalytic therapy are applicable to the retarded child. The cognition of internalized conflicts does not involve the entire cortical function. Working through the transference may modify pathological structures and defenses through new identifications.

REFERENCES

Blos, P. (1972).The Function of the Ego Ideal in Late Adolescence. *Psychoanal. St. Child*, Vol. 27, New York: Quadrangle Books, pp. 93–97.

Bornstein, B. (1930). "Zur Psychogenese der Pseudodebilitat," *Internationale Zeitschaft fur Psychoanalyse*, Vol. 16, pp. 378–399.

Fenichel, O. (1945). *The Psychoanalytic Theory of Neurosis*. New York: W.W. Norton.

Freud, A. (1965). Normality and Pathology in Childhood: Assessment of Development. In The Writings of Anna Freud, Vol. 6. New York: International Universities Press

Freud, S. (1914). On Narcissism: An Introduction. (1914). *Standard Edition* 14, 1957.

‾‾‾‾‾‾ (1923). The Ego and the Id. *Standard Edition 19*, 1961.

‾‾‾‾‾‾ (1926). Inhibition, Symptoms and Anxiety. *Standard Edition* 20. London: Hogarth Press, 1959.

‾‾‾‾‾‾ (1933). The Dissection of the Psychical Personality *Standard Edition* 22:75, 1964.

Greenson, R. (1967). *The Technique and Practice of Psychoanalysis*. New York: International Universities Press.

Hartmann, H., & Loewenstein, R.M. (1962). Notes on the Superego. *Psychoanal. St. Child* 17:42–81. New York: International Universities Press.

Leland, H., & Smith, E. (1965). *Play Therapy with Mentally Subnormal Children*. New York: Grune and Stratton, p. 2.

Mannoni, M. (1972). *The Backward Child and His Mother*. New York: Pantheon Books.

Moore, T. (1971). Changing Concepts in the Infantile Neurosis and Their Implications to Psychoanalytic Theory and Practice in Child Analysis. *Bulletin of the Philadelphia Association for Psychoanalysis*21:129–144.

Spitz, R.A. (1965). *The First Year of Life*. New York: International Universities Press.

Woodward, K., Brown, D. & Bird, D. (1960). Psychiatric Study of Mentally Retarded Pre-School Children. *AMA Archives of General Psychology* 2:156–170, February.

CHAPTER 8

FAILURE IN THE TREATMENT OF A PSYCHOTIC MOTHER AND CHILD: ASPECTS OF TRANSFERENCE AND RESISTANCE[1,2]

[(1984). Psychoanalytic Review (71)(3):397–412.]

A constant object implies far more than the capacity to sustain love for another person... it implies above all that the object is perceived and represented as it is in reality, with a minimal subjective distortion

(Bak, 1971, p. 237).

The study of a case of treatment failure may not be a gratifying task for therapists; the shadow of doubt is cast upon their professional acumen and indeed suspicion doubting the efficacy of psychotherapy enhances the ranks of the disbelievers. If the reader can pardon the audacity of a reference to Freud's (1905) case study of a treatment failure, "Dora," there is much to be gained from an analysis of the negative therapeutic reaction. Freud's magnificent interpretation of Dora's dreams, the profound reconstruction of the past, his understanding of the symptoms and defense were of no avail as the powerful transference reactions defeated the embryonic analysis. Yet the analysis of Dora heralded Freud's (1912) early recognition of the power of the transference and its pivotal role in the methodology and

---

1 This paper was written with the support of the University Affiliated Facility program of HEW at New York Medical College.

2 I wish to express my appreciation to Mrs. Mary Lieber, the therapist of Mrs. M and J. Without her patient and sensitive treatment, this paper would not have materialized.

theory of psychoanalysis. It became increasingly apparent that making the unconscious conscious, or interpreting repressed wishes and conflicts, could offer only superficial resolution if the past, affectively reactivated and given fresh impetus in the transference, was not treated.

The purpose of this paper is to elaborate on the frequent difficulties met by psychotherapists working either in the more depressed ghetto areas where the personality disorganization parallels the social distress, or in an outpatient department of mental hospitals and mental hygiene clinics. It is hoped that some clarity will be gained by the examination of the problems of resistance (Spotnitz, 1969; Sternbach & Nagelberg, 1957). These problems include: the role of transference as it emerges in once or twice a week therapy, the means and mode by which transference can defeat treatment, the mechanisms involved in the establishment of reality testing, and the cognitive distortions in the delusional system. Whether we can learn to refine our treatment methods to treat the "untreatable" (Sternbach & Nagelberg, 1957) or simply gain greater perspicacity into the limits of treatment is indeed a challenging issue and a purpose-worthy of exploration.

Freud (1924) states that psychosis in contrast to neurosis represents a struggle between the ego and the external world, while the neurosis results from a struggle between the ego and the id. The external world maintains its representation in the ego in two ways: first, the present perceptions which are always renewable, and second, "by the store of memories of earlier perceptions, which in a shape of an 'internal world' form a possession of the ego and a constituent part of it" (p. 150). In the psychosis, the perceptions of the external world are rejected, and the storehouse of memories lose their significance due to the turning away of interest from the real world. The ego creates a new world based upon the fanciful wishes of the id. The motive for this new creation lies in the intolerable experiences of frustration of a "wish" by reality. The psychotic thinking is an attempt to repair the rent in the ego due to the withdrawal of cathexis from reality, a restitution based upon the imagined wished for gratification. The infant's "hallucinated milk" is an early prototype and forerunner of the restitutive cognitive process.

Psychosis has been compared with the thinking of children and primitive man. A fundamental difference must be noted, for in the child and primitive man the world of reality, the cause and effect of natural forces, had not been learned. The interchangeability of animal, man, inanimate objects are possible according to the laws of primitive psychological mechanisms. For primitive man, thoughts regarding world order are influenced not by the natural forces but by the dominance of wish-fulfilling fantasies (Freud, 1913). This is also true for children. Since primitive man organized wish-fulfilling fantasies into ideation which structured social and economic forces, we must regard this as the predecessor of scientific knowledge and the forerunner of logical thinking. These early ideations represent the development of man's intellectual history. When primary process is encountered in an adult, the late latency age child, or adolescent, it is due to a special creation of a *Weltanschauung* based not upon a logical approach to reality, but as a derivative of id functions, an attempt to gratify infantile wishes. This derivative represents a failure of narcissistic libido to attach or remain permanently attached to the object world. In the psychosis, Freud indicated that it is the regression to narcissism—id organization (Schur, 1966)—that is responsible for the psychotic ideation. Excessive narcissistic libido invested in either self, object, or body ego is less amenable to external perceptions. Magical thinking results from the attempts to gratify wishes or to reduce frustrations from the external world. Perceptions and behavior are influenced by the internal demands for pleasure and gratification and continue to exert an enormous influence upon the individual's relationship with the real world. The aggressive drive in this state is less likely to be modified by Eros; a state of ambivalence to objects prevails with the result that the drives are not sufficiently neutralized and are susceptible to drive defusion. The defense mechanisms of sublimation and neutralization are seriously compromised.

To understand the degree by which the psychotic process resists change may shed some light on why a change from a narcissistic to an object libidinal investment is fraught with difficulties. Greenson (1965) has indicated that resistance functions as an opposing force, a tenacious block to change. Resistance is a force fed by the energies of the id to maintain a homeostasis in the pleasure-unpleasure balance and at the same time provide for some mode of drive discharge. Narcissistic cathexis of the ego and of the ego ideal presumes a character structure more prone to frustration and therefore greater ambivalence to the object. The aggressive drive is less easily bound with narcissistic libido. Since narcissism presumes a more mobile state in search of gratification and pleasure seeking, aggression is readily evoked when frustration occurs. Investment in objects is secondary to self-gratification, thus preventing the neutralization of aggression by the libidinal drive. It is this process which interferes with a constant object representation and determines the degree of ambivalence to the object. The more developed form of identification with the object is restricted and early forms of incorporation, introjection, and imitation dominate the mode of self- and object-representations, which results in a weak and poorly synthesized ego.

Modification of the psychotic defense structure poses serious dilemmas for the ego's adaptive capacity. The danger of onslaught from the side of the drives for discharge and gratification and the demand for the synthetic functions of the ego (Nunberg, 1955) to respond appropriately to external reality threaten the already weakened integrity of the ego. The danger lies in the increased withdrawal of interest in the external world and regression to an earlier stage of gratification and adaptation.

CLINICAL PRESENTATION

Mrs. M was a heavy-boned, square-faced, black woman in her late 30s, unattractive in her premature aging. Her face and body seemed to deny sexuality and the square plaid coat exaggerated the squareness of her body. The mannish dress and bizarre tee shirt, with a picture of "Jaws," gave an unsettling impression.

Mrs. M' first sought help at the agency's preschool unit because of her son J's bizarre and unpredictable behavior. He was four and a half years old at the time of referral. In a Head Start Program, J was unable to relate to children; withdrawn and isolated, he would suddenly become seized by some inner fantasy, throw himself on all fours, "barking," as if he had been transformed into a dog, or "quacking," as though now he were a duck. This behavior occurred in school, the park, a bus, obviously motivated by some acute anxiety and the defensive wish to guard against this great discomfort.

At the age of five months, Mrs. M had sought help at a large metropolitan hospital over her concern that J had a peculiar manner of nodding his head. Nothing unusual was found, and he was followed in the health clinic for years. By the age of four, J was already a large, clumsy boy, awkward in gait, and speaking in a low, almost inaudible, staccato tone. Psychological tests revealed an intellectual functioning in the 70s — a borderline intelligence, though the clinical impressions indicated a child of functional retardation resulting from emotional and intellectual constriction. Three years later, J scored in the 90s. In decisive contrast to J stood his sister, two years his junior, an excellently coordinated child, bright, alert, aggressive, and quite beautiful.

The diagnostic considerations regarding J centered upon questions of a constitutional ego deficit resulting in childhood psychosis, or an atypical ego development due to grave disturbances in the early mother-child dyadic relationship, or a combination of both factors. A fourth consideration in this psychotic picture was the factor of identification—a considerable element in unrealistic thinking and behavior, resulting from identification with a psychotic mother (Pine, 1979).

Certain objections were raised by staff early in the treatment regarding the diagnosis of psychosis for the mother. It was asked legitimately, can one make this claim where no blatant distortions in thinking and orientation are present, or in the absence of delusions and hallucinations? Are we making a claim for psychiatry when the problems result from the domain of the cultural and social environment? Mrs. M has a strong religious orientation, a fundamentalist view of life. Like the Calvinist doctrine that views man's failings and fallen ways as a result of the power of the devil, Mrs. M considered the surrounding environment as evil, as the incarnation of the devil. The sexual promiscuity, drugs, alcoholism assaulted her sensibilities, and she was withdrawn and isolated in this world of "flesh." There appeared no escape for her, a poor black woman dependent upon public assistance, restricted in mobility by a prejudiced and class-striated society.

Mrs. M came to New York in her early 20s, leaving behind in a Southern town a three-year-old son from her first marriage, which resulted in divorce; a mother, stepfather, and seven siblings. Her father died when she was 10 years old. The history is scant, only idyllic reveries of her mother, a warm, beneficent loving woman, and a few repetitive screen memories of sitting on the front porch, sunshine, light, and flowers, in the presence of her mother, or waiting for the mother to return after a day's excursion in town, and the patient remembering her feelings of loneliness at the separation. A few scattered fears emerge, that of the graveyard near the home. A vague memory of the father was recaptured but emerged more like the remnant of a dream, a shadowy, male figure pushing her on a swing. No mention was made of the stepfather, though he assumed responsibility for the care of her son after her mother died.

Mrs. M's current isolation was extensive. Her personal relationships meager, she had few ties to any social structure. In recent years, she had developed a cardiac condition. Mrs. M refused to marry the father of her two children, J and M. She regards him as "irresponsible" and "tied to his mother." In spite of his wishes to marry her, and to visit the children, she has ejected him from visits to the home. For a brief period during the treatment, she permitted visits. At one point, Mrs. M joined in the family outings to the movies or park, but soon complained that the father made the children too rowdy, he could not be relied upon to visit when he planned, "Why do the children show such excitement when he comes, they show more love for him than for me" became a complaint, and finally when he bought the children a dog, he was subsequently driven away.

An educative attempt to enlist her understanding regarding the children's need for a father, an explanation as to why the absent love object appeared more desirable than the permanent object in the home was met with negativism and resistance. The failure to experience conflict, guilt, or doubt regarding her feelings or behavior toward this man, or to regard the needs of the children is indeed a striking example of the deficit in superego functions.

Resistance to treatment emerged at the onset; until J was assigned to the same therapist as Mrs. M, treatment was sporadic. Weekly sessions were rejected in favor of biweekly contact. It was clear that distance from human contact was required by Mrs. M. A female therapist was assigned in spite of J's need for a male figure of identification. It was considered that Mrs. M's aggressive feelings for the male would elicit immediate resistance and the treatment would experience defeat. The idealized image of the mother and the reverence portended the possibility of establishing a narcissistic transference reflective of Kohut's (1971) "idealized image." That which was anticipated did indeed occur. The patient became increasingly interested in the therapist, travelled in the therapist's neighborhood in search of her, and on one occasion met her in a neighborhood store. The patient wanted to buy a bicycle similar to the therapist's and in numerous ways exhibited a love attachment.

During the second year of treatment, Mrs. M moved from her high crime, delinquent area which bustled with drug peddlers to a quiet, sedate neighborhood, less offensive in drugs and delinquency and far more stable. A suggestion to move had never been made by the therapist nor had any aid been volunteered. It had been apparent from the inception of treatment that Mrs. M had sufficient capacity to manage this move at a point that change could be tolerated and that any suggestion would be met with resistance. The move was regarded as a reduction in the psychotic organization, for it represented a lessening of externalization of internal processes. Mrs. M required that the external world be "evil", as a source for displacement of her own inner feelings that she was evil. A horrendous environment provided a compromise solution for the underlying delusions; it is not "I that am evil, it is the world," and indeed it was a very evil world within those blocks. Freud (1913) stated that neuroses are "asocial structures, they endeavour to achieve by private means what is effected in society by collective effort" (p. 73). In the psychosis the "private means" are transformed into public means, the attempt is to change the social and scientific order of the world of reality. Therefore, the public change for Mrs. M from a "bad" place to a "good" place was viewed as a diminution of self-condemnatory feelings and a change in the capacity of the ego to tolerate libidinal and aggressive impulses.

The assumption was further made that some shift in the ratio between the aggressive and libidinal drive had occurred. In moving to a "nicer" neighborhood, the externalization of hate for the world was deprived of its source. While Mrs. M in no way involved herself with neighbors or community groups or church, she had a positive feeling for her new environs. The inanimate object world was invested with positive feelings. She fixed up her apartment, curtained the windows, took pride in its comfort and beauty.

Just as the therapist's office was comfortable and attractive, so Mrs. M strove to emulate this site in her home.

For a while it was thought that the treatment might ultimately prove successful. The move and the reestablishment of contact with the children's father had occurred in the same timespan. A momentary flirtation with a man further added to the hope that the libidinal investment in human objects was also occurring. These changes, unfortunately, could not be sustained; the father was chased away from his children in anger and jealousy; the man was soon viewed with suspicion. The isolation and withdrawal were reestablished.

Daydreams presented themselves. Whether they were hoarded from the past and continued to occupy conscious thought or were of a more recent origin, is unknown. Mrs. M fantasied that she was a wealthy woman residing in Hollywood; she imagined riding in a chauffer-driven car through the beautiful streets accompanied by her children. A second fantasy revealed her sailing an ocean liner and traveling around the world, a wealthy beautiful woman who dined at the captain's table. In contrast to the woman of elegance in the fantasy, Mrs. M would frequently arrive for her sessions in a black, "Jaws," tee shirt and plaid slacks.

After four years of treatment, Mrs. M announced quite suddenly that she would no longer come to see the therapist except on special request for J. She found the sessions "too upsetting"! What had occurred? In the next to final session, Mrs. M had related a series of incidences regarding a neighbor. For several weeks this woman had made it a habit to visit Mrs. M in the evening with her children. The neighbor, hungry for friendship, had attached herself to Mrs. M, who must have exuded some form of friendliness. The woman talked to Mrs. M of her sexual problems, difficulties with men, money, children, life in general. One evening, on hearing the expected knock at the door, Mrs. M herded the children into the bedroom where they remained huddled in a corner, silent and waiting for the woman to depart. This behavior occurred for two or three nights following, until there were no more evening visitations. In describing this event, Mrs. M became agitated and finally revealed to the therapist her belief that the woman was an agent of the devil, sent to tempt her in the ways of the damned and to destroy her. The session following this tale, Mrs. M announced her decision to terminate treatment.

The psychotic response to the neighbor was not surprising. These delusions had always been present in a dormant state and did not invade the ideational content provided Mrs. M maintained her isolation and protection against external stimuli. As long as the incursions from the external world permitted a balance between the aggression and libido or left the narcissistic idealization untrammeled, Mrs. M could suppress the psychotic organization. Since delusional thinking was ego syntonic, why should this current delusion drive the patient from treatment, from the idealized love object?

Several possibilities present themselves. First, Mrs. M may have unconsciously sensed the therapist's shock at the story. For the first time, the therapist experienced the full impact of the patient's illness. While nothing was said, an unconscious communication may have been perceived. The patient, sensing these feelings, could have withdrawn to protect her sense of self-esteem and to hold onto a benign love object. The patient, unable to tolerate the awareness that she was psychotic or so perceived by the therapist, withdrew. A second point to be considered is that the patient's improved functioning indicated some improvement in reality testing. It can be postulated that the intellectual functions, less invaded by drives and wishful fantasies, are more receptive to reality. When the patient related the tale, her capacity to observe and judge the quality of the distortions confronted her with the sense of the illness. Since the ego was not yet able to tolerate the results of these observations and perceptions, the patient withdrew in a defensive flight to prevent further narcissistic injury and a more pervasive psychotic regression. These two suggestions are certainly worthy of consideration, and yet it is my contention that a third consideration provides the core from which the above factors received their impetus.

A strong transference had already been established and it was precisely the transference that was responsible not only for the dissolution of the therapy but also accounted for the delusional response to the neighbor. It was the "return of the repressed" that was ultimately the basis for the resistance and the delusion. A strong erotic attachment had developed to the therapist. The tee shirt which Mrs. M sported was not just an anomaly of modern times, it represented unconscious wishes of oral incorporation. J uninhibitedly gave expression to these wishes as he made large, beautifully shaped sharks while verbally expressing his thoughts, "I want to be a shark; I want to eat you, to become white and strong like you. I want to eat up mommie; I want to be eaten." The theme to eat and to be eaten are early normal infantile wishes, and they constitute the benign games between mother and child. For Mrs. M the unconscious wishes expressed an oral libidinal mode of incorporation in regard to the therapist. An examination of the two fantasies produced by Mrs. M will further confirm these transference feelings. Mrs. M dreams of driving in a chauffeur-driven car with her two children through the streets of Hollywood. Hollywood represents fame and fortune. When is the child most famous and fortunate? As an infant loved, adored by the mother riding in her pram through the streets and admired by all the passersby. The wish is to return to that period of infancy when the child and mother are united in a state of narcissistic bliss and enjoyable exhibitionism.

In the fantasy of the "ocean voyage," we observe Mrs. M again in a moving vehicle, a boat, dressed in a long gown, a veritable femme fatale who dines at the captain's table, a select seating for the most prestigious guests. Does not this fantasy also evoke infantile wishes, to be rocked in the mother's arms? The pleasurable experience of feeding at the mother's breast is the thinly veiled wish of eating with the captain, and the beautiful woman is again the beautiful and admired baby.

The strength of infantile wishes and fantasies in this patient pervades current ideation and ego functions. Fantasies that can play a constructive, adaptive and sublimatory role in ego development continue in an almost undisguised manner reflective of infantile life, unrealistic and maladaptive. They encourage withdrawal and delusion.

The fantasies also give some indication of oedipal wishes; the captain, the chauffeur, one a man of command, the other to be commanded. At the same time that Mrs. M has fantasies of strong, powerful and "manly" men, she humiliates them. Her wish that J be strong, courageous, is constantly contradicted by her harsh orders, dominance, and total surveillance of his life and body. The oedipal position is indeed weak. There is evidence of a negative oedipal constellation as indicated by the masculine demeanor, her rivalry and hatred of men. In spite of these oedipal signs, the men must be viewed rather as substitutes for the wished for mother. The rage and hate is a displacement from the rage at what was experienced as the disappointing and ungratifying mother who is maintained as a loving object by a process involving idealization. Contrary to Kernberg's (1976) conceptualization that the idealized mother is maintained by the defense of splitting the good and the bad objects, it is my contention that idealization results both from object representations occurring at various developmental phases (Spiegel, 1959) and the defense mechanisms of repression, denial, and projection. In the psychotic patient, idealization is structurally maintained by a primitively developed ego ideal, which maintains the early idealized parental imagoes and infantile grandiosity unmodified by reality. The objective world is internally processed through a narcissistic ego organization; all perceptions and experiences are dominated by wishes and magical thinking. What is lost is the capacity to invest the world with object libido, therefore reality testing is seriously compromised.

The stories of the neighbor discussing her sexual affairs undoubtedly provided the stimulus for the patient's thoughts regarding the therapist's sexual life. We know that the patient made forays into the therapist's neighborhood frequently to shop or walk and she asked numerous questions regarding the therapist's personal life. Unconscious wishes of a negative oedipal nature toward the therapist were undoubtedly provoked: The wish to love the therapist as a man naturally would be frustrated by the therapist's real or imagined relationships with men. Hidden beneath the oedipal fantasies are the more dangerous infantile wishes, the wish to be the sole love object of the therapist, that is, the transference mother, and also the wish for unity, to incorporate the therapist-mother. The failure to separate in time, place, or the object has an almost delusional quality in the affective state.

Just as Mrs. M experienced frustration in childhood with the birth of siblings, the loss of the mother to the father, the father to the mother and then the stepfather, the present frustrations are experienced not only as current ones but evoke the powerful affective states and memories of the past which flood the ego. There are qualitative and quantitative aspects to the mode by which frustration is experienced. The earliest perceived anxieties of the infant relate to the fears of loss of the mother, not as an object in her own right (Speigel, 1959; Spitz, 1965), but as a minister to the needs of the child. What is feared is the anticipated increase in drives and anaclitic needs (Freud, 1911) which the infant cannot gratify without the mother. Frustration understood in this frame of reference can arouse earlier memories of actual loss or anticipated loss of the mothering object. In a rapid regressive state, current frustration is associated with threatened object loss. Mrs. M, by a very loose associative process, relates neighbor-mother-therapist as one unit. The past and present are merged in time and condition. In order to maintain some ego integrity a withdrawal not only from the therapist in reality, which is from the treatment, but from the libidinal investment is necessary. The withdrawal alone apparently was not an adequate defense. To prevent further regression, a delusional state as restitution was utilized. If we recognized that the stimulation from unconscious wishes is too powerful for the ego to tolerate, then the "return of the repressed" either creates a situation of absolute withdrawal and stupor as observed in catatonia or a delusional ideation which permits contact, though distorted, with the real world. Mrs. M, under the stress of the transference wishes, could protect herself only by the withdrawal from treatment and the delusion which represents a restitution.

Werner (1978) has pointed out that external stimuli affect the total organism. "Any stimulation, whether it comes through exterioproprio-, or interoceptors, is sensory tonic in nature" (p. 195). Perception may be affected equivalently by various kinds of sensory stimulation, and the perceptual properties of an object depend on the way in which stimuli from a physical object affect the organism and on the specific and active manner in which the organism reacts to it. Further, Werner states that if the stimuli interfere, or are incommensurate with the organismic state, there emerges a tendency in the organism to alter its state in the direction toward establishment of equilibrium between body and object. What Werner expresses in the language of developmental psychology is echoed in Freud's (1911) proposition that delusions and hallucinations occur in order to establish some harmony between the psychic structure and the external world—to maintain psychic homeostasis.

Since hindsight provides us with valuable theoretical insights, the postulate is that initially, treatment for Mrs. M was an unnecessary invasion into her established precarious balance between the world of wishes and reality and ego integration and disintegration. Were it not for the needs of J and his continued need to separate from Mrs. M, to find a means of discharge for the aggressive drive in reality, rather than in the fantasies of sharks and monsters, Mrs. M would have been best left to her isolation and idealizations. The requirements of mother and child run in contradictory avenues. The task at hand may find a solution in the ability to enlist the cooperation of the mother in small but important steps that will gradually permit some separation, such as summer camp, an after school group, bus travel. Whether these changes can effectively interrupt a psychopathic mental structure already formed is a troubling question. The most primitive mechanisms of ego development continue to operate in the boy, oral incorporation of the mother and of the object world being the dominant mode. Since the ambivalence and aggression to the mother is powerful, the object representation and identifications cannot be retained. He must constantly incorporate because of the loss; this sieve-like state augurs poorly for psychic success. The mother is to be devoured by J. The shark, or the shark mother, devours him; he wishes to be fat like "mommie" to have "fat arms like mommie." Since "mommie" views him not only as an extension of herself but as a defective self, the incarnate of the female-male identification, his sense of defectiveness is suffused by his defensive identification with the powerful animal world of sharks, dinosaurs, and primeval black bears. He continues to be dominated by primary process; reality is too threatening to his narcissistic integrity. Just short of delusion, the powerful wish to be these animals assumes the form of what Anna Freud (1936) refers to as "denial in fantasy."

Certainly, if one were to ask J if he were a shark, the response would be a negative. Yet the affective state dominates his judgment and relation to real objects. Whether this is to be considered a thinking disorder is questionable. Since the reality is perceived, and exists side by side with wishes, the affective derivative of the drives, it would perhaps be more correct to view this as a "splitting mechanism" in the process of defense (Freud, 1940; Greenson, 1965; Kernberg, 1976; Kohut, 1971; Knight, 1940; Nunberg, 1955; Peuman, 1963; Pine, 1979; Schur, 1966). As physiognomic thinking has not been adequately relinquished, and bodily processes easily define physical and inanimate behavior and structure, the danger lies in dominance of the ego by the id. Magical thinking and primitive wishes can be countered only with difficulty due to ego weakness and the enormous frustrations experienced by him in reality. The defense of splitting which maintains contact with perceptions as they exist in the real world can easily be replaced by the more dangerous mechanisms of denial and projection. Excessively frustrating or anxious situations will readily call forth these mechanisms to create a new internal and external reality.

CONCLUSION

The individual treatment issue of what is the measure of success must at some point be subsumed under the larger question of what the agency can afford, and for what return, and who is also waiting at the door for service. That there is evidence of change for J and some movement in Mrs. M is not in doubt. J no longer "denies in act" that he is a human; only in fantasy does he make claim to change into sharks and monsters. Though withdrawn in school, he is learning, and he has one positive relationship with a boy. Toward the other boys who are cruel and aggressive, he adopts a feminine attitude; he blows kisses at them. Only he and I know that these kisses represent his wish that he could create poison in his body, and the "blow kisses" are currents of poison with which he kills them—a very thin line between reality and delusion, but reality continues to hold sway in conscious awareness. The treatment can claim success for this ability to perceive the meaning of his wishes and to tolerate some separation from the mother. As for Mrs. M, the physical move to an improved environment is viewed as the only sign of change. Indeed, this is not terribly significant when viewed from the strength of id's relationship to the ego and the ego's compromised relationship to reality. And, yet, who can turn away a boy who is desperate for help and a mother who, in spite of her fears, brings her son twice a week for psychotherapy.

REFERENCES

Bak, R. (1971). Object Relationships in Schizophrenia and Perversions. *Int. J. Psycho-Anal.* 52:237.

Freud, A. (1936). *The Ego and the Mechanisms of Defense.* New York: International Universities Press.

Freud, S. (1905). Three Essays on the Theory of Sexuality. *Standard Edition* 7:125–248, 1961.

———— (1911). Formulations on the Two Principles of Mental Functioning. *Standard Edition* 12:213–226, 1961.

———— (1912). The Dynamics of Transference. *Standard Edition* 12:97–108, 1961.

———— (1913). Totem and Taboo. *Standard Edition* 13:1–164, 1961.

———— (1924). Neurosis and Psychosis. *Standard Edition* 19:149–156, 1961.

———— (1940). Splitting the Ego in the Process of Defense. *Standard Edition* 23:271–278, 1961.

Greenson, R. (1965). *The Technique and Practice of Psychoanalysis.* New York: International Universities Press.

Kernberg, O. (1976) . *Object Relations Theory and Clinical Psychoanalysis. New* York: Jason Aronson.

Kohut, H. (1971). *The Analysis of the Self.* New York: International Universities Press.

Knight, R. (1940). The Relationship of Latent Homosexuality to the Mechanism of Paranoid Delusions. *Bull. Mennin. Clinic* 4:149–159.

Nunberg, H. (1955). *Principles of Psychoanalysis.* New York: International Universities Press.

Peuman, J. (1963). Role of Transference in Case Work with Public Assistance Families. *Social Work* 8:47–54.

Pine, F. (1979). On the Pathology of the Separation-Individuation Process as Manifested in Later Clinical Work: An Attempt at Delineation. *Int. J. Psycho-Anal.* 60:225–242.

Schur, M. (1966). T*he Id and the Regulatory Principle of Mental Functioning.* New York: International Universities Press.

Spiegel, L. (1959). The Self, the Sense of Self, and Perception. *Psychoanal. St. Child* 14:81–109.

Spitz, A. (1965). *The First Year of Life.* New York: International Universities Press.

Spotnitz, H. (1969). *Modern Psychoanalysis of the Schizophrenic Patient— Theory of Technique.* New York: Grune & Stratton.

Sternbach, O. & Nagelberg, L. (1957) . On the Patient-Therapist Relationship in Some "Untreatable Cases." *Psychiatry* 5:3.

Werner, H. (1978). *Developmental Processes: Heinz Werner's Selected Writings (Vol. I, General Theory and Perceptual Experience).* S.S. Barten & M B. Franklin (Eds.), New York: International Universities Press.

CHAPTER 9

FREUD'S TREATMENT OF THE "RAT MAN": A POLEMIC WITH HIS CRITICS

[(1998). Psychoanalytic Review (85)(3):373-397.]

To propose a discussion on Freud's treatment of the Rat Man, when much has already been said on the subject (Kanzer & Glenn, 1980a & b; Lipton, 1977, 1979; Mahoney, 1980) sets up the anticipation of a repetitive foray. The case histories have been the object of meticulous scrutiny and it would seem that there is little to gain by this essay. Nevertheless, any renewed study of Freud is bound to produce some revelation, for his genius often showed itself in his biblical-like expositions—a capacity to state in elliptical form an idea of profound theoretical or methodological import. There is scarcely an idea or aspect of theory in our current discourse that cannot be found either explicitly or implicitly in Freud's writings. The Ran Man resonates with much that contemporary treatment issues are concerned with such current ideas as the dialogue between patient and analyst, and the immediacy of experience (Poland, 1992; Chused, 1992) are evident in Freud's treatment of Paul Lorenze. His remarks regarding the process of psychoanalysis and discussions, that at time take on the tone of an educational or intellectual exercise, were in essence a dyadic dialogue that contributed to the experiential mode for the unfolding of the transference. Though, true, Freud was not focusing directly upon transference theories in his theoretical exposition of this case, it is clear in the treatment and in Freud's terse comments that these issues were paramount to the work.

Undoubtedly, this case contributed to the development of his ideas in the technique papers (1910, 1912a, 1912b, 1913, 1914, 1915, 1919).

Poland's (1992) perception that, "dazzled by the past we have at times lost our bearings in the present, as if we could reach for the past without putting our full weight on the present," (p. 186) is an echo of Freud's (1912b) statement in relation to the transference:

> that they, and they only, render an invaluable service of making the patient's buried and forgotten love-emotions actual and manifest; for in the last resort no one can be slain in absentia or in effigy [p. 108].

Thus, to reclaim the dialogue on Freud's treatment of the "Rat Man," that seemed to exhaust itself in the 1980s, may contribute to the current discourse on transference and countertransference, resistance and defense, and the interrelationship between the patient and the analyst (Gill, 1993; Gill et al., 1974).

My discussion on the Rat Man will complement Lipton's ideas (1977, 1979), and is in general agreement with his critique of the rather stringent criticism directed against Freud for his treatment methods in the case. The nature of the criticism against Freud is both general and specific in kind. Methodologically, Freud's critics (Kanzer, 1980a & 1980b; Langs, 1980; Mahoney, 1980; Weiss, 1980) find fault with his technique in handling such issues as the establishment of an extratransference relationship, analytic neutrality, intellectualism, and finally with what they feel to be Freud's avoidance of the negative transference. The source of more virulent criticism, or better still, of major indictment in Paul Lorenze's treatment lies less with Freud's theoretical premise than it does with several particular acts, namely supplying the missing word in the second session, feeding him, and sending him a postcard.

Like Lipton (1977, 1979), I, too, feel compelled to respond to those who are critical of Freud's handling of the Rat Man analysis, but I find myself unable to agree with him that Freud's technique in the Rat man case was fully matured, and that the written works of 1910–1914 represented a codification of the theories that were already in practice. Rather, it is my opinion that at the time Freud was treating Paul Lorenze, psychoanalytic technique as well as the theories of transference and resistance were very much in the inception phase. They had yet to evolve through the reciprocal process by which theory and clinical practice were either complementary or divergent, such that one or the other had to be modified by a new understanding of the material.

I think it would be worthwhile to briefly consider the Dora case in relation to that of the Rat Man. A comparison would suggest that in the Dora case there was a very different level of conceptualization on Freud's part with regard to methodology. Here the dominant therapeutic endeavor was to render what was unconscious conscious. Freud felt that in freeing the unconscious wishes from repression, the ego's normative growth patterns would be restored. And once freed from the fears associated with infantile sexuality the energy bound in the defense could then be applied to a more creative solution. The recognition of resistance was not yet a potent weapon in Freud's arsenal. He was too enthralled with the labyrinth of mental mechanisms: the detours of the unconscious through the associative pathways, the function of primary process, and the role of condensation and displacement. By the time Freud began the treatment of the Rat Man the role of transference and resistance was clearly an important concept in his theories of technique. Still, he was, and continued to be throughout his life, primarily interested in mental structure and in psychic mechanisms. In Sulloway's term, Freud was a "biologist of the mind" (1979). His investigation of psychic mechanisms paralleled his medical training. For Freud, the study of anatomy and histology required the investigation of structure and function. Thus, technique did not loom large in Freud's writings. Perhaps he was too creative a spirit to be regimented by a list of rules on methodology. Yet, for their lucidity and their exactness, Freud's papers on technique remain unparalleled. And while it must be acknowledged that psychoanalysis has indeed elaborated the concepts of transference, and has even elevated the theory of countertransference to a kind of methodology, I do not believe that we have materially improved on Freud's concepts.

Having said this much, let us return, momentarily, to the critics of Freud's Rat Man case. Kanzer (1980a) speaks of Freud's brilliant, intuitive work, of his ability to glean unconscious meanings from rather innocuous material. Praise, though they may be, Kanzer's remarks are, in essence, veiled criticisms of Freud. It is Kanzer's belief that Freud relied on intellectualization, persuasion, and the "human influence" to achieve results in the treatment.

The demand to yield up a "picture of his lady" was, for Kanzer, an indication of a "stern" and intrusive act. Kanzer goes on to say that Freud did not "comprehend under the concept of transference and resistance," the patient's negative and ambivalent reactions, nor that the memories of death wishes toward the father were in actuality, and more importantly, death wishes toward Freud. Kanzer is equally critical of Freud's decision to feed the Rat Man, citing it as yet another instance of the break with therapeutic neutrality. According to Kanzer, Freud failed to understand and to deal effectively with the negative reactions which followed the feeding.

Langs (1980) has criticized Freud for creating a "sector of misalliance" with the Rat Man by feeding him and by writing to him. He is especially critical of the "egregious" error Freud committed when, in the second session, he completed Lorenze's sentence regarding the rat's penetration into the anus. Both Kanzer (1980a) and Langs (1980) regard Freud's "guessing" of Lorenze's thoughts as a transference gratification, a homosexual seduction, and as a "mutual acting out." In regard to the "sectors of misalliance," Langs states that Freud "consistently avoided the day residue and current precipitants of his patient's transference reactions, nor did he take cognizance of any realistic perception and reality based reaction to himself" (p. 218). Langs calls attention to the aggressive elements in Freud's interpretations and demands for material, and sees the feeding of the Rat Man as a "dangerous homosexual seduction and attack to which the Rat Man reacted with great mistrust and rage" (p. 277). Turning to Freud's technique, Langs (1980) writes that because Freud's primary focus was on

> the generic roots of symptoms and so-called transference fantasies, he almost entirely overlooked the current precipitants of the "Rat Man's" reactions toward him and had no extensive clinical experience in distinguishing his patient's primarily intrapsychically determined fantasies about him (transference) from their conscious and unconscious realistic, veridical perceptions (nontransferences). [p. 227]

Of course, Freud is not beyond criticism. Yet, what is this mode of censure that demands from Freud an almost prescient knowledge, and that assumes, in addition, that Freud should have been aware of all of the ramifications of transference? Freud, himself the discoverer of transference, is being taken to task for not anticipating the vicissitudes of a psychic phenomenon he was still in the process of discovering. Consequently, what we must notice in Lang's statement that Freud had no extensive "clinical experience" in distinguishing transference from nontransference perceptions is that his words betray an implicit, if not explicit, denial of historical progression. Indeed, these critiques of Freud are not offered from the perspective of retracing the process that Freud was involved with, a process that centered on, among other things, the problems in understanding the mechanisms of projection and displacement which underlie the transference, the power of infantile wishes, and, perhaps most crucially, the methodology of treatment.

The capacity to control one's responses, to act on consciously felt affects, to explore one's own unconscious in the nexus of the patient's unconscious is the continual labor of psychoanalytic theory. Nearly one hundred years have passed since the advent of psychoanalysis, and we are still grappling with the subtle modes of transference and countertransference. Undoubtedly, much of Freud's behavior in regard to the *Rat Man:* feeding him, praising his abilities, writing to him, and guessing his thoughts, is problematic and thus warrants critical investigation. Whether we can dismiss these methods or acts as anti-analytic, and, therefore, harmful to the progress of the treatment with absolute certainty, however, is questionable. But Freud's critics, bound by the rigidity of their own categorical imperatives, have left little room for query and flexibility in the treatment process.

We can, I think approach Freud's behavior in the Rat man case on many levels. Some of it clearly follows the cultural mores of the period. Freud, however, was far more experimental in his treatment methods than appeals to the palate of contemporary analysts. The assumption that Freud could have known what in his language or manner of presentation would lead to either a negative, eroticized, or positive transference reaction without a certain amount of exploratory activity is an idealism. Certain theories can and do evolve from an a priori premise, but there will always be those that must rely primarily on trial and error, itself a method of investigation. Therefore, to criticize Freud for failing to understand the negative transference, and for inducing negative feelings, and finally for countertransferential responses is, in my mind, largely gratuitous. Let us not forget that Freud did indeed modify what he perceived to be erroneous tenets in his work. There are a number of examples of this: the Dora case (1905), his concepts about the role of seduction in the aetiology of the neurosis (1897), and his ideas concerning the origins of anxiety (1923). That Freud, then, neither reappraised his treatment of the Rat Man nor repudiated the theoretical premises stated in the case suggests that he was satisfied with his methodological practices as they were in concert with his overall theories on psychoanalytic technique. Again, I do not mean to suggest that Freud is beyond criticism. Nor, do I think, would he. Freud was quite aware and quite comfortable with the knowledge that future research would both modify and expand some of the fundamental hypotheses of psychoanalysis (1905, 1915). Perhaps at that time it was more important for Freud to offer to posterity the evolution of a theory and the development of a methodology than it was to rewrite history for the sake of perfectionism.

Freud begins Lorenze's analysis by making him

pledge to submit to the one and only condition of the treatment: namely, to say everything that came into his head, even if it was unpleasant to him, or seemed unimportant or irrelevant or senseless" [1909, p. 159].

Surely, we are startled by this rather authoritarian demand—the requirement of a "pledge" of submission—from Freud. In response to such a pledge, we can imagine several possible reactions: rage at the demand, negativism, or that of a passive homosexual fantasy that had been stirred up in the patient by the analyst's actions. Given the possibility for such reactions, it is indeed curious for Freud to have begun his treatment of the Rat Man in this way. We can only wonder whether Freud regarded the positing of the fundamental rule of psychoanalysis as a necessary introduction to the analytic procedure. Freud frequently engaged in intellectual explanations on the nature of mental processes with his patients. With Lorenze, he often discussed the role of repression and the root of guilt in psychic reality, and various other aspects concerning defense and resistance.[1]

---

1 Freud felt that while these discussions were ineffective in modifying the defenses and the resistance, they could serve some useful purpose in abetting the process of free association.

But since Freud gives us no clue as to his rationale, we can only speculate at his motives from our own understanding of his conceptualizations, and from a hermeneutic reading of his text. The material that follows "the pledge" in no way shows the affects of rage, or of inhibition, or of constraint. It is my assumption that Freud considered his preliminary remarks as the means by which he could simultaneously educate Lorenze as well as reduce his excessive anxiety. And, I would further speculate that guiding Freud's actions here was the earlier principle of freeing the unconscious or preconscious material from repression. That this principle is both operative and of paramount importance in the Rat Man case becomes clear when we realize that Freud allied himself with Lorenze's unconscious against the strictures of censorship; in structural theory (Freud, 1923), we would characterize it as an alliance with the id against the superego and the ego. Also, in spite of Freud's admonitions against the dangers of suggestion, in practice he never abandoned this method as a necessary ally in analytic work (1940). I am aware, however, that there will be those who will not regard my comments as an adequate explanation for what Langs (1980) perceives to be Freud's autocratic character structure and his seductive nature. Yet, after making the pledge, Lorenze produces material relating to his early sexuality, and provides fundamental clues concerning the structure of his present symptomatology. Previously, however he had related an important fact: there were two men to whom he was attached. One was a current friend who provided him with moral support, and the other was a friend from adolescence who had betrayed him. From Freud's discussion, the ensuing transference meaning of these relationships becomes apparent. The very fact of the male analyst as an authority, together with Freud's command that Lorenze submit to the fundamental rule of analysis, could have evoked both his wishes and his fears in relation to men. Here, we might wonder whether Freud was too interested in the nature of the obsessive mechanism, and the role of infantile sexuality in the etiology of the neuroses such that the emergent transference became a secondary consideration. But as Freud makes no comment concerning his introductory remarks at the beginning of Lorenze's analysis, we have no way of knowing for sure whether he even considered that his initial statement about the fundamental rule of analysis influenced Lorenze's subsequent associations.

Langs (1980) accuses Freud of neglecting the transference which, in his view, is already present in the second session. However, it is necessary to distinguish between transference-like reactions and transference which is specifically experienced toward the analyst (Greenson, 1967). Freud was indeed aware of the homosexual meaning of Lorenze's recitation regarding both his "friend" and the tutor of his adolescence, making it inconceivable for him not have considered this as an element in the emerging transference. Freud (1912) had always considered the positive transference as a sublimation of erotic feeling, and it would be in keeping with this postulate for him also, to consider that the homosexual current could contribute to the establishment of positive affects (1921).

Over the course of the second session, Lorenze tells Freud of his rat obsession. As he relates the story told to him by the "cruel captain" his agitation increases; he jumps from the couch, paces the room, and finally is unable to complete the tale of the cruel punishment: that of the rat boring into the prisoner's anus. Lorenze begs Freud "to spare him the recital of the details." Freud replies that

> I myself have no taste whatever for cruelty, and certainly had no desire to torment him, but that naturally I could not grant him something that was beyond my power. He might just as well ask me to give him the moon. The overcoming of resistances was a law of treatment, and on no consideration could it be dispensed with [p. 166].

This rather startling statement seems to suggest that both the patient and the analyst were in the grips of the analytic process which needed to be obeyed at all costs. Yet, this type of command is compatible with the obsessive compulsive neurosis from which there is no escaping the demands of the compulsions. For Freud and for Lorenze then, the "laws" of psychoanalysis presented a means for displacement of the obsessional mechanism. But, while one may want to conclude that the compulsion to obey the laws of free association was Freud's way of providing the Rat Man with a secondary line of defense, there is no evidence that this is what occurred.

An intellectual idea always has the capacity to evoke an emotional response, and it is conceivable that Freud's statement provided a reassuring note to the analytic process. It is not only to the analyst that the patient establishes a positive transference, but also to the process (Greenson, 1967). Perhaps, it was this positive transference to the analytic process that reduced the impact of Freud's personal authority. The sublimation of eroticized object love as it was transferred onto the psychoanalytic process created a situation wherein both Freud and Lorenze became participants in the method or the "idea."[2] Thus, not only does Freud become an equal ally in the analysis (Poland, 1992), but, as he tells Lorenze, he "would do all [he] could, nevertheless, to guess the full meaning of any hints he gave me" (Freud, 1909, p. 166). Freud's remark here follows a prior discussion he had had with Lorenze concerning the nature of "resistance." But we need to pause here and consider whether Freud is himself participating in a somewhat seductive act with his patient, a coy sexual arousal the result of which is "sadomasochistic" pleasure (Langs, 1980). It is my impression that quite the contrary is true. Freud informs Lorenze that he is in the grips of powerful unconscious forces which are infantile in nature. At the same time, however, Freud communicates to him that he will join forces with Lorenze's

---

2 Freud elaborates this concept in his paper on "Group Psychology" (1921).

ego against the censorship or repressing forces, as well as against the arising sexual impulses. We are all aware that the intent of the therapeutic act may be variant from its result. The analyst, as it were, may be likened to a double agent; he supports the reality ego and the defenses while simultaneously encouraging id pleasures and the undoing of repression (Greenson, 1967). Does Freud increase the Rat Man's eroticism when he completes the sentence of the rats boring their way in the "anus?" Clearly, he is aware of the Rat Man's erotic arousal. He comments on the "strange, composite expression" of Lorenze's face, saying, "I could only interpret it as one of horror at pleasure of his own of which he himself was unaware" (p. 169). Freud also remarks that the

> patient behaved as though he were dazed and bewildered. He repeatedly addressed me as "Captain," probably because at the beginning of the hour I had told him that I myself was not fond of cruelty like Captain N., and that I had no intention of tormenting him unnecessarily [p. 169].

Certainly, Freud, himself the master of recognizing reversals, understood that the Rat Man had reversed this statement in his unconscious and took it to mean that Freud, or someone, was in favor of cruelty. I have deliberately used the pronoun "someone" here because in Lorenze's state of "deliria" Freud, the Rat Man, and Captain N. are a composite figure.

The question of whether by supplying the word "anus" Freud both heightened the erotic transference and transposed the transference into a reality situation is also at issue. Both Kanzer (1980) and Langs (1980) consider that Freud complicated it and was, indeed, seductive in his behavior toward Lorenze. A secondary consideration in this case refers to the use of scatological language by the analyst. While anus is a technical term, it does have the power of inducing erotic ideas. Thus, in this context, the word anus evokes a scatological referent. Does Freud's use of the word, then, increase the drive stimulus, or does it in fact serve to reduce the eroticism? We have recognized that language may serve the function of stimulating the drives, but at the same time language, as a derivative of thought, has the capacity to sublimate and reduce in quantity the drive and shift the aim (Freud, 1911; Shapiro, 1979).

The charge that Freud not only had created a dangerous seductive environment for Lorenze (Langs, 1980), but also had shifted the transference from an internal template to an external reality perception that interfered with the transference and the therapeutic work, is, I believe, without merit. To speak of transference in a second session has its own set of complexities. The critical meaning of this second session does not arise from the issue of transference, but rather from the confused state: "the deliria," from which Lorenze attempts to ward off the prohibited wishes. Further, it is important to remember that Freud did not believe that every transference response needed to be interpreted as long as the patient produced material without resistance (1912b, 1913). After Freud helped the Rat Man complete the exciting but unacceptable tale—they bored their way in—by uttering the words "into the anus," there is no interruption in the material or constriction in Lorenze's behavior. In fact, Lorenze goes on to relate another obsessional idea which points to the underlying aggression he felt toward his "girl" and his father. Lorenze states

that "suddenly" a thought occurred to him as the cruel captain told his rat story: that "at that moment this was happening to a person who was very dear to me" (p. 167). Somewhat later in the session, he acknowledged that he had this thought about his father who was already dead.

Both Kanzer (1980) and Langs (1980) believe that Lorenze's thoughts that the rat punishment was happening to his "girl" and his father are essentially transference wishes toward Freud, and that Freud did not understand this, once again missing an opportunity to investigate the transference. If all material presented by the patient from the very inception of treatment is determined by transference, then Freud did, indeed, miss the basic meaning of the rat story. Consequently, he would have to take responsibility for his own contribution to the patient's anal sadistic fantasies (Langs, 1980). On the other hand, if Freud's completion of the sentence enabled the patient to deal with highly charged and prohibited material, then what we have here is an example of the analyst's role in overcoming his resistance. And nothing in the text suggests to me that Freud aroused Lorenze's passive homosexual wishes, nor does the text support the thesis that the sadistic wishes aroused by the memory of the captain's tale have currency in regard to Freud's behavior at this point in the treatment. We need to consider whether anything would have been lost if Freud had not volunteered his assistance. Though not likely, it is conceivable that his assistance allowed for a greater accessibility of the lascivious, hostile, sadistic, and masochistic wishes into consciousness. This very participation enabled Lorenze to view Freud as a more benign superego representation, and also may have helped to reduce his resistance (Kestenberg, 1980). While a particular act of the analyst such as Freud's helping Lorenze with hints may never be subject directly to an analysis, it is anticipated that this aspect of the patient's resistance and transference reactions will eventually admit to analysis. For a transference interpretation to be effective, a collectivization of the patient's experiences are necessary (Freud, 1912b, 1913; Fenichel, 1941; Greenson, 1967). There are a multitude of transferential reactions within the analytic session, and the constant interpretation of these reactions would only create a sterile environment for the analysis.

But many of Freud's actions in his treatment of the Rat man are liable to raise a quizzical brow. At one point, he requests, nay, insists, that the Rat Man produce a photograph of his lady because he wants him to give up his reticence about her. He begins his notes for October 11 with the following:

> ... violent struggle, bad day. Resistance, because I requested him yesterday to bring a photograph of the lady—Conflict as to whether he should abandon the treatment or surrender his secrets. His Cs far from having mastered his oscillating thoughts [p. 260].

Freud does not indicate how he handled the resistance, nor does he comment on the effect his request had upon the transference. Nor, for that matter, does Freud give us any clue as to how he handled the Ran Man's threat to terminate the treatment. It is not, however, beyond our power to conclude that Freud did not consider the issue of the photograph as a specific transference issue, viewing it rather as part of Lorenze's desire for secrecy regarding his lady, and generalized resistance (A. Freud, 1966; Greenson, 1967). Still, Freud's insistence upon the photograph is mysterious, and necessarily serves to provoke our curiosity. But as he did not elaborate his thinking on this point, we can only judge by the subsequent material as to its negative effects if any.

In the session of October 27, Freud stated that "so long as he makes difficulties over giving me the lady's name his account must be incoherent" (p. 272). He goes on to say that "after I had persuaded him to reveal the name of Gisa Hertz and all the details about her, his account became clear and systematic" (p. 273). Freud is referring here to the material which has emerged from repression. And it is from this material that we learn about the Rat Man's ambivalence toward his lady, and about his obsessive prayer "Hapeltsamen"—which is shorthand for a prayer that could not be said without the intrusion of an aggressive thought. In subsequent sessions the material centers on masturbation, sexual activity, suicidal thoughts, as well as thoughts about prostitutes. Kanzer (1980) and Langs (1980) have labeled Freud's demand for the photograph intrusive and authoritarian, and yet it is precisely this intrusive and authoritarian act which led to Lorenze's rather extensive line of associations. In spite of Kanzer (1980) and Langs (1980) proclamations that Lorenze experienced Freud's request negatively, in my mind a more plausible interpretation of Lorenze's behavior is that he felt a sense of relief from the superego prohibitions. He had internalized the demands of his father, who opposed his liaison with Gisa. Following from this, then, it seems likely that Freud's insistence on both seeing the photograph and learning the lady's name would have given acceptance to Lorenze's genital wishes to marry. However, whether these acts of Freud together with his interpretations were experienced by Lorenze as support for his genital wishes in the conflict between the anal and the genital phase is something we can never know. But, it is a likely consideration. And finally, I would again suggest that Freud understood that Lorenze's vagueness in telling him Gisa's name or in showing him the picture was not a resistance to the transference, but rather a resistance to life (A. Freud, 1936).

Both from the session on November 21 and those following, it becomes possible to observe the emergence of a powerful, though negative, transference. Lorenze told Freud that he should "turn him out, [that] the most frightful thing had occurred to his mind while he was riding on the bus" (p. 281). It was only after Freud interpreted the vengeful feelings and the gratification he would achieve in giving up the treatment that Lorenze was able to relate that the thoughts concerned Freud's daughter. Obviously sexual in nature, Freud regarded Lorenze's thoughts as a displacement from incestuous wishes and actual sexual activity with his sister, Julie. Continuing, Lorenze admitted to fantasies about Freud's mother, fantasies in which "swords [were] eaten by Freud and the children." He also had fantasies of Freud's daughter performing fellatio on one of the deputy judges—Freud notes that Lorenze himself "wishes" to become a judge.

Again, we must pause to ask whether Freud defused the transference by his focus on Lorenze's current conflictual situation and genetic constructs. Freud's critics seem to feel that he underestimated Lorenze's powerful negative reactions toward him. Kanzer (1980) states that it was his intuitive genius that achieved success in spite of his countertransference and intellectual treatment. I rather think that Freud's genius lay in his capacity to differentiate the point at which the transference defended against the infantile and unconscious wishes as well as the point at which the infantile material was used as a defense against the transference (Greenson, 1967). Freud did not appear to focus on the transference as the dynamic vehicle for interpretation with the Rat Man. Stone (1984) has indicated that there are

> many who, if not in doubt regarding the great value of transference interpretations, are inclined to doubt their uniqueness and to stress the importance of economic considerations in determining the choices as to whether transference or extra-transference may be indicated [p. 96].

Furthermore, Stone addresses the importance of the extra-analytic life of the patient. I do not believe that Freud was unaware of the negative transference; certainly, he himself comments on it. But to have laid stress on the transference would in all probability simply have lent support to Lorenze's obsessive symptomatology. Lorenze's thoughts regarding Freud and his family resemble his obsessive rat fantasies. They are alien, and they impose themselves on his thinking. In short, the rat fantasies are defense manifestations against conflicts which Lorenze cannot face. The true affects and wishes were not directed toward Freud, but were related to his lady, his sister Julie, and his parents. Freud understood, and I think rightly so, that Lorenze's anxiety was caused by his conflicts about "marriage and copulation." The transference thoughts served the purpose of a displacement from the guilty affect over his hostile wishes toward Gisa and his incestuous wishes toward Julie. Only with great resistance was Lorenze able to admit to his rage against both Gisa and his father. Though his incestuous wishes as well as his sexual and seductive behavior toward Julie were quite manifest in the material, they were isolated from his affects. In his note for November 17, Freud wrote that Lorenze's pathological changes could be explained by his sexual assault on Julie after their father's death. For Freud, the unconscious and preconscious conflicts provided the dynamic material in the working through of the defense and the resistance. And in economic terms the transference was the lesser source of resistance. Throughout the treatment, Freud utilized both the unconscious material regarding the loved and hated objects in Lorenze's life and the transference as a means of working through the defense and the resistance.

The session on November 22 reveals an intensification of the negative transference. Having killed off Freud's mother in fantasy, the Rat man leaves a card with the words "pour feliciter" rather than with the expected ones "pour condoler." Freud understood this transference material as a defense against the murderous wishes Lorenze had toward his own mother. The transference served as a defense against the current affect state. When Freud made this interpretation Lorenze responded, "you are taking revenge on me—you are forcing me into this, because you want to revenge yourself on me" (p. 283). He then confessed to Freud that he was walking around the room because of his fear that Freud would beat him. The emergence of this beating fantasy indicates a shift in the associations and affective state in the session from transference reaction as defense against unconscious material to an acting out of the transference neurosis—a wish to be beaten by Freud. This repetition of infantile wishes does not indicate a negative transference, in fact, quite the contrary. I believe that it speaks of the positive erotic wishes of a masochistic nature. Lorenze's sessions from November 23 to November 30 are replete with sadomasochistic fantasies: rat-killing, cat-skinnings, shootings, and anal intercourse. Freud's interpretation of Lorenze's murderous wishes toward his mother freed his sadistic impulses from repression, and despite the claims of Freud's critics, these are not transference wishes induced by Freud's behavior but the remnants of the Rat Man's infantile sexuality which had been freed from repression. On the other hand, in the November 30 session, Freud makes it abundantly clear that he recognized Lorenze's defensive mode against the transference. He remarks that Lorenze had collected more rat stories in order to evade the transference fantasies (p. 289).

Freud has been further assailed by critics for inducing passive homosexual fantasies in Lorenze by his autocratic behavior (Langs, 1980; Kanzer, 1980). His demand for a photograph of Lorenze's lady, as well as for her name almost brought about the end of the treatment; Freud himself admitted that his final success in persuading Lorenze to identify his lady and to reveal all the details about her came about only after a long struggle. But to "persuade" and to "struggle" is not the same as gaining insight or undoing repression, rather it has an element of autocracy and a demand for compliance. The question, however, still remains; did Freud, as Langs (1980) has determined, induce a passive and submissive response in Lorenze, perhaps even in response to Freud's own unconscious homosexual wishes (Langs, 1980). Again, we can only conjecture, but I see no evidence for these critical evaluations. I would argue that the beating fantasy was aroused by Freud's perspicacity in recognizing Lorenze's defense against the rage at his mother and his lady. Further, Lorenze's unconscious wishes for the powerful male, and his sadomasochistic homosexual wishes are activated in the transference by the act of interpretation. The lifting of repression extended not only to the area of the aggressive affects, but also had associated effects in regard to other unconscious wishes, especially that of his homosexual love for his father which was reexperienced in the transference.

Freud commits two other acts in the Rat Man case which warrant our attention: the feeding of the Rat Man, and the sending of the postcard. What were Freud's motivations for feeding his patient, and, more importantly perhaps, for sending him a postcard? Lorenze complained that the card, which Freud signed "cordially" was "too intimate." In the session of December 8, Lorenze excoriated Freud for sending the card, referring to him as a "filthy swine" who needed to be taught manners; he accused him of picking his nose, and told him that Frau Professor Freud should "lick his arse." In addition, he claimed that Freud was trying to turn him into a son-in-law. Were these responses a direct reaction to the postcard, an aggressive defense against what many consider a seductive act by Freud? Again, we have no direct means by which we can understand why Freud sent the card.

While these transference reactions may well have been a direct result of the postcard—an overly friendly act by Freud that aroused threats of seduction in Lorenze—we can, I think, consider another explanation. Freud stated that "he developed a great irritation with me which was expressed in insults" (p. 293).

Lorenze, however, only became irritated and insulting after Freud made the interpretation that he found it intolerable that his father had given up his love for money when he married into the Rubensky family. Lorenze, of course, was confronting the very same dilemma; like his father he could either marry his lady, who was poor, or he could marry the Rubensky's seventeen-year-old daughter and acquire wealth and position. His rage at Freud, which he expressed by calling him a "filthy swine," and by telling him that Frau Professor Freud "should lick his arse," simulates the temper tantrum of one who has been caught at a bad deed and then by identification acts as the aggressor. Thus, it seems to me, that the transference reaction can only be accounted for by the interpretation which exposed his unconscious conflicts, and his wish to betray his love object. But, as I have previously indicated, a transference reaction does not have the same quality of a transference neurosis (Greenson, 1967). Lorenze's comment that the postcard Freud sent him "was too intimate" raises issues regarding the transference neurosis. Regrettably, other than the standard documentation of the facts, there is no commentary from Freud on this incident. That he recorded it at all, however, is certainly an indication that he recognized the role that it played in Lorenze's associations as well as its role in the overall progression of the treatment. In all likelihood, it was the postcard which evoked the transference wish in regard to his father with whom he had a strong love relationship and identification, but toward whom there was also powerful ambivalent feelings. Though a loving and kind man, his father was crude and rough, and often offended Lorenze's sensibilities. On the other hand, Freud not only had all of Lorenze's father's more gentle qualities, but he also had the added advantage of education and refinement. Freud's postcard probably evoked the wish—the family romance wish—of an oedipal constellation for a different father. This perhaps, may explain Lorenze's comment that the card was "too intimate." The sense of intimacy may have evoked a series of untenable conflicts: the wish for Freud as the substitute father, and thus, guilt toward his own father, and the struggle between the heterosexual and homosexual wishes. Also, and of primary importance, was the conflict between Lorenze's wishes and those of his father which accounted for his pathological symptoms, therefore necessitating that the uncovering of Lorenze's unconscious conflicts toward his father become the major emphasis of treatment. Thus, Freud was not amiss in omitting the transference interpretation in the session on December 8. Economic shifts between the infantile object and the analyst are a constant concomitant in the analytic hour (Poland, 1992).

A caul of mystery surrounds another act of Freud's. I am speaking here of his decision to feed Lorenze. Stating merely that Lorenze "was hungry and was fed," Freud gives us no clue about why this occurred. We have no indication from Freud that he considered feeding a patient as part of his technique (Lipton, 1977). Anna Freud has remarked that it was not uncommon for a patient to be fed if he had no opportunity to eat or if he had traveled a great distance (Lipton, 1977). Therefore, we would not be altogether misguided in our thinking if we were to look upon this simply as an ordinary custom of the times, or even as an act of civility on Freud's part. But is it equally possible that this act represented an aberration in Freud, a "misalliance," if you will. During the session in which it took place, there appears to be no conscious or latent reaction to the feeding itself. Biegler (1975), however, has pointed out that the session was longer than any of the other sessions with the Rat Man that Freud reported on. Biegler has suggested that Freud's having fed Lorenze "provoked and emotional storm by its breach of the patient-psychoanalyst therapeutic barrier." What emerged in the session was "primarily oedipal material [which] then induced an anal regression through which Freud was able to make important discoveries concerning anal passivity" (p. 283). Biegler, however, acknowledges that in spite of this breech in the analytic barrier, Freud's genius lay in his ability to successfully use the material in the best interest of his patients. While I must admit that I find Biegler's argument to be cogent, I do not find the quality of a "transference storm" in Lorenze's reaction. Rather, I suspect that we can attribute the session's lengthy documentation to the importance of the material produced, e.g., both his masturbatory fantasies and their bizarre enactment, his ambivalence toward his father, the range of his obsessive and compulsive behavior toward Gisa, and finally, and perhaps of ultimate importance, his suicidal impulses.

The following sessions, December 2 and January 1, contain evidence that the "feeding" stimulated a transference response. In them Lorenze told Freud of his fantasy that

between two women—my wife and my mother—a herring was stretched, extending from the anus of one to that of the other. A girl cut it in two, upon which the two pieces fell away (as though peeled off) [pp. 307–308].

This rather strange fantasy seems to resemble a dream rather than a daytime reverie. But much of Lorenze's thinking is permeated by these dreamlike fantasies, and they are fantasies which appear to reflect the loosening of the barrier between the id and the ego. In the herring fantasy, the bizarre quality of the reverie reflects the influence of primary process such that we can locate the characteristic role of condensation, displacement, visual image presentation, and finally the distortion of reality. However, neither regression alone nor the emergence of primary process functions can fully account for the strange ideational quality in Lorenze's fantasy. Rather, I would suggest that a major factor in the distortion of reality is the mechanism of isolation of idea from idea (Eissler, 1959). For while the idea of a wish and the idea of the real are separated spatially, or put another way, separated by a different level of libidinal phase organization, it remains possible for them to exist side by side without a threat of opposition. Freud assigns this quality of coexistent libidinal phase organization to the system unconscious (1900, 1915), and it is operative in structural regression where different levels of ego organization are juxtaposed in temporal relationships (Modell, 1968). Lorenze's fantasy of a herring extending between two women can be understood as the amalgam of genital and anal sadistic conflicts and wishes which, like a cubist painting maintain their composite but separate images by means of isolation.

Grunberger (1966) has commented elaborately on various aspects of the Rat Man's regression to an anal sadistic phase. Unable to sustain the genital organization, Lorenze, according to Grunberger, maintains his phallic wishes by searching for anal penises which in the fantasy cited above are represented by the herring. In Grunberger's view, the women with the anal penis suggests the presence of a defense against castration, and he points to the role of the diffusion of the instincts within the anal sadistic component, i.e., the separation between the anal eroticism and control, about which he says that "this control [is] devoid of all libidinal elements" (p. 165). For Grunberger, the analization of the libido has resulted in a "part object" relationship to the object world such that the Rat Man substitutes the "faeces" as a representation of the object. It is my impression that the mechanism of isolation (Eissler, 1959) which separates idea and affect, and libido and aggression, i.e., affect from affect, is for Lorenze, a fundamental defense against his ambivalence, and that there is no question of his libidinal cathexis to the "whole object." The relibidinization of "faeces" did not in essence replace object libido with ego libido, this suggesting that a narcissistic regression occurred. Rather, in spite of the regression, the structure of the genital-phase organization was maintained.

I have presented here a somewhat circuitous discussion on the nature of the Rat Man's fantasy as a means of indicating the nature of the connection between Freud's act of feeding him, the fantasy which resulted, and the primary meaning of the fantasy's latent content. As I have indicated elsewhere in this paper, the criticism of the "feeding" is essentially concerned with illustrating that the seductive nature of Freud's act served to compromise Lorenze's genital position and exacerbate his passive wishes. It is my opinion that, in much the same way day residue behaves as a stimulus for dream formation, the "feeding" acted as a precipitant for the Rat Man's herring fantasy. But it was not the feeding itself which prompted the reverie, rather, it was the actual herring he was served and the woman who served it to him. In the analysis, Freud treats this day fantasy as he does dreams in general. In the fantasy, the herring behaves like a centrifugal force from which anal wishes of penetration, women with anal penises, worms (the equivalency of the anal penis), early memories of anal eroticism, and finally the defense of disgust emerge. In my opinion, the transference was not the dynamic component in the fantasy, nor did the feeding provoke emotional turmoil or result in a homosexual submission to Freud. The material associated with the fantasy followed a continuous plane, leading from both the regressed voyeuristic and exhibitionist components of the anal phase and the aggressive attributes of these partial drives (Grunberger, 1966) to the conflicts over rivalry and rebellion, and between homosexual and heterosexual love in the oedipal phase. The fundamental problem for Lorenze continued to be centered around his ambivalent relationship with his father and with his lady.

There are a number of other significant issues present in Freud's treatment of Lorenze which require examination from a theoretical and methodological perspective. The first is Lorenze's relationship with his mother. Barely alluded to in the formal history of the case, it is only from Freud's own written notes that we learn anything significant either about her character or about her relationship with her son. Freud has been duly criticized for his apparent neglect both of their relationship and the role it played in the etiology of his patients illness. He does, in fact, allude to Lorenze's incestuous tie to his sister Julie, as well as to the probable sexual relationships he engaged in with his sisters. In a brief footnote (p. 209) Freud does indicate that these relationships may be partial displacements from his incestuous relationship with his mother. Freud did not find it at all curious that a grown man with an independent income would postpone agreeing to treatment until after he had discussed the matter of the fee with his mother. Later in the treatment, Freud does make note of Lorenze's identification with his mother, but he did not consider the identification nor the resultant conflicts as an aspect of Lorenze's ambivalence about marriage.

The second issue we need to consider is the curious silence on Freud's part in regard to Lorenze's relationship with his sister Katherine, and the meaning her death may have played in his suicidal acts and wishes. Five years his senior, Katherine died when Lorenze was approximately five years old. There are two rather poignant references to her. One is in a transference fantasy which emerges after he admits to a wish to be beaten by Freud. In the original record of the case, Freud quotes Lorenze as saying, "now you'll turn me out," and then goes on to make the following comment:

> It was a question of a picture of me and my wife in bed with a dead child lying between us. He knew the origin of this. When he was a little boy (age uncertain, perhaps 5 or 6) he was lying between his father and mother and wetted the bed, upon which his father beat him and turned him out. The dead child can only be his sister Katherine, he must have gained by her death [p. 284].

It is in this session that Lorenze has the fantasy that Freud's mother had died and that he left a condolence card with the words "pour feliciter." Lorenze's preoccupation with death and the displacement of a dead sister and mother onto Freud's family is indicative of a rather powerful defense against what might be an incomplete mourning for Katherine. But an even stronger indication that Lorenze had not fully worked through Katherine's death and that it continued to exercise a powerful motif for his suicidal ideation occurs in the following dream which Freud recorded and dated December–January 1907:

> I was in a wood and most melancholy. The lady came to meet me, and looking very pale. "Paul, come with me before it is too late. I know we are both sufferers." She put her arm through mine and dragged my away by force. I struggled with her but she was too strong. We came to a broad river and she stood there. I was dressed in miserable rags which fell into the stream and were carried away by it. I tried to swim after them but she held me back; "Let the rags go!" I stood there in gorgeous raiment [p. 268].

Lorenze's associations, or better still, his own interpretation of the dream, does not elucidate latent meaning. He says that the "rags meant his illness and the whole dream promised him health through his lady." In view of his regard for the dream as the "royal road to the unconscious" Freud, according to his notes, surprisingly enough, neither pursued nor interpreted this dream. The original record of the case reports a large number of dreams that either were not interpreted or else whose interpretations were not expounded upon in the text of the case. In his record of the October 18 session, Freud noted that a dream went uninterpreted, explaining that "it is in fact only a more distinct version of the obsessional idea which he did not dare to become aware of during the day." In comparison with the Dora case where dreams had been the pivotal focus of the treatment, Freud has clearly modified his technique in the treatment of Lorenze. Where with Dora it was precisely the interpretations of dreams which, as they prematurely exposed her unconscious wishes, aroused her resistance, with Lorenze, it was almost a paucity of dream interpretation which confronts our analytic mindset. Freud, however, has indicated that dreaming could itself serve as a resistance, and it is clear that he regarded them in this light.

My purpose in writing this paper is to demonstrate that the critiques directed against Freud for his handling of the Rat Man case have essentially overstated the case. In conclusion, I would like to repeat that the criticism against Freud for neglecting the transference, for ignoring the negative transference, and for inducing a passive and submissive attitude in Lorenze is largely the result of a too rigid and too pristine application of the theories on transference and resistance (Lipton, 1977). The constant reference to transference issues in both the original record of the case and the original published case history clearly indicate that Freud recognized that the transference was a central factor in the analysis. I have made the distinction between transference as a reenactment in the transference neurosis and transference reactions themselves. Transference reactions can serve a specifically defensive purpose (Greenson, 1967) where the transference is used as a defense against current unconscious conflicts. I have suggested that Freud recognized the defensive role of the transference reactions in Lorenze's affective responses. It is my contention that the so-called transference "storm reactions" (Langs, 1980) were aroused by Freud's interpretation of Lorenze's current ambivalence regarding Gisa and his aggressive affects toward his mother and deceased father. Lorenze was reacting with rage to "having been found out" by Freud who, in a sense, disclosed his subterfuge of the present by raising past issues.

In respect to the criticism directed against Freud for feeding Lorenze and for sending him a postcard, I again suggest that it ignores the social and cultural mores of the period. Freud's critics have found evidence of induced passivity, of submission and of rage toward Freud for these acts. My own investigation of the text in no way supports their findings, just the opposite: there was a progressive modification of the ego's defensive structure due in part to the lifting of repression. Lorenze's ambivalence and aggression were central to his pathological symptom formation, and Freud's genius lay precisely in his ability to work through the defenses and the resistances. Yet, as I said before, Freud is not beyond criticism.

As Mahoney has stated: "The 'Rat Man' case is a majestic fragment." And in his view the case history is suggestive of theoretical achievements that, on the whole, have been neglected. "For instance," he writes

here and there Freud hinted at a whole semiotic range and contiguity and isolation in obsessional neurosis, from relationships with the body schema, to separation of affect from ideation, to the substitution of the visual function for physical touching, and finally to the temporal disconnectedness that can keynote obsessional articulation [p. 214].

In ending here, I can only agree with Mahoney: that the "Rat Man" is indeed, a majestic fragment. The case stands as a testimonial to Freud's exploratory mind, to the clarity of his style, and perhaps most significantly, to the breadth of his historical perspective.

REFERENCES

Biegler, J. (1975). A commentary on Freud: Treatment of the rat man. Annual Psychoanal., vol. III. Chicago Institute for Psychoanalysis, New York: International Univ. Press pp. *271–86.*

Chused, J. (1992). The patient's perception of the analyst: The hidden transference. *Psychoanal. Q.,* 61: *161-184.*

Eissler, K. (1959). On isolation. *Psychoanal. St. Child,* 14:*29–60.*

Fenichel, O. (1941). *Problems of Psychoanalytic Technique,* Transl. D. Brunswick, New York: The Psychoanalytic Quarterly.

Freud, A. (1936). *The Ego and the Mechanisms of Defense.* New York: International Universities Press.

———— (1966). Obsessional neurosis: A summary of psychoanalytic views as presented at the congress. *Int. J. Psycho-Anal.* 47:2–3, 116–122.

Freud, S. (1897). September 21. In J. Masson, Ed., *The Complete Letters of Sigmund Freud to Wilhelm Fliess.* (1985). Cambridge, MA, & London: Harvard University Press.

———— (1900). The interpretation of dreams *Standard Edition* 4.

———— (1905). Fragments of an analysis of a case of hysteria. *Standard Edition* 7.

———— (1909). Notes upon a case of obsessional neurosis. *Standard Edition*10.

———— (1911). Formulation of the two principles of mental functioning. *Standard Edition* 12.

_____ (1912a). The employment of dream interpretation in psychoanalysis. *Standard Edition* 2.

_____ (1912b). The dynamics of transference. *Standard Edition* 12.

_____ (1913). Further recommendations in the technique of psychoanalysis. on the beginning the treatment. *Standard Edition* 12.

_____ (1914). Further recommendations in the technique of psychoanalysis. Recollection, repetition and working through. *Standard Edition* 12.

_____ (1915). Instincts and their vicissitudes. *Standard Edition* 14

_____ (1919). Turnings in the ways of psycho-analytic therapy. *Standard Edition* 12.

_____ (1921). Group psychology and the analysis of the ego. *Standard Edition* 8.

_____ (1923). Inhibitions, symptoms and anxiety. *Standard Edition* 20.

_____ (1940 [1938]). An outline of psychoanalysis. Standard Edition 23.

Gill, M. (1993). On 'enchantments': Interaction and interpretation. *Psychoanal. Dial* 3:111–122.

_____ Meislin, J., & Hyman, L. (1974). Early interpretation of transference. *J. Amer. Psychoanal. Assn.* 24(4):779-794.

Greenson, R. (1967). The Technique and Practice of Psychoanalysis. New York: International Universities Press.

Grunberger, B. (1966). Some reflections on the rat man. *Int. J. Psycho-Anal.* 47:2–3; 160–168.

Kanzer, M. (1980a). Freud's human influence in the rat man. In M. Kanzer & J. Glenn, eds., *Freud and His Patients*. New York: Jason Aronson.

_____ (1980b). The transference neurosis of the rat man. In M. Kanzer & J. Glenn, Eds., *Freud and His Patients*. New York: Jason Aronson.

Kestenberg, J. (1980). Ego-organization in obsessive-compulsive development. A study of the rat-man, based on interpretation of movement patterns. In M. Kanzer & J. Glenn, Eds., *Freud and His Patients*. New York: Jason Aronson.

Langs, R. (1980). The misalliance dimension in the case of the Rat Man. In *Freud and His Patients.* New York: Jason Aronson.

Lipton, S.D. (1977). The advantages of Freud's technique as shown in his analysis of the rat man. *Int. J. Psycho-Anal.* 58:255-273.

Lipton, S.D. (1979). An addendum to the advantages of Freud's technique as shown in his analysis of the rat man. *Int. J. Psycho-Anal.* 60:215-216.

Mahoney, P. (1980). *Freud and the Rat Man.* New Haven: Yale Univ. Press.

Modell, A. (1968). *Object Love and Reality. New York:* International Universities Press.

Poland, W. (1992). Transference: "an original creation." *Psychoanal. Q.* 61:185-205.

Shapiro, T. (1979). *Clinical Psycholinguistics.* New York: Plenum.

Stone, L. (1984). *Transference and Its Context.* New York: Jason Aronson.

Sulloway, F. (1979). *Freud: The Biologist of the Mind.* New York: Basic Books Inc.

Weiss, S.S. (1980). Reflections and Speculations on the Psychoanalysis of the Rat Man. In M. Kanzer & J. Glenn, Eds., *Freud and His Patients.* New York: Jason Aronson.

CHAPTER 10

THE MEANING OF SILENCE FOR THE HOLOCAUST CHILD SURVIVOR: THE ROLE OF FAMILY ROMANCE AND RESCUE FANTASIES

[(2006). Psychoanalytic Review (93)(6):903–922]

History is no stranger to human aggression, yet, the Holocaust (1940–1945), a magnum opus of deliberately planned destruction, defies comprehension. Historians, philosophers, and social scientists have tried to make sense of this disaster. Psychoanalysts, likewise, have contributed an impressive literature to an understanding of individual behavior and group dynamics during the Nazi tyranny and its aftermath (Bergmann, 1982; Kestenberg, 1980; Krystal, 1988; Niederland, 1981; Ostow, 1982; Pines, 1986).

Much has changed in the past sixty years. Individual survivors who previously maintained. an "epic silence" have begun to speak, to acknowledge the horrors, the trauma, and losses that they experienced. The world, albeit reluctantly, has acknowledged its crimes and denials of this catastrophic event. In spite of this change, we have a history of shattered lives among the survivors, and serious difficulties for their children (Yale Holocaust Video Archives; Holocaust and Genocide Studies, University of Minnesota). The question that we must address as psychoanalysts is by what diagnostic norms are we to judge a people so brutalized and traumatized by the social structure? How are we to understand the psychology of the survivors when the norms of a "good-enough" society no longer applied? How realistic an assessment can we make when the structure of their society, the organization of family life, and the moral value of human relationships disintegrated under the planned extermination by the Nazis? [Wannsee Conference, 1942].

There is a vast psychological literature on the subject of the Holocaust survivor; nevertheless, I hope to add some additional insights that may be relevant to the study of present-day trauma victims especially children (in Darfur, Bosnia, Rwanda). My concern is with the nature and meaning of a particular syndrome of the child survivor, that is, the phenomenon of silence.

The clinical picture of the "child survivor" is that of depression and massive repression which is characterized by "silence" that until recently was rather pervasive and appeared to be typical to the trauma. To describe this pattern as solely pathonomonic would be to deny the impact of the postwar society on the survivors. For those who could talk and for those who needed help to talk, the world was unwilling to hear or to help. The psychological responses of the survivors were not simply an expression of defense, but reflected the dictates of the social order—to remain silent. Fundamentally, we witnessed a *folie à deux*, a complicity between the individual and the external world. The unspoken demand by society for almost two decades required "silence"; to speak was experienced by society as an accusation against its failure to act, to rescue these people.

In an informal discussion regarding the difficulty in speaking about the Holocaust, a survivor with a wry smile turned and confronted me with the statement:

Why do you need such fancy theories? It is so much simpler; nobody wanted to hear. I went to Chicago to visit my six uncles—they welcomed me with open arms—I wanted to talk—to tell them what had happened to me and to my family; I was the only one left, but every time I tried to talk, they would not listen. They did not want to hear, so I gave up trying; I remained silent.

The enlightened world could not hear what had happened to the six million Jews and to the other groups who had perished in the camps and the ghettos. To hear is to know, and the knowledge imparts a demand for reflection and understanding. What could possibly be gained by reflection, except the awareness of guilt and betrayal (Laqueur, 1980; Wyman, 1984)? Thus, in this social climate, for the survivors to talk meant the creation of another hostile environment; perhaps, inner distance is preferable to ostracism. To remain silent, not to threaten the society that offered refuge, at least provided some emotional solace; by this collusion between the individual and the society, the survivor could physically and psychically heal.

Social guilt is more easily assuaged than individual guilt; without talking or writing about the Holocaust the event faded from memory and from history. Social conscience, implied here only in a descriptive sense, is rooted in its collective writings; it does not have the driving or punishing force as that of the individual conscience. The social corollary to individual repression is omission and distortion. It requires a collective effort of will by groups of people to arouse social consciousness, but this is not so for the individual. The individual psyche in the course of development has created a superego that carries on its functions regardless of conscious will (Freud, 1923).

Despite the impact of society that commands silence on the psychological responses of the survivor, and despite my aforementioned doubts as to how to categorize the psychological behavior of the survivors, I do believe that psychoanalytic theory can provide some significant insights. Silence reflected a specific internal purpose, motivated by a sequence of unconscious meanings. One of the primary meanings of silence emerged in relation to the "survivor syndrome," which we have frequently described as almost synonymous with "survivor guilt"—an internalized attack upon the self for having remained alive when everyone—parents, siblings, relatives, and friends—was destroyed (Rosenberg, 1993). Various aspects of this guilt have been studied from a divergent range of clinical and theoretical perspectives (Bergmann, Martin, 1982). One central explanation is based upon both the derivatives of the oedipal conflicts and the role of unconscious aggressive wishes which, harmless in themselves, take on an ominous character in the midst of familial destruction (Bergmann, 1982; Jacovy, 1982; Kestenberg, 1980; Krystal, 1985; Nederland, 1981; Ostow, 1982). In conjunction with the psychological impact of external reality, the roles of the superego as the internalized parental authority and the receptacle of abandoned infantile narcissism (Freud, 1914, 1923) are particularly important. The superego does not necessarily reflect a current appraisal of what is real, but maintains its evaluative procedures based upon past wishes and thoughts, and is a strident agent in the creation of survivor guilt. Since the misdemeanors of childhood can no longer find expiation in subsequent loving approval from the parent, the superego as a self-referent becomes harsher than the admonitions of the parental objects (Freud, 1923). An additional perspective by Bergmann and Jacovy (1982) call attention to the characterological effects of traumatization upon the already existing psychic structure. They have raised the question whether what appeared to be a specific symptom formation related to the trauma of the Holocaust could maintain credibility without reference to earlier genetic influences. Therefore, silence as a symptom formation must be understood from this bifocal perspective.

It is important to stress at this juncture that the Holocaust, though understood as a major social failure and traumatic assault upon whole groups of people, nevertheless must also be understood from its impact upon already developed psychic structures as well as its impact upon those individuals whose psychic structures were in a state of *statu nascendi*. From this perspective, it is possible to understand the formidable difficulties that existed for the Holocaust survivor in resolving major phase specific tasks. Processing of libidinal and aggressive drives, self and object representation, and preoedipal and oedipal issues had been derailed by these cataclysmic events.

My focus concerns the problems arising from difficulties in resolving certain oedipal conflicts that have affected the child survivor's ability to function successfully in his or her adult life. I hope to add to the understanding of child survivor guilt an additional dimension, that of the role of the family romance and rescue fantasies, normal ideational components in child development that became pathological agents in the Holocaust trauma. These factors, as they might have influenced the psychological development of the child survivor, continued to impact negatively on the now-adult defense structure.

OEDIPAL DYNAMICS

Family romance and rescue fantasies play a useful role in the child's continuing endeavors to master the oedipal phase. By creating a phantasmagoric family or narrative, unconscious oedipal conflicts are enacted in a new scenario, removed from the parental objects. Therefore, guilt over sexual and hostile wishes are reduced. They also provide a creative means, an important sublimatory vehicle, to dispose of the oedipus complex (Beres, 1958, 1972; Kris, 1955). The passivity that is experienced by the child's ego, the sense of helplessness in contrast with the parental activity and power, is magically reversed in these sagas. Replacement of the family of origin by a new and edifying family in fantasy raises the child's self-esteem, and is used defensively to master the humiliations and helplessness of childhood. To sustain these fantasies, to receive narcissistic gratifications while simultaneously accepting the reality of the real parents, helps to modify infantile grandiosity and is an important element in the successful resolution of the oedipus conflict (Freud, 1909).

Family romance and rescue fantasies secondarily enable the ego to successfully master the ambivalence toward the primary objects of identification (Esman, 1987; Freud, 1923; Loewald, 1979). This is accomplished in neutralizing aggression by means of elaboration in fantasy. Thus, to replace an object in fantasy while simultaneously continuing to love the object, albeit with some ambivalence is a common ego state. This ambivalence within the ego—a split between love and hate, fantasy and reality—is temporary and resolves itself with the normal resolution of the oedipal conflicts. Object loss in fantasy is essentially play, as the object is easily reinstated; of course, this is contingent upon the level of ambivalence directed toward the internalized representations (Roiphe, 1979; Roiphe & Galenson, 1973).

When object loss occurs in reality during crucial developmental phases, what had been a harmless family romance fantasy for the child can appear to the superego as an act attributable to the wish to get rid of the parent (Ferenczi, 1913). To believe that one may have killed a parent through wish, in spite of the reality, interferes with accepting that the object is gone. To mourn an object that you feel you have killed and to relinquish libidinal attachment from that object is a double burden. Under these conditions, the ability to transfer libido to another object even in adulthood increases the level of guilt due to the role of murderous thoughts and feelings of betrayal.

What then is the internal state of the child survivor who has lost the primary love object at too young a psychological and emotional age, and how does the process of internalization proceed? Initially, the child is confronted with the loss of a love object for which he or she can only find a substitute in the most optimum conditions. The sense of self is depleted by the loss of the love object and the identificatory object (Bibring, 1953; A. Freud, 1967). In this state, the ego has great difficulty in relinquishing the object, and mourning, a crucial ego mechanism, cannot achieve what needs to be accomplished, that is, the decathexis of the object relationship and the cathexis of mnemonic traces of the object (Freud, 1917). Rather than a normal mourning process, a perverse reaction occurs, the former world is created within the ego, and a new aim is established, that of retaining the deceased object (Bowlby, 1966). By means of this resurrection, the child's need for protection and love can find some satisfaction, albeit in a fantasy world.

Since so much of the inner world of child survivors is constructed by the illusionary, unconscious thinking is dominated by narcissistic and grandiose ideals. Unfortunately, the failure to realize these omnipotent fantasies in reality subjects the child survivor to added feelings of incompetence. Furthermore, the child's unrealistic perception of so-called parental inadequacies not only reinforces normal ambivalence toward the internalized imagoes, but interferes with a positive identification and self structure (Kohut, 1971). If we consider even normal maturational assaults to preoedipal ego development, we can see that the ego's ability to tolerate excessive assaults at the oedipal phase will be proportionately affected. In concert with these harmful experiences both to the self and to the object, the normal unfolding of the identificatory process suffers adversely (Bibring, 1953). The mixture of fantasy and reality is difficult for any child to distinguish (A. Freud, 1936), especially at a developmental phase when the ego-ideal may exert a more powerful influence upon ego structure.

In this state, the child survivor, unable to realize his or her rescue fantasies, experiences shame and guilt. Depression is further exacerbated by residual guilt, a reaction to normal oedipal conflicts. To lose a parent, particularly an oedipal rival, complicates the battle, because the rival parent is also a loving parent, a source of support and identification. What then is lost is an important aide in traversing the oedipal phase, resolving conflicts, and establishing realistic identifications. Survival of one parent may even reinforce guilt, especially if it is the parent of the opposite sex. Thus, the imagined possibility of an oedipal victory, the realization of the family romance wishes, leads to a new set of anxieties. With the oedipal rival extinct, the unconscious oedipal wishes appear to dominate reality.

Guilt, depression, shame, and humiliation are common phenomena for the child survivor.

Clinical observation reveals the residual effects of this object loss for the child survivor. First is the magical role of words to create a new reality (Ferenczi, 1913). Second is the inability to complete the identification process; subsequently, the real object is replaced by a fantasy object. The result is often a poorly defined self and object representation. Andre Green (1972) discussed the problems for ego function and structure that develop as a result of the ego's incapacity to establish inner representation. He also emphasized the difficulty in developing symbolic functions when a significant object has been lost. The correlative distinction between symbolism and fantasy lies in the concretized wish-gratifying aspect of fantasy; symbolism is a cognitive process utilizing abstraction that enhances intellectual and emotional comprehension. While fantasy may utilize the symbolic process, its essential aim is to gratify wishes, and it may give expression to the wish without symbolic overtones. For the child survivor, unfortunately, fantasy too often assumed the concretization of the wish and thus, distorted reality (Kestenberg, 1980; Ornstein, 1985; Vegh, 1979).

Consequences of object loss can be observed by the rupture in establishing important identifications. Parental loss during the first diphasic phase of the oedipus complex impairs the ego's capacity to synthesize conflicting modes of reality perceptions and to integrate divergent perceptions of the self and the object (A. Freud, 1967; Sandler & Rosenblatt, 1962). The ability to compromise between wish and reality requires some mode of gratification (Freud, 1905); since the object is no longer able to both gratify and to teach, fantasy is often substituted for reality. Narcissistic gratifications also necessitate a real object; thus, parental loss interferes with the modulation of narcissism (Freud, 1920).

In an attempt to salvage both object representation and self-worth, rescue fantasies, though regressive in nature, provide some psychic relief.

Unfortunately, these fantasies fail in their corrective psychological task. They attempt to enhance grandiose ideations in order to defend against harsh reality. The narrative of rescue fantasies remains an undercurrent in the emotional and social interactions of the child survivor, and continue to influence the character structure of the grown child survivor (Vegh, 1979).

Even in those situations that appear as a fortuitous act of fate, such as placement in a protective home with substitute parents, the child survivor was beleaguered by psychological tensions, as that which should have eased the child's fears and torments, unfortunately, often increased guilt. In reality, the child survivor was given a new family who may have been more effective than his biological family. Further, emotional abandonment of the parent by the child in ordinary circumstances is a cause for guilt; it completely disobeys the most basic tenets of Judeo-Christian morality: "to honor thy father and thy mother." When the child removes love from the parent and displaces that love to another object, especially in an atmosphere where parents are subjected to cruel and inhumane suffering, one can only anticipate that the aggressive forces of the superego will assault the ego.

At the developmental phase where the family romance ideation was particularly powerful, any possible realization of these wishes made what was imaginable turn into the unimaginable. In case studies of the child survivor whom we now can only know as an adult, we witness the rather pervasive feelings of ego weakness existing side by side with feelings of grandiosity. For these children, what could have been a normal phase in the use of fantasy had assumed a new dimension. This Sophoclean exchange of families turns to tragic retribution.

Langer (1991) has pointed to the confusion in the child survivor as to his role in the hand of fate: Was it the hand of the other that destroyed his parent, or was it his own hand?

Rescue fantasies are multifaceted in their psychological contribution to ego structure. Anna Freud (1936) has pointed to the relationship between them and altruism. The wish to rescue in conjunction with identification promotes the ego's desire to both retain and care for the object. To interrupt this fantasy, to lay bare the helplessness of childhood, to victimize the child and parent by an overpowering aggressor, impedes healthy development. Altruistic defenses play an important role in the development of social mores and social values. Rescue fantasies not only have an ameliorative effect upon the aggressive drive, but also, by turning destructive wishes into the opposite, a wish to rescue, provide the ego with an important social and interpersonal mode of relationship to the other.

Having already referred to various factors that converge to create the phenomenon of survivor guilt, I now consider the role of identification and object love in relation to guilt. Freud (1923, 1930) developed the theoretical constructs of identification and object love. Ferenczi (1909) and Abraham (1924) have added to the concepts of introjection and internalization, and more recently Sandler (1987, 1960), Schafer (1960, 1990), and Meisner, 1981) made additional contributions to our thinking on internalization, and superego ego development. Kohut (1971) has indicated that the capacity to integrate a realistic self-representation is directly related to the internalization of modified idealized parental imagoes. For the child survivor, unfortunately, the natural stages of psychic development regarding identification have been adversely affected by the Holocaust experience. Identification and object love are processes that have their inception at the onset of infancy. Both processes establish the template for self and object representation. Sandler (1987) suggested that there is a "persistence" of the "genetically earlier primary confusion" between the self and the object, and it is the persistence of this genetically early state that must surely provide the basis for feelings of empathy. Furthermore, he stated that "in connection with what we call secondary identification, we would suggest that the bridge to these processes is the persisting momentary state of primary confusion or primary identification which occurs before the process of 'sorting out' or disidentifying occurs" (pp. 25–26).

I suggest that the object from which self and object representation derive can assume internally equal valence with the self, and it is this concept that gives survivor guilt its potency.

For self and object maintain that diffuse state that existed in infancy, that oceanic feeling when the object and self are felt as one (Freud, 1930). In the course of psychic development, the object becomes separate from the self, yet it can still maintain equal emotional value with the self. Therefore, to experience guilt at the loss of the object is not an aberration in psychic development. While failure to save the object has elements of narcissistic thinking, and the remnants of infantile grandiosity (Freud, 1914), the basic identifications of the preoedipal phase maintain a predominant force in psychic structure. This capacity to place the concerns for the object before self concerns are part of ontogenetic development and independent of reaction formations. Kestenberg (1982c) stated that

> One could no longer trust one's neighbors. Trust had become an undesirable commodity and survival often became associated with utter dehumanization. The feeling of being left all alone, perhaps even by God, was degrading enough, but one of the most poignant indignities that one might endure was the feeling of guilt for surviving perhaps at the expense of others… [p. 53].

As I have indicated, survivor guilt is multidetermined, and no one factor can account for the depth and pervasiveness of this internal affective state. Nevertheless, there are perplexing aspects to these guilt feelings. Particularly poignant is the question of why one experiences guilt over one's own survival in respect to the stranger—the unknown? This response is especially striking when we consider the frequency of aggression in the history of mankind toward those who are strangers (Freud 1919, 1920). One explanation may be found in the complexities of the oedipus complex. Here I turn to the great interpreter of the unconscious, Sophocles, and his Oedipus story. Myths, folklore, and parables are embodiments of human psychology expressed in socially accepted representations. In the play, the stranger whom Oedipus kills is Oedipus' father, Laius, the ambivalently loved and hated rival. Through projective mechanisms, the stranger may either assume the role of the hated or of the loving father or parent, and thus becomes the recipient of these variable emotions. This viewpoint adds another dimension to Freud's (1919) explanation, in "The Narcissism of Minor Differences," of why aggression is directed to strangers. In "survivor guilt," remnants of the early oedipal conflict reemerge through transference—a ubiquitous mechanism—activated both in individual and group relationships, and the stranger in the Holocaust trauma represents the loving father (Freud, 1912; Greenson, 1967; Loewald, 1988) who is killed. Infantile conflicts continue to play a significant role in survivor guilt, and these conflicts by association and abstraction are transferred to the unknown victims of the Holocaust, the strangers.

Guilt in the Holocaust environment is kaleidoscopic, and the situations that arouse guilt range from the innocuous to the portentous. From this perspective of multiple determinations, I focus on a particular aspect of the aggressive drive. Aggression in this atmosphere of perennial destructiveness is easily aroused. Often there is confusion as to the appropriate recipient, and aggression can as easily be directed both to the aggressor and to the victims, including oneself. In an atmosphere of aggression, it is not easy to maintain one's equilibrium. Blame and anger are often directed to the victim for his lack of appropriate response, and sadistic feelings toward the victim can be engendered despite emotions of sympathy and comradery. The realization that aggressive feelings can be directed equally at the victim and the aggressor must result in a sense of dismay regarding one's moral and ethical integrity. In this multidimensional foray of aggression, the superego targets the helpless ego for its intractable responses. This occurs despite the reality that the aggression is a silent emotion and most often not acted upon (Freud, 1908). In this state of pervasive aggression, the child survivor experienced himself or herself as a "murderer" rather than a victim.

This discussion of the nature of survivor guilt based on a number of multidetermined factors (Waelder, 1936) aims to portray the dynamic conflicts in the child survivor and to provide some additional understanding regarding the underlying basis for silence, this most pervasive and indomitable defense. Silence, in the child survivor, has the effect of leveling the emotions to a monotone; it coats human relationships with distance and obscures the past from the present (Langer, 1991). To break this silence is to effect a major modification in the defense structure. One of the primary purposes of the silence is to protect the fantasy object from destruction, to maintain the existence of the lost object as a reality. In this context, silence maintains a constant unshakable image of the continued existence of the object. The word, or rather the silent word, has become the equivalent of the real; it is the magical use of language. By means of this concretization, the survivor who uses language is in danger of losing the illusion (Greenacre, 1970). For children, words and reality are coequal and, depending upon the age, symbolic language is easily destabilized (Ferenczi, 1913). Silence, then, as a bridge to the unconscious is an attempt to reinvent the existence of the lost object; it becomes an enabler for the ego to maintain restitution of the object by means of language. In this situation it is the negation of language (Freud, 1915, 1924; McDougal, 1989) in order to maintain the "yes" to the parent's existence. By severing the word connection with the mnemonic traces, silence maintains a protracted imagining of the existence of the lost object. This is not a psychotic process, nor does it result in a hallucinatory system. The process is maintained by the functions of topographic regression (Freud, 1900; Modell, 1978; Schwartz, 1996). Past and present objects seem almost to maintain the same emotional space with evenly directed cathexis. Kestenberg (1982b) speaks of maintaining a double existence where past and present comingle as a single entity. Freud (1900) refers to this process as the "psychical locality," and Shatan (1974) calls this phenomenon "perceptual dissonance."

Silence in this situation is closely related to mechanisms of denial. Not to speak is not to know; it is the isolation of the external event from the psychic impact. For the child survivor to remain silent is another mechanism by which the ego is spared the knowledge of repeated humiliations, embarrassments, and shame for oneself and one's objects. To be robbed of home, possessions, employment, profession, ridiculed in public, and forced to leave that which you have regarded as "yours" must affect the quality of self-esteem and endanger identifications. Anna Ornstein (1985) pointed to the loss of identifications for the child survivor and the detrimental effects upon self structures. Material possessions and psychological possessions such as ideas, ego-ideals, and object representations are often symbolic equations of the physical body. To have been robbed of one's internalizations is to stand naked and helpless before the world (Ornstein, 1985). To be seen psychologically and physically naked by your self and by your family is a humiliation almost beyond repair. Kestenberg (1980) indicated that the degree of deprivation and the resultant helplessness compounds the assault upon the ego, and the toll for the ego is a state of perpetual mourning. Silence, though, is essentially unable to eliminate the ever-present desire for the lost objects nor reclaim narcissistic idealizations.

Claudine Vegh (1979), a French psychiatrist, herself a child survivor, documents much of what I have elaborated theoretically in her research thesis, "I Didn't Say Goodbye." It is with an exquisite and searing exposition that she relates the stories of adult persons who had been child survivors. The words that were finally spoken to her had been denied utterance by many for thirty-five years. Both author and interviewee were often emotionally bereft when the words poured forth. Thus, when Samuel, a grown man in his forties, admits to deep shame over his father permitting himself to be deported, he attached himself with guilt—and breaking into sobs calls out, "Daddy, Daddy" (p. 73). Then he admits that "since my father left, I have never been able to cry. I felt walled in. I had forgotten that I was even able to cry!" (p. 74). The author, too, longs for her father and tells us "that to keep one's word was sacred; now, he had promised me that he would come back. And for many years, I too refused his not coming back" (p. 29).

The theme of silence as a restorer of the lost object repeats itself with every interview. Andre states

France is liberated. I wait for my father with total confidence. It never crossed my mind during all those years, that he would not come back.... I never speak of my father to anyone, he is within me, that is all, that is enough.... I asked my mother nothing, and strange as it may seem now, she explained nothing to me. When I say nothing, I mean nothing.... I called my eldest son after my father. I must admit that I never speak of my father to anyone. He is inside of me, that is all, that is enough. I never look at photographs of the past [pp. 44–45].

Sonia, married with children, confesses that she runs after a woman in the street, thinking "She's your mother, and then she turns around and everything collapses." And Robert states: "You know, sometimes I would glimpse someone that reminded me of my father, and in-spite of myself, I would follow or run after him, and not so long ago either" (p. 157).

Words as derived from thoughts are a trial action for the instinctual wishes (Freud, 1911); they make possible a preliminary exploration of reality. Perhaps the word already represents a sublimation—a change in the aim or goal (Kris, 1955). For the survivors to speak the words of their experience, to rekindle memory, is itself a trial action; it confronts the memory with reality. Since the wish for the lost parent is so strongly imbued within the unconscious, to recall the past is to immediately invoke the highly cathected image of the lost object. Memory is specific to a time sequence; it is past (Klein, 1966), but if past and present become comingled, then something in the psychic apparatus has lost its orderly progression. We know from the psychosis that this is a common occurrence due to regression, a shifting of cathexis from present to earlier mental structures wherein wish and reality are confused, and primary process dominates the psychic apparatus. Yet, when Samuel cries out "Daddy, Daddy," he has not lost his tie to reality; there is a fleeting regressive process, topographical in nature (Freud, 1900), that has occurred under the aegis of a powerful wish.

For the survivor who cannot speak, there is an existence in two worlds: one, the present real world, and the other, the realm of fantasy—the persistent daydream that attempts to capture the lost infantile objects. Almost universal among the child survivors is the need to maintain the "silence" as a preserver of the past. Vegh (1979) relates a statement from a friend:

> Not to talk about the past is not to blot it out, on the contrary, it is perhaps to try to preserve it in the depths of one's being, like a secret which cannot be shared…the only possible legacy when you have only a blurred image of your parents, and not even a photograph to help retrieve that image [pp. 29–30].

I think that it is more than the preservation of the memory that is at issue; the need is to revive the past by means of active wishes—a persistent daydream—and like all daydreams, not easily accessible to scrutiny by reality. Thus, silence not only restores the past, but keeps the past in parallel association with the present.

By utilizing this regressive mechanism, the ego constricts its relationships with current objects. The child survivor, I believe, re-creates the past, holds to a wish as a present action. Thus, when a woman of sixty-two, ill with the flu, sobs bitterly and cries out "Mama, Mama," she is re-creating what Freud (1900) describes as a "psychical locality." The current experience stimulates either a past event or a series of associations that, rather than remain within the realm of memory, emerge as current experience, a loss of the time factor and secondary revision. This aspect of regression, the temporal quality that is easily accessible to consciousness, is what constitutes the perpetual daydream of the survivor.

The age at which the loss occurred influences not only the character structure but also the accessibility of memories (Klein, 1966). The nature of the object relationships is also determined in part by age and specific libidinal-phase development. Thus, loss at the phallic or latency age interferes with an adequate oedipal resolution. The failure to resolve this complex can result in fixation to the infantile object, and more often than not, in an unrealistic image of the object. Further, a second chance to rework the oedipal conflicts in puberty is very difficult. Loewald (1979) indicated that one of the major problems in resolving the oedipus complex lays not so much in the required repression but in the capacity to work through the guilt. If the object is lost before this guilt can be adequately worked through, then fixation to the object maintains a powerful self-destructive and object-destructive component. The superego, while empowered by earlier narcissistic, omnipotent fantasies and identifications, has at the same time the disadvantage of an ambivalently internalized imago.

These factors are evident in many of Vegh's (1979) interviews. Thus, Robert, caught in the grips of a strong emotional spasm, relates:

In fact, I don't know what it is to live. I live in the past, and worst of all, when I hear children say their parents were wonderful, it hurts because I don't have that consolation. I blame them, do you understand? Yes, I blame the dead who paid for my life with their own! [p. 156].

Robert, who accusingly blames his family for going to the "slaughter house like sheep," is speaking as the phallic child full of fantasy ideas of heroism.

Madeline exclaims in great turmoil: "I am going to admit something appalling to you. I can't forgive him; I can't forgive my father for letting himself be deported without trying to escape his fate" (p. 57). Joseph, her brother, states with great sorrow: "I lost my home and my mother at one go. I consider my mother to be my mother only in name, but that is all... my real mother is my Swiss mother, as I call her" (p. 65).

Helene exclaims: "But what I am saying is absolutely disgraceful... was it necessary to save us at all costs, for us to live afterwards without parents, with the impression of always being abandoned..." (p. 134).

Paul gives vent to a myriad of conflicts:

I have the feeling that it is not worth thinking about, especially that period. I've never talked about it, not even to my wife, and especially to my mother, and I try never to think about it.... Besides... I think of my father as a "poor devil." Deep down, I can't forgive him for being so stupid as to let himself be trapped like an idiot, you see he ought to have thought more carefully! I think that is what upsets me the most [p. 51].

Lazare, who was eight at the time of his father's deportation, in retrospect states:

You see, my father answered the summons to protect us, his children, and it was he who...in a way, sacrificed himself so that we could live. I think it is always possible to find a solution; but the one my father found was perhaps not the best; that is all.

I would have done anything to survive; I am a fighter-back. I resist. He must have had his reasons for reporting back to the police. The proof is he did protect us—We almost owe it to him that we are all alive. I missed my father; I missed my father a lot. But I came through all right. Didn't I? [pp.].

Lazare's questioning of his father's judgment in answering the police summons might conceivably attest to a realistic appraisal of the historical past, but from the nature of his associations and the judgmental quality, it is more than that. When he states: "It is always possible to find a solution.... I would have done anything to survive; I am a fighter-back, I resist," this clearly points to a comparison between father and son, a negative criticism, irrespective of the objective criteria. The son is smarter than the father; he is the victor, both emotionally and with life. The death of the father leaves him as the "oedipal" victor, and he has survived with his mother. Yet it is a traumatic victory, for not only has he lost an important love object, and an important source for identification, but he is also left in a situation that creates psychic danger. The relationship to the mother can be fraught with incestuous complications. Loss, bereavement, and guilt plague Lazare with unremitting assault, thus neutralizing any narcissistic triumph he experiences.

CONCLUSION

To understand the phenomena of silence in the child survivor requires a multidimensional approach. The role of the external world as a participant in this silence and in the reinforcement of denial mechanisms has been clearly established. The internal need to remain silent is largely determined by the wish to reclaim the lost object, to maintain that relationship to the first and primary object of identification and love. Furthermore, the role of rescue fantasies and family romance ideation are significant in survivor guilt syndrome. These fantasies are latency-age related, and they serve as both a defense and sublimation for oedipal conflicts (Loewald, 1968). Functionally, they act as a means of reclaiming for the ego some solace for the narcissistic injuries deriving from the oedipus complex (Esman, 1987). If the family romance ideation appears to find some basis in reality, as it did for many of those who survived, the child survivor is oppressively bereft by the loss of the parental object and suffers guilt over the loss.

The inability of the child survivors to realize in actuality their rescue fantasies generally resulted in depression. Furthermore, the persistent belief by the child survivors that they were capable of surviving when the parent failed tends to increase the depressive affects and guilt. Completion of the mourning process for the child survivor is extremely difficult. Mourning implies acceptance of loss, while the child survivor continually struggles against this acceptance, and, by silence, attempts to maintain the existence of the lost object.

REFERENCES

Abraham, K. (1924). The influence of oral eroticism on character formation. *Int. J. Psychoanal. Psychother* 6:393–406.

Bergmann, M. (1982). The oedipus complex in childhood survivors. In M. Bergmann & M. Jacovy, eds., *Generations of the Holocaust*. New York: Basic Books Inc.

_____ & Jacovy, M. (1982). *Generations of the Holocaust*. New York: Basic Books Inc.

Beres, B. (1958). Viscissitudes of Superego Functions and Superego Precursors in Childhood. *Psychoanal. St. Child* 13:324–351.

_____ (1972). Ego autonomy and ego psychology. *Psychoanal. St. Child*, 26: 324–351.

Bibring, E. (1953). The mechanism of depression in affective disorders. In P. Greenacre, ed. *Affective: Disorders*. New York: International Universities Press.

Bowlby, J. (1966). *Attachment and Loss*. New York: Basic Books Inc.

Esman, A. (1987). Rescue fantasies. *Psychoanal. Q.* 26:263–270.

Ferenczi, S. (1909). Introjection and transference. In S. Ferenczi, *First Contributions to Psychoanalysis*. London: Hogarth Press 1952:35–57.

_____ (1913). Stages in the development of the sense of reality. In S. Ferenczi, *First Contributions to Psychoanalysis*. London: Hogarth Press 1952:123–239.

Freud, A. (1936). *The Ego and the Mechanisms of Defense*. New York: International Universities Press, 1946.

_____ (1967). About losing and being lost. *Psychoanal. St. Child* 22:9–19.

Freud, S. (1900). The interpretation of dreams. *Standard Edition* 4, 1953–1970,

_____.(1905). Three essays on the theory of sexuality. *Standard Edition* 5.

_____ (1908). Character and anal eroticism. *Standard Edition* 9.

_____ (1909 [1908]). Family romances. *Standard Edition* 9.

_____ (1910). A special type of object choice made by men. *Standard Edition* 11.

_____ (1911). Formulations on two principles of mental functioning. *Standard Edition, 12.*

_____ (1912). The dynamics of transference. *Standard Edition* 12.

_____ (1913 [1912–1913]). Totem and taboo. *Standard Edition* 11.

_____ (1914). On narcissism. *Standard Edition* 14.

_____ (1915). Thoughts for the times of war and death. *Standard Edition*14.

_____ (1917). Mourning and melancholia. *Standard Edition* 14.

_____ (1920). Beyond the pleasure principle. Standard Edition 18.

_____ (1921). Group psychology and the analysis of the ego. *Standard Edition* 18.

_____ (1923). The ego and the id. *Standard Edition* 19.

_____ (1924). The dissolution of the oedipus complex. Standard *Edition* 19

_____ (1930 [1929]). Civilization and its discontents. *Standard Edition* 21.

_____ (1933). Why war. *Standard Edition* 22.

_____ (1939 [1934–38]). Moses and monotheism: Three essays. *Standard Edition* 23.

Green, A. (1972). The analyst, symbolization and absence in the analytic setting. In *Private Madness.* Conn: International Universities Press.

Greenacre, P. (1970). The transitional object and the fetish: With reference to the role of illusion. In P., Greenacre, *Emotional Growth,* Vol. 1, New York: International Universities Press.

Greenson, R. (1967). *The Technique and Practice of Psychoanalysis,* Vol. 1, New York: International Universities Press.

Kestenberg, J. (1980). Child survivors of the holocaust: Case presentation and assessment. *J. Amer. Psychoanal. Assn.*, 28(4):*275.*

_____ (1982a). Analysis of children of survivors. In M. Bergmann & M. Jacovy, eds., *Generation of the Holocaust.* New York: Basic Books.

_____ (1982b). World beyond metaphor. In M. Bergmann & M. Jacovy, eds., *Generation of the Holocaust.* New York: Basic Books.

Klein, G. (1966). The several grades of memory. In Loewenstein, Newman, Shur & Solnit, eds., *A general psychology*. New York: International Universities Press.

Kohut, H. (1971). *The Analysis of the Self*. New York: International Universities Press.

Krystal, W. (1988). *Integration and Self Healing: Affect, Trauma, Alexithymia*. Hillsdale, NJ: Analytic Press.

_____ (1985). Trauma and the stimulus barrier. *Psychoanal. Inquiry* 5(1):131–162.

Laqueur, W. (1980). *The Terrible Secret: Suppression of the Truth About Hitler's Final Solution*. Boston: Little Brown.

McDougal, J. (1989). The dead father: An early psychic trauma and its relation to disturbance in sexual identity and creative acting. *Int. J. Psycho-Anal*. 70:205–219.

Orenstein, A. (1985). Survival and recovery. *Psychoanal. Inquiry* 8:99–130.

Roiphe, H. (1979). A theoretical overview of pre-oedipal development during the first four years of life. In *Basic Handbook of Child Psychiatry, Vol. 1*. New York: Basic Books.

_____ & Galenson, E. (1973). Object loss and early sexual development. *Psychoanal. Q*. 42:73–90.

Rosenberg, B. (1993). *To Speak At Last*. University of Illinois Press.

Sandler, J. (1987). *From Safety to Superego*. New York: Guilford Press.

_____ (1960). On the concept of Superego. *Psychoanal. St. Child*, 15:128–162.

_____ & Rosenblatt, B. (1962). The concept of the representational world. *Psychoanal. St. Child*, 17:128–135.

Sandler, J., Holder, A., & Meers, D. (1963). *Psychoanal. St. Child*, 18:139–158.

Schafer, R. (1960). The loving and beloved: Superego in Freud's structural theory. *Psychoanal. St. Child* 15:163–190.

Schwartz, C. (1996). Regression: A reconsideration of topographic theory. *Psychoanal. Review* 83(6):813–25.

Shatan, H. (1974). Through the membrane of reality: Impacted grief, perceptual dissonance in Vietnam combat veterans. *Psychiatric Opinion* 2:6–15.

Veigh, C. (1979). *I Didn't Say Good-Bye.* New York: E.P. Dutton, Inc.

Waelder, K. (1936). Principle of multiple function: Observation on over determination. *Psychoanal. Q.* 5:45–62.

Wannsee Conference. (1942). Wannsee, Germany.

Wyman, D. (1984). *The Abandonment of the Jews.* New York: Pantheon Press.

CHAPTER 11

AGGRESSION AND THE PURPOSE
OF ANTI-SEMITISM

The history of Anti-Semitism is a long and disastrous tale for humanity. Jews have suffered the consequences of this form of hatred and revile for centuries. I will attempt to demonstrate that the hatred of the Jews reflects both bio-psychological mechanisms and the effects of social structures. Basically, hatred derives from aggression, a biological instinct, universal for all humanity. All Societies must organize and synthesize this aggressive drive in every aspect of their structure and function. Aggression has both positive and negative qualities and has been utilized by societies as both a protective and destructive force in order to maintain their integrative functions.

Peter Gay, (1993) a scholar of both social history and psychoanalysis, wrote a very erudite book, *The Cultivation of Hatred,* in which he indicated that:

> The scars that aggression have left on the face of the past are indelible. Wars and rumors of war, class struggles, clashes between religious denominations or racial and ethnic groups, rivalries for place and power in politics and business, the hatreds generated by nationalism and imperialism, the ravages of crime, the confrontations of private life from marital discord to family feuds—all these, and more offer pervasive testimony that aggression has supplied most of the fuel for historical action and historical change. The search for the

origins, meanings, and implications of aggressiveness—threatening or adaptive—has always been, and must always be, a pressing preoccupation for local magistrates, social reformers, military planners, and political theorists [p. 3].

Certainly, the very idea that societies cultivate hatred suggests an anomaly. Why should any person. group or society want to cultivate hatred? Is this not the very emotion we would like to eradicate from our lives? Yet Gay suggested that hatred was not just an emotion that erupted spontaneously in our society, but rather, social organizations utilized hatred for very specific purposes, as he indicated, hatred derives from aggression, an instinctual drive that is inherent in all humans and which expresses itself in both negative and positive behavior.

That hatred is often viewed as a separate emotional entity from aggression is a theoretical error. It is a derivative of the aggressive drive (Freud, S. 1920) and derives its qualitative characteristics both from this drive and the negative experiences in life. Whether we wish to conceive of aggression from a Darwinian concept that of "survival of the fittest" or a Freudian understanding that aggression is instinctual in nature, it is essential that we understand how civilizations have utilized and organized the pervasive nature of this aggressive drive. Societies have early recognized that in order to preserve human life, they had to control and structure the expression of aggression as it emerged in individual and group behavior. Thus, by legalistic means and cultural mores, societies established a code of external controls and social patterns. We may well ask: What is the nature of this aggressive drive that plays such havoc with the functioning of civilization and, simultaneously, appears as a necessary correlate to its survival? From the earliest development of mankind, aggression provided a protection against destruction of the self and the group. It is a protective device, without which we could not survive.[1] Man's early history was a constant struggle for survival both from the animals of prey, and his own species. In genetic terminology, we refer to the concept of the survival of the fittest genes. That the struggle of genes to survive and to win in the internal biological warfare must influence human biological functioning is a given. Certainly, we can observe this in animal behavior. Though man developed beyond the beasts of prey, the inherent force of aggression did not recede. It is important to note that aggression does not always imply a negative quality. Aggression is also a positive attribute in man's functioning. It accounts for our creative pursuits both in work and personal relationships. The tillers of soil, the artists, the cooks, the mothers and fathers all utilize this aggressive drive for the well-being of society and personal development. Yet, that there also exists a negative aspect to this drive, a primary focus of this paper, is most apparent. A perusal of the daily papers or the TV news provides conclusive evidence—a father shoots his two young sons; a police officer is murdered. In fact, killings are committed daily; wars and destructive acts have abounded throughout history. We are both witness to and captive of aggression, whether perpetrated by external sources or internal conflagration. In fact, a primary factor in the history of civilization is the history of war and social conflicts.

Civilization, if I may anthropomorphize, has long recognized that the force of aggression cannot be eradicated, nor is individual or group control easily achieved. Issues of right and wrong succumb to revenge, and to kill one's enemy often assumes a moral imperative. We may well ask why this aggressive drive that plays such havoc with a peaceful development

---

1 Freud in his 1920 paper, "Beyond the Pleasure Principle," now viewed aggression as a compliment of the Death Drive as opposed to his former position that the aggressive drive derived from the sexual instinct. In my paper, "Beyond the Pleasure Principle: A Dilemma for Psychoanalysis," I have proposed that the Aggressive Drive is independent of the Death Drive and stands as the primary instinct while a concept of a death drive is more reflective of a biological principle. (Schwartz, C.).

of civilization cannot be better controlled. As noted earlier, from the earliest history of man, aggression provided protection against personal destruction. As one of the basic biopsychological drives along with the sexual drive (Freud, 1920, Schwartz, unpublished paper), aggression serves as a protective, affective behavior without which mankind could not survive. "That aggression has not receded nor given way to the demands of a new social order is indeed a dilemma. Unfortunately, that which once served a practical purpose, the survival of the individual, still holds within it the seeds of its own destruction. If to save oneself one had to kill the other, then the other became a constant source of danger to the self. Though laws were devised whereby it was possible to both protect the individual or group and to punish the predator, it has not been possible to adequately control this aggressive drive. Society essentially systematized a legal system and social responses by which civilization both controlled and still gave expression to aggression. No longer do we view mankind as barbaric but, rather we have created a social structure to give credence and respectability to that aspect of aggression that perpetuates killing and death. Thus, to reiterate, the aggressive instinct is basically qualified by the nature of social interaction, economic, political behavior, and a wide range of social ideology. Further, it is necessary to reiterate that society has devised many methods of organizing group attitudes to discharge aggression. One such devise if I may use a euphemism—was to find a "convenient Other."

Freud had indicated this concept in his paper *Moses and Monotheism* (1939 [1934–1938]). He had stated that one of the grounds for hating the Jews is

the circumstances that they live, for the most part, as minorities among other peoples, for the communal feeling of groups requires, in order to complete it, hostility towards some extraneous minority, and the numerical weakness of this excluded minority encourages its suppression (p. 90).

Gay has also expostulated that, "Nothing seems more natural than the case in which humans claim superiority over a collective 'Other'" (pg.68). For many reasons, the Jews have served the role of the "convenient Other," a legitimate rationale by a society's ethos in order to protect its own cohesion. By dispersing aggression outward to the Other, the stranger, society attempted to minimize internal strife. In essence, social organizations have incorporated individual psychological mechanisms, specifically the mechanism of displacement. Of course, I am again anthropomorphizing society. This mechanism of discharging aggression to the other is in no way limited to the unruly mob or the less educated. Our great hero of the enlightenment, Voltaire (1878), was as vituperative towards the Jews as the common man on the street, in his entry "*Juifs*" written for the *Dictionnaire Philosophique,* he stated "In short we find in them only an ignorant and barbarous people—Jews were the enemies of mankind." And Marx (1867), who was himself Jewish, distorted the "Jewish" role in society and referred to them with venom. He rhetorically asked, "What is the object of the Jew's worship in this world? Usury. What is his worldly God? Money" (p. 37).

The diatribes against the Jews, the hatred, the poisonous lies of "Blood Libel, the Protocols of Zion" were spewed from the mouths of the educated, the Popes, the Church ministers, and the literati. Unfortunately, we are all harbingers of aggression. Jews are not exempt either. Do they not claim their selection from all other people by God? Have they not also fought wars to subjugate other countries? We are all bound by this innate aggressive drive. The task is to recognize the seeds of irrational and destructive desires. How we control ourselves and, more importantly, how societies devise controls, is essential.

At this juncture, I wish to discuss two psychological mechanisms that can enlighten our understanding of Anti-Semitism. Both derive and are complimentary of the instincts that Freud, revised from his former instinctual concepts, the sexual and the ego instincts. In his paper "Beyond the Pleasure Principle" (1920,1923), he postulated the Ego Instincts and the Death Instincts as now fundamental in psychic and somatic structures. The aggressive drive was now a compliment of the death drive. Both primary drives are basic to psychological theory. The first of these concepts that is pertinent to our understanding of Anti-Semitism, and derive from the ego instincts, is identification. Identification represents the capacity of a person to perceive aspects in another that resemble oneself or the reverse, aspects of oneself in the other, and are pleasing to one's emotional state. We can either internalize those common elements as feeling part of the self or externalize them and project them onto the other. In either case, we feel a sense of identification. This process also applies to negative aspects of the self and other, and in this situation the identification can assume a hostile and rejecting quality. Either of these emotional responses are aspects of identification and result either in a sense of *simpatico* with another or a feeling of rejection. This mechanism is primary in all human relationships, and it is an element that operates in all biological life. We observe this in how animals respond to their duplicate other and mate within the same species. The explanation of why similar genetic species or psychological sameness seek each other is essentially a teleological answer. We may conjecture that this mechanism, identification, supports survival of the species from a reproductive standpoint, and from a psychological position of binding people together.

That we observe identification in individual relationships likewise extends to group functioning. The group is bound by a community of ideas, similarities in looks and behavior, powerful leaders that confer sameness, and other features with which one identifies with. Thus, this binding of the group makes it possible to view the "other" as a different species. Freud (1914) spoke to the concept of "narcissism of minor differences," by which he meant that minor differences could result in an injury to our sense of self. Differences seem to disturb our psychic equilibrium. I do not believe that this is simply a learned response that is taught because of political or economic reasons, even though hate for the other is used to further social goals. Hate or rejection of the other is a basic psychological response of distress, essentially caused by the unfamiliar.

Furthermore, the concept of identification helps to understand how aggression to the "other" is permitted by the social order. We tend to love, to want to bond with, the similar, and to reject that which appears different. Observe babies and their reaction to a stranger; there is initial fear, anxiety, and withdrawal. We refer to this as "stranger anxiety," a second psychological mechanism that is inherent in the function of the ego instincts. This component drive emerges from the instinct for survival, a component of the Ego Instincts (Freud,1920, 1923), and is inherent in all individual development. Perhaps, this is a very primitive survival mechanism that is no longer adaptive in our current social development. Yet, the outsider continues to be experienced as threatening to the individual, and unfortunately, is likewise replicated in the larger group's affective responses. Thus, to have an enemy solidifies a group, and at the same time provides an outlet for aggression. By banding against the stranger under the sanctification of society, by discharging destructive aggression, the entire social structure is spared the plague of conscience. And yet, that aspect of control, of maintaining a balance of the aggressive drive between the positive and negative aspects, has proven problematic for civilizations throughout history. Wars with other nations are chronic; killings within families are abnormally high; class conflicts, gang wars, criminality—all elements that can bring about the downfall of a particular society or destruction of a group—are axiomatic for social existence.

I will again speak in anthropomorphic terms by suggesting that society operates with unconscious mechanisms. We are all aware that society does not have an unconscious, it is rather organized by its history of written and oral traditions, and attitudes reflected in its social and legal systems. Freud (1934–1938) had also indicated that "introducing the concept of a "collective unconscious" gains us little theoretical accuracy," and yet he does state: "The content of the unconscious, indeed, is in any case a collective, universal property of mankind" (p. 132). Thus, we shall speak of society's unconscious. It appears that this social unconscious behaves on two levels: the cognitive and rational, and an opposite state of conflicting attitudes, prejudices, and destructive behaviors of which it is seemingly unaware. It is with this latter that it handles aggression and the mechanisms that infuse and diffuse this drive.

By exalting society with an unconscious process, I want to point to a condition that appears harmful to its well-being. The very idea of perceiving the Jew as vermin has given societies throughout history a sense of righteous killing. To hang the Jew, to burn him, to exile him without any sense of conscience are strange phenomena when the entire oeuvre of these societies bespeaks of kindness, love one's neighbor, morality, justice, and the sanctity of human life. How can we understand this contradiction?

Perhaps we can provide one answer by introducing the concept of defense, a psychological mechanism that operates in the mind as a means of maintaining psychic equilibrium, coherence, and a method of hiding the unpleasant. In Anti-Semitism, we can observe a defensive functioning that permits contradictory states to exist in the psyche. "This particular defensive mechanism, referred to as isolation, or more commonly called splitting (Freud S. (1940 [1938], Eissler,1959) permits the mind to keep apart ideas and behaviors that are in opposition to each other, and to act one way or the other without undue distress at their apparent contradiction. That not all behavior can be entirely consistent, and we cannot always evaluate every act or word and maintain optimal functioning is a truism. In splitting we can observe how this mechanism makes possible thinking and behavior with the least amount of exertion. It serves to conserve energy. Even killing that is absolutely justified requires this mechanism to operate. One must split off from his conscience that which can emotionally destroy, debilitate, or inhibit functioning. Unfortunately, we have corrupted this mechanism to permit murderous aggression. Thus, the Church Fathers, the Voltaire's, can act with impunity and not assail their conscience.

Another aspect of the role by which defenses operate can be observed in the defense mechanism of projection. As we observed the role of negative identification, that is, those negative aspects of ourselves that we reject, we can see how the defensive role of projection plays out in Anti-Semitism. By projection, we observe ourselves but not in a conscious manner, and thus, we attempt to put into the other those characteristics that we reject. These psychic qualities that are viewed as bad—hateful factors that we wish to eliminate are easily projected onto the "other." Since these hated qualities are frequently unconscious, that is, unknown, we tend to try to throw them away, or we may also transfer them onto another or a group. As we evaluate the role that Anti-Semitism plays in a society, we can observe how the defense of projection plays a protective role in order to maintain a personal and social sense of integrity. The Jew has become the repository of all the worst qualities of mankind. He has been called rapacious, selfish, a usurer, and other adjectives reflecting human abhorrence. Thus, the "convenient other" is closely allied by identification but is a negative "other" —the one whom you deny in yourselves.

At this point, we may also speculate that, due to ancestry of the Christian religion from Judaism, the parent had to be maligned in order to enable the separation, and to continue to maintain their independence. Initially, the role of anti-Jewishness in the separation process had served emotional and political purposes, but unfortunately, it was later exploited and justified itself as a righteous cause. And though this separation has long since been established, it continues to contain the seeds of hatred. As I have suggested, Anti-Semitism serves psychological, political, and economic purposes. It bolsters the power of the Catholic Church, other religious groups, and political hierarchies. The Jew, "the other" is the alien, the hated one, a very suitable object for the aggressive drive.

As a further enumeration of the defensive structures in Anti-Semitism, I want to discuss the role of generalization that belongs somewhere on the mental and psychological continuum.

Generalization is a cognitive function. It is an organizing principle by which we make order of our perceptions and thinking processes. Specific observations and thoughts are categorized into similar units so that each does not undergo a laborious mental process in order to ascertain where it belongs or what it means. Our minds require the ability to go from the general to the specific and back. (Vygotsky, 1965 [1934]) We tend to group people by their affiliation, their race, religion, and nationality. In conjunction with identification, we apply characteristics from the specific and ascribe them to the group. If some Jews are nasty, usurious, or show any other negative quality, then all Jews by identification suffer these nasty qualities. If some Jews are college professors, Bankers. or statesmen, then all Jews pretend superiority, and we both envy and hate them. You may well query: What has this to do with Anti-Semitism? Well, the answer lies in the way we generalize specific characteristics of an individual. We tend to group people by their affiliation, their race, religion, and nationality. In conjunction with identification, we tend to take characteristics from the specific and ascribe them to the group or visa-versa. This is what psychically occurs in Anti-Semitism. Thus, generalization has been used by humanity to perpetuate specific myths about the Jews, and most often for psychological means to both control and destroy them.

I shall now add another psychological construct to my premise regarding the role by which Anti-Semitism has been utilized by Societies. I will suggest that Anti-Semitism is modern day civilization's *Totem and Taboo* (1913). That part of the totem which early societies revered and hated is no longer recognized in consciousness, but is well hidden in our psychic structures, and in the annals of society. What is evident are the taboos. And the Jews are taboo. Freud has pointed out that taboos represent "certain persons and things which are charged with a dangerous power which can be transferred through contact with them, almost like an infection," they are "dangerous and unclean". (pp. 21–22). Freud, further quotes the theorist Wundt (1906, p. 308), who indicated that "Taboo is nothing other than the objectified fear of the 'demonic' power which is believed to be hidden in a taboo object" (p. 24).

Perhaps, what is most salient, in Freud's discussion of *Totem and Taboo,* is his contention that totems give expression to mankind's fundamental ambivalence between love and hate—that is aggression. Thus, the Totem and the Taboo represented a means by which early societies attempted to control destructive behaviors between persons, and especially their rulers. Of course, the conscious use of totems is long gone, but relics exist, and I am proposing that Anti-Semitism is a modem expression of the ancient "Totem and Taboo relics."

THE HISTORY OF ANTI-SEMITISM

To date the history of the beginnings of Anti-Semitism is not easy. Some have claimed its origins almost from the earliest period of the Jews settling in the land of Canaan, that the wars and hostilities were an expression of Anti-Semitism. Yet, I would claim that Anti-Semitism as a form of specific hatred and antagonism—a modern taboo—had its origins after the Roman conquest of Palestine in 70 AD. Jews were exiled and dispersed in the diaspora—that is, to various foreign countries. When living in a state of independence, composed of people with similar characteristics and religious beliefs, and ruled by their own Jewish leader, or under the control of another country, it is difficult to conceive of the general attitude toward them as Anti-Semitism. As an independent country, a subjected country, or tribal units, they too, were guilty of wars and conflicts with other tribes and countries. Their kings and leaders such as David, Saul, and Solomon were renowned throughout history. Thus, I will contend that the history of conflicts with the Jews when they had their own land, a consolidated country, or tribal area, should not be referred to as Anti-Semitism. Rather, this was a time when warfare among countries, as it is today, represented a general hostility among different countries that fought for power, land, and economic supremacy. I contend that Anti-Semitism represents a qualitative psychological difference in its relationship to the Jews when they become a minority group within a specific country. The aggressive drive takes on a different quality in its means of discharge and purpose. As stated earlier, Anti-Semitism serves a protective device against aggression directed against the self, that is, the group, and is rather directed to the "other." The Jews, as a minority population in the various foreign countries, served a utilitarian purpose; they were "the other," the taboos, utilized in order to protect the indigenous population from self-destruction.

That the Jews have endured Anti-Semitism and resisted assimilation throughout history is quite a remarkable feat. What is there in the culture and the religious beliefs that have sustained this group identity? The Spanish Inquisition, the expulsions from many European countries, the Ghettos, and finally the Holocaust, all have unleashed the destructive side of the aggressive drive against the Jew, and yet the Jew has maintained its internal group cohesiveness.

Is it the power of identification that maintains the group's cohesiveness, or the power of the positive aggressive drive that protects the individual against destruction by the other, or the strength of their convictions that they were the "Chosen People," and their stringent belief in one God? Perhaps, we may hypothesize that a combination of many factors contributed to the strength of their convictions. Perhaps some thoughts from Freud in *Totem and Taboo* (1913) will help elucidate that sense of being Jewish, and survival amid hatred, killings and assimilation in the diaspora:

"What is left to you that is Jewish? Answer: 'A very great deal, and probably its very essence.' He (the Jew) could not now express that essence clearly in words; but some day, no doubt, it will become accessible to the scientific mind'" (Preface, Freud,1913).

In conclusion, I want again to reiterate how the role that the discharge of aggression i.e., the aggressive drive in the form of hatred, has played in Anti-Semitism, and the means by which organized societies have deliberately utilized this hatred as a displacement from within the group to the 'other.' Various psychological mechanisms have been co-opted as vehicles for the discharge of aggression to the 'other.' Unfortunately, individuals will always be driven by the aggressive drive that emerges in the form of hatred, rivalries, murderous wishes, and distortion of reality. It is the task of society to apply the laws of justice and reason that can exercise appropriate controls over the destructive aspects of the aggressive drive. Unfortunately, society has not done an adequate job in either controlling wars, hatred or Anti-Semitism.

REFERENCES

Darwin, C. & Keber, L. (1859). *On the Origin of Species.* J. Murray, London.

Eissler, K. (1959). On Isolation. *Psychoanalytic Study of the. Child* 14:29–60.

Freud, S., (1901) Three Essays on The Theory of Sexuality. *S.E.* 7, 1905.

_____ (1909). Five Lectures On Psychoanalysis. *S.E.*11, 1910,

_____ (1912–1911). Totem and Taboo. *S.E.* 13, 1913.

_____ (1914). On Narcissism: An Introduction. *S.E.* 14.

_____ (1920). Beyond the Pleasure Principle. *S.E.* 18,

_____ (1923) The Ego and the Id. *S.E.* 19.

_____ (1932). Why War (Einstein & Freud). *S.E.* 22, 1933.

_____ (1934–1938) Moses and Monotheism: Three Essays. *S.E.* 23, 1939.

_____ (1938) Splitting of the Ego in the Process of Defense. *S.E.*23, 1930.

Gay, P. (1993). *The Cultivation of Hatred.* New York & London: W.W. Norton.

Marx, K. (1867, 1885, 1894). *Das Capital.* Berlin, Germany: Verlag von Otto Meisner.

Schwartz, C. (2024). Beyond The Pleasure Principle, The Death Instinct: A Dilemma for Psychoanalysis, p. 119 in current volume.

Voltaire, M.de (1878). Juif, *Dictionnaire Philosophique.* Ed. Garnierr-Towe.

Vygotsky, L. (1934). *Thinking and Speech.* MIT Press, 1962.

Wundt, W. (1927). *Taboo. Volkerpsychologie.* 4th edition. 10 Vol. Leipzig: Krovernn Abstract-Aggression and the Purpose of Anti-Semitism.

CHAPTER 12

LANGUAGE AS ARTISTRY: IN THE TREATMENT OF A BORDERLINE PSYCHOTIC PATIENT[1]

[(2009). Psychoanalytic Review 96)(1):1–20.]

I propose to examine the process by which the therapist experiences difficulties in selecting, from a multitude of ideas, a specific one that conveys a particular meaning for the patient. This, of course, necessitates an inner exploration to find the right words that can translate the idea into a meaningful experience both emotionally and cognitively. Poland (1986) noted that it is precisely "through words that an analysis comes to life, has power, and becomes a talking cure" (p. 244). Language thus assumes the "importance of major and powerful action" (Poland). It is the "wide range of the analyst's words" that can contribute to the "maintenance of the regressive and analytic nature of the dyadic balance" (Poland). Glover (1955) indicated that through our words we "supply word bridges" (pp. 132–133) that establish communication between the unconscious and the preconscious systems; speech is therefore our fundamental communicative link to the patient (Loewenstein, 1956).

My case discussion will focus on the confluence of thought and words, and the difficulty in transmuting thoughts into meaningful language that is acceptable to the patient. Further, I will address the sublimatory process in the analyst and the artistry involved in our use of language.

---

1 I would like to thank Drs. Daniel Schwartz and Marvin Hurvich for their valuable theoretical contributions.

Greenberg (2002) called attention to the problems of the "analyst's tension" in the analytic work. He noted that tension is omnipresent in the analyst at every step of the therapeutic process. This tension is rooted in the dichotomy between "analytic goals" that is, ideal theoretical constructs, and the praxis of therapeutic engagement. Between goal and practice, there exists the reality of the patient's character organization, transference, resistance problems, and the act of practice that may differ or come into conflict with theoretical goals and "so-called correct" treatment practice. The analyst's "tension" is not a negative in the analytic work, and it should not be a factor to be eliminated. For Greenberg, it represents a creative and productive mode of functioning.

I propose to complement Greenberg's thoughts with a parallel concept, the role of sublimation for analytic work. Sublimations are an integral part of our character structure, fortify our work capacity, and provide the empathic understanding by which we connect with patients. When we address theories of sublimation, we generally are concerned with the sublimatory process in the patient. By introducing the role of sublimation in the analyst's affective repertoire, I wish to focus on a defense mechanism (A. Freud, 1936, S. Freud, 1915/1963a) that is central to the analyst's function. I am aware that my formulation of the role of sublimation may conflict with the current understanding of countertransference as the main medium through which the analyst's affects are transformed into emotional response and behavior.[2]

---

2 Countertransference was initially characterized as unconscious conflicts in the analyst that impinged on the patient's emotional sphere and interfered with or disrupted the analytic work (Fenichel, 1945; Freud, 1912/1958; Glover, 1929; Little, 1957). The concepts of countertransference have gone through successive constructs that increasingly view it as the medium through which the analyst perceives the patient's unconscious meanings. Countertransference in this theoretical frame has become the major analytic tool by which the analyst understands, interprets, and uses himself or herself as the subject/object in the analytic work. My usage of countertransference will refer to the former construct, granted a narrower understanding that views countertransference as a product of unresolved or conflictual areas in the analyst that both arise and are enacted in the transference. From this perspective, I interpose the importance of sublimation as a necessary correlate to the

Loewald (1988) indicated that

> ... when psychoanalysts consider human creativity, whether on the plane of daily living and ordinary work, or on the plane of higher cultural pursuits, and original thought, and imagination, they have recourse to the idea of sublimation [p. 8].

Creative activity in the analyst exists in the realm of thinking, and the artistry of psychoanalysis emerges through the medium of language. The import of language usage for the analyst therefore reflects a need supraordinate to the subjective interaction with the patient, a need best described as evolving from the sublimatory process that has its own laws of appropriate functioning (Loewald, 1988).

Despite the ubiquity of countertransference in the analytic setting, I am suggesting that countertransference is not the only way by which we gain insight into the world of our patients. Tensions in the analyst are not always caused by unresolved conflicts or induced countertransferences. Freud (1909/ 1955, 1912/1958) made it quite clear that a significant amount of analytic work occurred beyond transference and countertransference. Obstacles that occur in our therapeutic work may arise from a variety of factors related to skill, knowledge deficiency and inexperience. Further, tensions may arise when the sublimatory processes in the analyst are thwarted by either the patient's defense and resistance or character structure. I suggest that we need to view the range of affective response in the analyst as multileveled and to recognize that even a response as emotionally laden as "frustration" need not indicate an unresolved psychic conflict nor an imperative demand upon the patient to perform for the analyst.

---

current usage of countertransference. I propose that we approach the work of analysis from a multi-layered perspective of emotional, cognitive, intellectual, and creative work inherent in the analyst's function.

Sublimation in the analyst is a critical tool in analytic practice. Mechanisms of identification, displacement, and empathy are constituent components of sublimation that affect the analyst's therapeutic ability (Hartmann, 1955). Sublimation was initially defined by Freud (1915/1963a, 1923/1961) as a vicissitude of an instinct, a mechanism of defense. The instincts' capacity to "function in a wide variety of arenas far from their original purposive actions" and their capacity to change objects are indications of sublimation. Freud viewed sublimation as desexualized libido, displaceable energy, and sublimated energy. Anna Freud (1936) indicated that sublimation converts drives to a "higher" state of mental function. As a defense, sublimation in the narrow sense functions as a mechanism within the ego; yet in the wider sense, sublimation infuses all mental functions: affecting id, ego, and superego structure and drive energy (Hartmann, 1955); they can be total or partial; can represent a deflection of drives from their original aim and object; and can affect ego aims and ego functions (Freud, 1923/1961b; Hartmann, 1955). I want to call particular attention to the ideas of Hartmann regarding the difference in sublimation of aim and sublimation of function. It is precisely this distinction that is paramount in analytic work. As analysts, we may have achieved the most noteworthy aims in our work, but we can be flawed in our analytic function. Drive derivatives, sadism, masochism, exhibitionism, and voyeurism or more direct overt acts of aggression or sexuality may intermittently intrude on our practice. When this occurs, we concomitantly observe a failure in sublimations coequal to superego problems and countertransference enactments. Sublimations are clearly reflected in our use of language, which is the purveyor of our understanding and our wishes. We may give direct expression to drive activity or drive derivatives in the very words we utter. Language may express through metaphor and symbolization a range of ideas and emotions that represent the transmission of sublimated drives; for example, understanding, friendliness and *sympatica*, a reflection of a "higher order" of mental activity

(Freud, 1915/1963a). Sublimation involves the mechanisms of identification, displacement, and projection, all of which contribute to the analyst's capacity for empathy. Analytic work flows between emotion and cognition, that is, the fulcrum through which the "other" is comprehended. Sublimation and empathy, primary requirements for analytic work (Hartmann, 1955; Loewald, 1988), are proximal mechanisms that aid in transforming drive derivatives from direct gratification to a level of function whereby the aim shifts from wish fulfillment to understanding (Fenichel, 1945; Loewald, 1988).

Language is the connective tissue between patient and analyst; it is the primary tool of the analyst. Though language is an autonomous function, genetically derived, initially, it is suffused with drive energy and essentially serves the purpose of drive discharge. Stone (1967) indicated that early speech is instinctually dominated. It is used to ingest the mother with whom the infant seeks to reunite in order to undo the separation of birth and growth processes. Within the analytic situation, speech for the patient can regress to a drive state in which meaning and understanding are overshadowed by the desire for drive gratification. In this case, the function of speech as communication loses its metaphorical and symbolic functions; it shifts the aim from understanding to drive discharge and gratification. For the analyst, however, speech must retain its sublimatory mode; otherwise, the analyst and patient both succumb to enactment and drive gratification. In this context, language acquires a creative hue; it translates the concrete into the abstract, turns the general into a meaningful specific, and gives life to construction by turning the here and now into the past and future. Clearly, it is self-evident that interpretations proceed through meaningful language, and affects are understood through the affective use of language.

CASE MATERIAL

In the following case material, I emphasize the nature of sublimatory processes in the therapeutic work and the means by which language as a factor in this process aided communicative understanding with the patient. I will also demonstrate the difficulties that arose for me from inhibitions of language imposed by the nature of the patient's pathology. The focus on my internal thought processes and action in words during a number of sessions with my patient will demonstrate, I hope, how my use of language effected some important emotional discharge for the patient and resulted in some modification in the ego's defenses. Further, I shall discuss the patient's resistance and show the technical difficulties in formulating verbal communication with her. I will present transference and countertransference aspects of the work, the interrelationship between them, and my own explicable reactions to both the patient and my own conflicts.

In presenting this case, I shall also discuss problems that may arise for those patients for whom analysis of the transference can induce a disorganization of the ego, with the possibility of both regression and psychotic ideation. In these cases, projection of the hated and guilty self and paranoia as a defense against narcissistic ego insults are not uncommon. A disruption of the treatment can result if these regressive and projective processes are not contained. To interpret the transference for this patient was clearly antitherapeutic. Rather, it was important to establish displacements so that the patient's fragile, narcissistic ego structure was not challenged. Similarly, as in child treatment, we often treat the child's ideation as concrete and do not interpret because it may pose a threat to the developing ego or the fragile ego structure. The task was thus to maintain a supportive environment.

My patient, Jane H., a borderline psychotic personality, with underlying paranoid features,[3] was seen four times a week for 4 years. She was an attractive 45-year-old woman who had never married and had intermittent, short-term love affairs. These affairs generally ended badly, with her feeling abandoned by the man. She was a commercial artist whose work history was erratic; at times, she achieved commercial success, at other periods she struggled financially. In part, this was a result of the economic problems in her field; however, the difficulties also resulted from her persecutory ideations and negative behavior.

The patient was the youngest of three sisters. An older sister was described as psychotic; the middle sister seemed the healthiest and was married with children. There was little involvement between the patient and this sister. Her mother appeared to be a depressed, withdrawn woman with little warmth, while her father was described as a bon vivant, a man involved in various business enterprises, and moderately successful. He worked long hours so that Jane saw little of him during her developing years, but he did spend Sundays with the family. Her fondest memory was riding with her father and the family in his flashy convertible.

The treatment with this patient was supportive psychotherapy. The fragility of her ego structure and the underlying paranoid structure mitigated against insight therapy. The aim of support was to provide the ego with more elasticity by essentially listening with an accepting ear and focusing on her inner suffering, fears, and anxieties. When possible, I would attempt to objectify the external world to make it less threatening than the subjective perceptions of her inner representations and paranoid projections. I had to be extremely careful not to imply criticism or to appear overly supportive of

---

3 My usage of the term borderline psychotic personality follows the criteria established by Knight (1954), who treats psychosis as on a continuum. In this schema, borderline occupies a space between neurotic and psychotic, and given undue stress from either external or internal demands, psychotic ideation and processes will occur.

others. The narcissistic transference was highly ambivalent. It could easily become a negative transference, and, indeed, this occurred numerous times and endangered the treatment.

At one point in the treatment, I contemplated a fee increase. The fee was moderate, and I had already reduced it due to a change in the patient's economic situation. There had been a substantial improvement in her income, and I felt that after a 6-month period it would be appropriate to raise the issue with her. Yet I found myself in a quandary because of her paranoid features that were bound to arise. For several months, I delayed discussing a fee increase. This delay and rethinking certainly suggests strong countertransference issues. Was I struggling with the fear of losing the patient; a feeling of rejection resulting from the patient's negative transference, the fear of the patient's aggression, and therefore my own hostility; or could it be guilt over what I regard as my greed, my wish to make more money?

I knew that all of these factors were operating, and the difficult task for me was to isolate and understand my countertransference in the analytic work. I will subsequently elaborate on the inner process of dealing with them. But there was another issue that I considered more pressing: how to proceed with the therapeutic work when I would probably disrupt the patient's equilibrium with my request, and possibly disturb the therapeutic work by evoking an excessively strong aggression. The question then became a matter of technical efficacy, a correct method at this time in the treatment. Further, I knew that I had to carefully select my words; I felt frustrated because the selected words seemed inadequate for the patient's psychic situation.[4] I was aware that I was

---

4 Martin Bergmann in a private seminar remarked "that as we listen to a patient, we formulate numerous ideas before we ultimately choose the so-called right one." I would add that these ideas and wordings often occur rapidly or remain somewhat quiescent and may also become obsessional. In this situation, we alternate between countertransference issues and technical skill.

experiencing a work blockage. At this juncture, I want to stress that I am drawing a distinction between countertransference difficulties and those difficulties presented by the technical medium of our work. To this extent, I am focusing on the craft of psychoanalysis that employs concepts of skill, technique, and knowledge.

Raising the patient's fee brought into focus these two considerations: the countertransference factors and the therapeutic skill. At times, a fee increase can be an important treatment method for dealing with transference issues, but clearly we gratify the needs of the therapist. Whether the act of increasing the fee comes under the realm of countertransference is an issue outside the scope of this article, but certainly it is not an improper question to consider. As I considered the fee increase, a number of thoughts repeatedly emerged in my internal dialogue. I remembered Freud's (1909/1955) realization that the Rat Man lied regarding his income and underpaid him. Yet apparently this did not become an issue in the treatment. Further, I recalled Eissler's (1974) paper on fees and his questioning the propriety of raising fees once treatment has commenced. Did my inner debate, my obsessing, represent a means of discharging aggression? I considered that my feelings in this situation arose not from the frustration of a wish but rather from the frustration over the inhibiting effects of language. In this sense, my feelings did not reflect derivatives of ungratified wishes but rather frustration in finding a "correct" approach to the issue.

The task for me was to control my language, so that the patient did not feel criticized or subjected to what could be experienced as an act of aggression on my part. At all costs, any invocation of guilt required special care. I recognized that my dilemma existed within a constricted emotional atmosphere wherein the selection of language was of enormous importance.

I considered, first, exploring with the patient the meaning of her continuing to delay payments for treatment. This had been previously dealt with in the context of her fears that "I would make her submit to me." I know that she has "felt powerless" in her relationships, that everyone seemed to dominate her, and that they could have their needs met while she felt helpless to meet her needs.

The displaced transference interpretation was a vehicle to explore current conflictual relationships and internalized images. The nature of her relationship with me was consciously taken out of the focus of the treatment. I did not elaborate on other meanings of her withholding payment: that she views me as an aggressor and thus acts in accordance with her identification with the aggressor, or that she wants to induce in me the same feelings of helplessness that she experiences, and further that she derives some sadistic pleasure by withholding my fee. To interpret these factors in the context of her actual acts of aggression toward me would result in narcissistic injury and might lead to projection, rage, and narcissistic injury. Her ego structure could not tolerate any recognition of her aggression toward me. I recalled from past sessions when I had inquired as to her thoughts regarding her late fee payments the stony silence and then, with my help, the outburst of rage: "I am mad; I resent your question; I always pay; if you want your money, ask for it." At that moment, I am lost to her as an external object and only with great difficulty, in the grip of the negative transference, can she hold onto me as an internalized and trustworthy object.

Some 10 minutes into a session, I am quite surprised to hear myself announce that "I am raising my fee as of January" (two months from the date). The patient asked what the new fee would be, and I simply told her. In this short interim, many thoughts raced through my mind: Shall I ask what her thoughts are? What does she think the increase should be? But this train of thought was dismissed.

For this patient, any emotional speculation arouses powerful primitive emotions that must be defended against. Speculation about ideas can have a purpose similar to signal anxiety; it permits anticipatory behavior or understanding. Anticipation in my patient becomes actual, concretized, and traumatic (Hurvich, 2000). Thus, I decided that a direct and simple statement was the most efficacious and would reduce the projective mechanisms by providing myself as the frustrating external object.

Rather quickly she responds, "Why do you do it now?"

Again, I decided to respond directly without any investigation of her thoughts: "I have delayed raising your fee until I felt that your income was stabilized."

"This is not fair," the patient states, "I finally make some money—in three months I can be out of work," then, silence.

I ask, "What are you thinking?"

"You are mercenary. A fee should not be changed in the middle of treatment. Once you expect to pay a certain fee, it should not be changed. You are unprofessional."

Her voice is brittle, sharp, and raised. She repeats again how unfair I am; treatment has not really helped her, her life is still miserable. She has no man, no real career; "I hate my work, you know that, I have always hated it." She implies that I do not appreciate how she is tied to a profession that she detests, she has no status, others get opportunities in which they can achieve greater artistic expression, she is stuck, nothing has changed in the 3 years of therapy.

"I am ambivalent about this therapy anyhow. I can't quit. I seem to be stuck to this in the way I have been to men who were bad for me. I am not getting better. I should quit coming here."

Then, as if raising the gauntlet, she asks, "What will happen if I am not working. I am a freelancer. I can't count on a steady income."

Here I blunder—a countertransference reaction—I remind the patient that I have reduced her fee in the past. At this point she replies, "I don't want to bargain with you; this is not a bakery where it is cheaper by the dozen. You are not fair; I don't like your manner." She then withdraws into silence.

Why do I blunder; is it because of conscience, the wish to prove that I am a kind, considerate therapist? Am I subtly telling the patient that she does not appreciate me?

Patients know their therapists, and if they choose to deny their knowledge, to negate a perception, telling the narcissistic, the borderline, or the psychotic patient is usually harmful to the treatment. The patient wanted to see me as selfish and wicked, to prove that I did not empathize with her inner world, which was full of destructive object representations; that I had no sense of her inner poverty. The more success she experienced, the poorer she felt. In part, this was a result of a negative therapeutic reaction, an unremitting attack by her primitive, destructive superego, and in part due to her masochism. Yet, at this point in her treatment, her need to experience herself as poor and a failure was a defense against her guilt over not wanting to pay me more money. It is an issue of "distribution of wealth"—how much to relinquish her oral wishes, the id's struggle against the external object. Had I remained silent at this juncture, it would have been the better part of "valor." All that was technically necessary was for me to help her express her rage.

The patient's rage was vented in the language of primitive ego mechanisms. I had to carefully construct my response to her anger, for she experienced words as concretizations, and she internalized meaning through projective mechanisms. For her to understand the meaning of my verbalizations could be experienced as a threat, for they would be at variance with the way she wished to perceive her own meaning. Further, the process of understanding meaning, that is, her motivations, her desires and needs (Vygotsky, 1934/1962), was too threatening. To apply thought to perception and to supply meaning to words could weaken her denial mechanisms. The genetic factors behind these primitive defenses lay in the nature of her ambivalent relationships to the object. If words lost their connective meaning to the object, then she could be spared the recognition of her own hatreds and the projective identifications.

She was able to establish concrete object relationships, but she was limited in her ability to maintain an inner positive object representation; and thus, her capacity to find loving objects was impaired. Words, like objects, undergo a developmental sequence in relation to meaning (Rycroft, 1986; Vygotsky, 1934/1962).

O'Shaughnessy (1983) discussed a patient for whom the mutative moment, that is, the real gain in insight, was recognized "with the active functioning of the patient's ego in working through in words." For my patient, the development of language was fixated on early phases of object relationships. The fixation was at that phase of development when the object was essentially a need-gratifying one, and thus her words were expressed in the language of oral wishes. It was not possible at this stage of the treatment for language to represent a "working through" process. Further, her language was essentially discharge language, not symbolic or metaphoric (Renik, 1993); she did not attempt to use language to derive or to convey meaning, for language was used essentially as a means for affective discharge (Winnicott, 1960). Not that she was volatile or spoke with heated passion; quite the contrary, her tone was rather soft.

Ferenczi (1913) spoke of the magical meaning of words for the child. It is precisely this magical function of words that I witnessed in my patient. If I could not give her what she wanted with my words, she became rageful and withdrew. I had to be exceedingly careful with my choice of words, in fact, with my sentence structure. For example, to introduce the idea of anticipation[5]—a means by which she could begin to develop the idea of an anticipatory response in a given situation—I would formulate a series of

---

5 Vygotsky (1934/1962) indicated that language plays an anticipatory role in the way speech transfers "social collaborative forms of behavior to the sphere of inner-personal psychic function" (p. 19).

possible events, similar to a "mock trial." I might say, "If you called Bob and invited him to the movies and he accepted, you might not know if he came because he cares for you or because he had nothing better to do." She might then interpret this as my saying that "he doesn't like you," thus a projection; or she could experience her doubts that "he really doesn't like me," and blame me for bringing it to her attention. Either way, she would become enraged at me for making her "feel bad."

For me to work with this very careful selection of words involved a constant structuring and restructuring of words and sentences. The difficulty in the work was not only an indication of countertransference reactions but also that of finding the necessary skill, the technical competence or inspiration, to help her develop a more realistic perception of external and internal reality. My emotions and my wishes were secondary in this sublimatory mode, for I was in search of a good therapeutic method.

Whether I could succeed in disengaging reality from wish in the patient would depend on her mood, that is, the state of her ego in relation to internal objects (Jacobson, 1964). If she could not tolerate the perception that Bob was not seriously interested in her, but simply regarded her as a friend, then she experienced my tentative inquiries as a narcissistic injury. I made her "feel terrible"; I indicated that he does "not like her." "How dare I presume to analyze him." At some other time if there were more gratifications in her life, it was then possible to introduce anticipatory thinking. With this patient I did not offer suggestions; I only examined possibilities that were derived from her explicit statements. There was no suggestion of choice; it was for her to choose, and thus I could only try to help her anticipate the consequences of her choice.

Clearly, when words are so infused with magic, and when frustration is a frequent ingredient in Jane's life, my choice of language was as difficult for me as that of selecting medication for a highly allergic person. With my patient, the requirement was to come as close as possible to magical gratification with language. Because language for her was not used as a reflection of reality by verifying thoughts, she distorted the use of language for the sole purpose of gratifying wishes. Unfortunately, this wish generally resulted in frustration, as Vygotsky (1934/1962) indicated: "gratification is not in the word only through the word" (p. 12).

When I attempted to help her anticipate the possible outcome of an affair with a man whom she liked but had doubts as to his interest in her, I had to sift through countertransference factors: "sleep with the man; it will be good for you to have even a sexual relationship (my wish to give her some pleasure in life); or "Don't sleep with him; you will be hurt and there will be hell to pay in the treatment." I had to guard against intrusion, value judgments, or any hint of suggestion. She wanted a lover, and by my exploration of her feelings she might act upon her wish and then accuse me of telling her to sleep with him; or if she had decided to sleep with him but no romance evolved, I was then responsible for the narcissistic injury.

"It was all your fault!" she bellowed at me.

As I have indicated, anticipating an affect with this patient was extremely difficult due to the concretization of language and its magical usage. For example, whenever I tried to help her anticipate the experience of "being hurt" to reduce the painful impact or to attempt to reclaim some of her past, the result was dubious. Anticipatory hurts were experienced as almost real and absorbed so much of her libidinal investment that memories of the past could not be elicited. This, I believe, resulted from excessive cathectic investment in present experience to gratify wishes. Thus, fantasy material was almost nonexistent and wish was translated into repetitive, obsessive thinking. The failure here of sublimatory thinking made it difficult for her to consider the past independent of the present and to maintain impartial judgment. Each new experience had inadequate historical referents; the representational object was marred with too much ambivalence so that unsatisfied libidinal wishes proved more powerful than the reality of an object relationship. For this patient, the attempt to find a totally new object that could gratify the infantile longing was primary, and any attempt to reexamine or refine an "old object" to contain memory and infantile wishes was experienced as too frustrating.

At times, I attempted to make a connection between the past and the present. I would point out that in regard to some acquaintance, "this woman feels so similar to your sister to whom you felt such allegiance and always had to please and to obey her whims even to the point of giving up every man as you felt they all belonged to her." I attempted to discredit her current perception of the person as a concretization of her sister. I would try to give her a depiction of the past as past so that she could begin to understand her behavior, her motivations.

If I could help her separate from the infantile objects and retain them as past affective object relationships, then perhaps we could deal with certain structural problems, such as her archaic superego. I may have been able to point out that "you felt you had to be submissive to your sister; she was the only one permitted to have a man." In this way, I could indicate that underlying some of her difficulty with men was the belief that she had robbed her sister, and that her self-hatred and self-criticism stemmed, in part, from her oedipal desires. Her sister, who had taken on the mothering role, represented a displacement from the mother. The patient was not as threatened by relating to oedipal issues and deficits in the mothering processes as by the attempts to help her understand the nature of her defenses and oral demands.

My interpretations were attempts to shift her thinking from the concrete experience to a contemplation of experience, to provide word meaning, and thus to change the motoric end result of a word, which is considered essentially segregated thought and is "incapable of changing anything in life" (Vygotsky, 1934/1962). When I attempted a partial interpretation, I had to carefully examine whether at that moment I was not a displacement from the sister transference. It may appear paradoxical that on the one hand I felt it necessary to guard against my becoming a transference object and, on the other hand, to recognize the importance of using the transference as a vehicle for change. Because the patient had difficulty with the "as if quality to the transference (Greenson, 1967; Nunberg, 1948), it became a question of understanding the narcissistic balance, the ego's capacity to tolerate drive derivatives, the traumatic results of transference affects, and transference interpretation.

One of the tasks of transference with this patient was to establish a sense of reality by providing a displacement from an inner representation to an external object, and then to subject that external object to corrective judgment by examining the nature of the drives and the derivative wishes. For the narcissistic, the borderline, and the psychotic patient, transference often exceeds the parameters of the symbolic, and the whole of the new object can become the old object. Thus, at times I felt on shaky grounds with this patient. Will I overstep the delicate balance between the negative and the positive transference, and between the real and the unreal? Will my interpretive words be taken as a criticism and therefore enrage her? Are her shifts from hate to love based on shifts in mood (Jacobson, 1957) that reflect my ability to gratify or to frustrate her preoedipal wishes? What I was hoping to achieve was a structural change that could endure the vicissitudes of the negative transference and maintain the constancy of our object relationship.

Renik (1995) addressed the role of intersubjective communication between patient and analyst. The analyst must find some resonance within the patient's ego structure to effect a mutual intercommunication. I would add that I needed to translate this intersubjective communication into an empathic identification with my patient, and in my patient with me. I hoped this identification would enable the patient to tolerate the demands of her inner world, subject her self-perceptions to more realistic appraisal, and modify her ego ideals. The plasticity of her ego and self-formations was always the primary consideration in any clarification or attempts at interpretation. This plasticity was necessary to ensure a more developed and mature mode of libidinal gratification and object relationship. If she could internalize, then I believe it would be possible for memory to remain as the past referent for the current experiences, irrespective of frustration.

Around the time of my vacation, I faced the problem of a probable negative transference reaction and an increase in rage that threatened the internalized object cathexis. She had to deal with my leaving by acknowledging that she could be affected or have some concerns of being left, yet that would not unnecessarily result in a denial of her feelings and, further, lead to an increase in pathological defenses. My patient had always protected herself from experiencing any affects by isolation, denial, repression, and withdrawal.[6]

In the past, she would respond to my return from vacation with "I did not think of you at all; in fact, I did not miss you; there is no point in my continuing the treatment."

When I had attempted to consider any emotional reaction before my vacation, she generally responded with anger at any assumption I would make: "Why should you assume that it bothers me?" Thus, I decided to deal with this vacation with a statement that included "we" in an attempt to undo the separation of affects between the patient and myself. I tried to indicate that her troubles, her affects, her feelings are not only my concerns for her but also are indicative of my struggles with the separation.

When I said, "What shall we do when I go on vacation, for this is a difficult time; so much is going on in your life and we have so much work to do," I wanted to frame her emotions within the analytic context of both parties—analyst and patient-struggling with emotional material. Her

---

6 Vygotsky (1934/1962) indicated that language plays an anticipatory role in the way speech transfers "social collaborative forms of behavior to the sphere of inner-personal psychic function" (p. 19).

struggle was to maintain her defenses as a protection against oral wishes and narcissistic injuries, and my struggle was to gently overcome her resistance, enabling her to deal with her frustration and anger. I do believe that there is a strong element of support (or what Freud, 1937/1964a, 1940/1964b referred to as suggestion) in the mode by which we identify an affect with a patient or in the means by which we give indirect reference to the affect. In effect, I believe that the analyst is conveying a belief that the patient can tolerate the conscious awareness of the affect and the meaning of the affect. Further, by using the "we," the analyst supplies another's ego as referent that can tolerate emotions. This is a concept similar to one advanced by Settlege (1993), who referred to the analyst as acting as an "auxiliary ego." I am aware that this formulation, that is, my reference to "we," can have the effect of reducing the separation between the patient and myself (O'Shaughnessy, 1983). I acted as though her feelings, her troubles, were also my troubles. There is some danger in undoing the separation between the analyst and the patient in that inadvertently I could re-create the desired "oceanic feeling" (Freud, 1930) that underlies her primitive wishes. A related danger is that for a patient with weak boundaries, the "we" becomes an invitation to merge, which could trigger panic over fear of a loss of a separate sense of self (Hurvich, 2000). On the other hand, there is the danger that I will arouse a sense of betrayal in her belief that I only simulate concern: I am going on vacation; I leave her to her own devices; in essence, I abandon her.

Rycroft (1986) indicated that "language is derived from external objects and contains within it precipitates of past psychological experiences and theories which may lead to hatred and suspicion of words themselves" (p. 246). I must find the words to convey a meaningful affect on my part so as to sustain the object relationship while I am away. I hoped to effect the cognitive awareness of my presence, even in my absence, through the cathectic memory traces of our past work together. A second purpose in formulating the concept of my leaving in this fashion was to reduce her denial mechanisms and reaction formations as much as possible—"I don't need you. I won't miss you. Who do you think you are that you mean so much to me?" Because this patient could not sustain an "as if quality" to the transference, the transference object became too real for her, creating the danger of merger.

My choice in phrasing was indeed a delicate issue, for I was always in danger of creating more frustration and rage. I want to stress that I do not regard this as only a countertransference problem but also as a problem that depends on sensitivity, skill, and understanding of the transference mood at the particular moment. The major problem was how not to overload the transference. By introducing the word "we," I hoped to create an identificatory process whereby she could also identify with me and my tasks and thus enhance her observing ego.

I hope I have not conveyed that the very sentence or the words themselves, even the most empathic of verbalizations, is fully responsible for psychic change. This would certainly bring a magic quality to language. Yet to deny the place of language in psychic change is an error, for, as Rycroft (1986) has indicated, psychoanalytic therapy shows that words can be used to express and resolve infantile conflicts.

THEORETICAL DISCUSSION

In presenting both theoretical and clinical material, I hope to explicate the multilayered range by which words must both reflect and transport meaning for the patient. Further, in distinguishing the role of sublimation as separate from countertransference, I want to reintroduce other factors that influence our function as analysts. I am suggesting that what may occur outside of the countertransference are the sublimatory activities performed by the analyst that can best be understood as an aspect of creativity and skill. Perhaps I can best present an explanation of the sublimatory process by quoting the words that Freud (1910/1957b) used to describe the creative processes of Leonardo Da Vinci:

> His [Leonardo] affects were controlled and subjected to the instinct for research; he did not love and hate, but asked himself about the origin and significance of what he was to love or hate. Thus, he was bound at first to appear indifferent to good and evil, beauty and ugliness. During his work of investigation love and hate threw off their positive or negative signs and were both alike transformed into intellectual interest. In reality Leonardo was not devoid of passion; he did not lack the divine spark which is directly or indirectly the driving force—*il promo motore*—behind all human activity. He had merely converted his passion into a thirst for knowledge; he then applied himself to investigate with the persistence, constancy and penetration which is derived from passion, and at the climax of intellectual labor, when knowledge had been won, he allowed the long restrained affect to break loose and to flow away when its work is done [pp. 74–75].

REFERENCES

Eissler, K.R. (1974). On some theoretical and technical problems regarding the payment of fees for psychoanalytic treatment. *Int. Rev. Psycho-Anal.* 11:73–101.

Fenichel, O. (1945). *The Psychoanalytic Theory of Neurosis.* New York: Norton.

Ferenczi, S. (1913). Stages in the development of the sense of reality. In (Ed.), *First Contributions to Psycho-Analysis.* London: Hogarth Press, pp. 213–239, 1952.

Freud, A. (1936). *The Ego and the Mechanism of Defense.* Milton Park, Abingdon, UK: Routledge, 1992.

Freud, S. (1909). Notes upon a case of obsessional neurosis. *Standard Edition* 10, 151–320, 1955.

———— (1910), Leonardo da Vinci and a memory of his childhood. *Standard Edition* 11 57–137, 1957.

———— (1912). The dynamics of transference. *Standard Edition* 12:97–108, 1958.

———— (1930). Civilization and its discontents. *Standard Edition* 2:57–145, 1961a.

———— (1923). The ego and the id. *Standard Edition* 19: *1–6,* 1961b.

———— (1915). Instincts and their vicissitudes. *Standard Edition* 14:*109–140,* 1963a.

———— (1915). The unconscious. *Standard Edition* 14: *159–215,* 1963b.

———— (1937). Analysis terminable and interminable. *Standard Edition* 2:209–253, 1964a.

———— (1940). An outline of psycho-analysis. *Standard Edition* 23:139–207, 1964b.

Glover, E. (1955). The transference neurosis (Vol. 2) pp. 123–137 In *The Technique of Psychoanalysis.* New York: International Universities Press, 1967.

———— (1955). The technique of psychoanalysis. In *On the early development of the mind.* pp. *91–107.* New York: International Universities Press.

Greenberg, J. (2002). Psychoanalytic goals, therapeutic action and the analyst's tension. *Psychoanal. Q.,* 77: 651–678.

Greenson, R.R. (1967). *The Technique and Practice of Psychoanalysis.* New York: International Universities Press.

Hartmann, H. (1955). Notes on the theory of sublimation. *Psychoanal. St. Child,* 10:9–29.

Hurvich, M. (2000). Fear of being overwhelmed and psychoanalytic theories of neurosis. *Psychoanalytic Review* 87:615–649.

Jacobson, E. (1957). On normal and pathological moods: Their nature and function. *Psychoanal. St. Child*, 12:72–113.

_____ (1964). *The Self and the Object World.* London: Hogarth Press.

Knight, R. (1954). borderline states. In R. Knight (Ed.) *Psychoanalytic Psychiatry and Psychology.* New York: International Universities Press, pp. 97–110.

Little, M. (1957). Countertransference and the patient's response. In *Transference Neurosis and Transference Psychosis.* New York: Jason Aronson, pp. 33–50.

Loewald, H. (1988). *Sublimation.* New Haven, CT: Yale University Press.

Loewenstein, R.W. (1956). Some remarks on the role of speech in psychoanalytic technique. *Int. J. Psycho-Anal.*, 37: 460–468.

Nunberg, H. (1948). Practice and theory of psychoanalysis. In *Nervous & Mental Disorders Monograph Series.*

O'Shaughnessy, E. (1983). Words and working through. *Int. J. Psycho-Anal.*, 64: 281–290.

Poland, W. (1986). The analyst's words: Their context and their formation. *Psychoanal. Q.* 55:244–272.

Renik, O. (1993). Analytic interaction: Conceptualizing technique in light of the analyst's irreducible subjectivity. *Psychoanal. Q.* 62:553–571.

_____ (1995). The analyst's expectations. *Psychoanal. Q.*, 43:83–94.

Rycroft, C. (Ed.). (1986). *An inquiry into the function of words. The psychoanalytic situation: The independent tradition in the British School of Psychoanalysis.* New Haven and London: Yale University Press.

Settlege, C. (1993). Therapeutic process and developmental process in the restructuring of object and self-constancy. *J. Amer. Psychoanal. Assn.* 41:473–492.

Stone, L. (1967). *The psychoanalytic situation and transference: Prescript to an* earlier communication. *J. Amer. Psychoanal. Assn.* 15:3–57.

Vygotsky, L. S. (1962). *Thought and Language.* Cambridge, MA: MIT Press. (1934)

Winnicott, D. (1960). The theory of the parent-infant relationship. *International Journal of Psycho-Analysis* 47:585–593.

CHAPTER 13

PERSONAL MYTHS SUPERORDINATE TO FANTASY: CASE DISCUSSION

To distinguish myth from fantasy as variants of internal psychic structure is a basic premise of this work. To understand and to give more credence to the role of myth in structurization of the ego is essential both for psychodynamic theory and treatment methodology. Myth in our theoretical structures has too frequently been conflated with fantasy. While fantasy has been conceptualized in several different ways; for example, as an aspect of creativity (Loewald,1975), and of self (Grossman,1988), or as a wish fulfillment tale (Kris,1956, Arlow,1969 a, b), myth generally has been understood to be a stabilized fantasy tale generally reflecting society's unconscious desires and wishes (Freud,1923).

More frequently, both concepts seem to interpose each other, to give mutual meaning to what Reik (1957) referred to as the emergence in distorted form of the original drives that have been disavowed, but "obtain a certain possibility of surreptitious expression" (p.85). I shall propose that the concept of the "personal myth" is both a correlate to fantasy, and simultaneously is a separate mental structure that differs from fantasy in the nature of its organization, stability of content, and permanence of characteristics.

My purpose in distinguishing personal myth from fantasy is to suggest that the personal myth as a cohesive unit organized by elements of unconscious and conscious fantasy, beliefs, and fables requires a separate consideration both clinically and theoretically. The "personal myth" as a narrative, a structured story, has established itself as the "real" memory of events, a consolidation of wish, fantasy, and belief that are condensed into a new fact, fortified by distortion and denial. Thus, representing a dialectic or syntheses of its component parts and results in an integration of fantasy and beliefs into a solidified mental structure, which tells a story (Segal, R. 1999, 2015) and tends to be very resistant to modification and influence by the "reality principle." The individual myth has been incorporated into the ego as a permanent story, while fantasies adhere more closely to the fluctuations of the id. Freud (1908a) indicated that the impulses toward "phantasy" are neither stereotyped nor unchangeable.

> On the contrary, they fit themselves into the changing impressions of life, alter with the vicissitudes of life; every deep new impression gives them what might be called a "date-stamp" [p.48].

He noted in "Creative Writers and Day Dreaming" (1908 [1907]) that myths are probably the "distorted vestiges of the wishful phantasies of whole nations," in "Family Romances" (1908b) he indicated that consciously remembered mental impulses of childhood encompasses the factors which enable us to understand the nature of myths. Though Freud made no clear distinction between myth and fantasy, it is apparent that the myth represented the social and cultural organized story of the more personal yet universal quality of individual fantasies.

Joseph Campbell (1959, Segal, 2015), the noted cultural historian, described the nature of myth from a literary and cultural perspective that interestingly veers close to a psychoanalytic perspective. According to Campbell, the myth represents mankind's attempts to understand his world, his birth, and death. Thus, all myths represent a biological-psychological structure that "is a function of the human nervous system, precisely homologous to the innate and learned sign stimuli that release and direct the energies of nature..." (p.42). Campbell stated that all societies, either in their religions or folklore, bear the primitive structure of myth and the same general outline of content but, that each culture embellishes and transforms myth according to the specific nature and development of its social and intellectual structure. Each, man, woman, and child through his

> maturing consciousness has come to know the world by means of the medium of this heavily loaded, biological based triangle of love and aggression, desire and fear, dependency, command, and the urge for release [Segal, p. 72].

A comprehensive review of the various theoretical positions on myth, fantasy, beliefs, fairy tales, and fables may provide greater understanding in our analytic discourse since as, I have already indicated, we are beset with a few conflated concepts that in and of themselves appear as excellent theories yet require a more refined distinction. By recognizing the role of myths as both an unconscious and conscious mode of defense and compromise formation in psychic structure that differs in function and structure from fantasies and beliefs, we can refine our treatment methods in dealing with certain resistances in our patients.

Though my focus is primarily on the difference between myth and fantasy, it is important to note that concepts such as beliefs, fables and fairy tales also form a mental organization. Beliefs tend to relate to issues of truth and untruth—right or wrong—about a subject (Wikipedia, 2019), and deal essentially with knowledge and epistemology. Fables and fairy tales that enter the content of fantasies and myth tend to serve a literary or social function and may have unknown origins, or are composed by specific writers. (Segal, R.,1999). They tend to express "elements of the fantastic." and magical acts, that express a moral lesson (March 23, Masters Review,

Internet), and generally contain unconscious wishes and fantasies, but are primarily recognized more as imaginative stories rather than a reality that exists or once existed.

The study of fantasy did not begin with psychoanalysis; it has had a long history, emerging from Aristotelian philosophy, and is an integral part of epistemological discourse. Psychoanalytic contribution to the study of both myth and fantasy has heightened the awareness of the unconscious, the role of drive and drive derivatives, in their content and origins. A number of theorists (Freud, S., 1908,1909,1911; Sharpe, 1940; Klein, 1946; Isaacs, 1949; Balint, 1959; Kris1956; Beres,1962; Arlow, 1969a) have further explicated the concepts of primary processes as central to understanding their role and aim in the structure of myths and fantasies.

Grossman (1982) indicated that fantasy is the dominant mode of internal organization and mental structure, and is at the core of the "self." Fantasy "organizes and directs behavior." As a fantasy, the details of the "self" may be elaborated, distorted, re-represented, repressed etc." (p. 927). He further posited that the "Self" depends on a person's view of himself, which, from a psychoanalytic point of view, means it is a fantasy. In short "the self" is a personal myth, a myth of which everyone has his own more-or-less original version. (p. 929). Thus, Grossman appears to conflate fantasy and myth as one and the same as he makes no attempt to differentiate the two.

According to Beres (1962) fantasy is a structured mental representation and "derives from instinctual drives cathected by the energies of the drives" (p.317). He considered that the relationship of fantasy as primary process mentation and its evolution to secondary processes, i.e., the reality principle, places fantasy in a bridge relationship between wish and consummation, wish and memory, and wish and reality. This brings us close to concepts between what is real, what is wishful ideation, what is fact and what is fantasy.

Erreich (2003) has stressed another element in the discourse of myth, fantasy, and belief, that of "compromise formation." In her lexicon, compromise formation has taken on the meaning of a structured content that is given meaning through the language of fantasy, and appears like a fantasy. "Compromise formations are the defensive operations on mental content, which then is represented via unconscious fantasy" (p. 567).

From the Kleinian perspective, it is, perhaps, Susan Isaacs (1948) who has presented the most detail defining "phantasy." The distinction had already been made between the spelling of "phantasy" with the *ph*, and the spelling "fantasy" with an *f*. Isaacs pointed out that fantasy spelled with "f", generally connoted conscious daydreams and fictions, while the "ph" spelling indicated predominantly unconscious phantasies that are phylogenetically structured in the unconscious. Phantasy in the Kleinian lexicon is a ubiquitous function of mental life in both normal and pathological states. Isaacs also indicated that phantasy is the mental expression of an instinct; it is the mental corollary, the psychic representative of instinct; "there is no impulse, no instinctual urge or response which is not experienced as unconscious phantasy" (p.9). She, further, indicated that the instincts conceived as a borderline psychosomatic process, which has bodily aims, are directed to concrete external objects, represented in the mind by phantasies. Phantasies are essentially derivative of the instincts, preverbal, and have a phylogenetic structure.

Freud (1908a) stressed that the motive force for all fantasies is unsatisfied wishes that belong to childhood. Fantasies tend to fall into two main groups, ambitious wishes or erotic ones, and frequently they are united. He pointed to the time factor in the development of fantasy. "It hovers" between three time periods, some current impression that then invokes some memory of an earlier experience in which the wish was fulfilled; and then creates a situation in the future wherein the wish will be fulfilled (p. 147).

Kris (1956) indicated that fantasies compose the personal myth, and what distinguishes the myth from the fantasy is the specific pattern that the fantasy develops and organizes into a fixed, biographical story. The story or narrative, that is, the myth, is usually an "autobiographical screen" that is highly structured, and whose defensive purpose is to hide or distort the true memory. He stressed that there is an "extraordinary investment in the past," and patients exhibit great difficulty in permitting exploration of the "autobiographical screen." The negative reaction to reconstruction and resistance to analysis of the myth, are indicative of the ego's heavily fortified defenses. From the perspective of the id, the resistance stems from the amount of pleasure derived from the fantasy, and what Kris (1956) referred to as a "valued and treasured holding." Personal myths do not reflect the true historical picture, and these myths are not borrowed "from a cultural tradition or any general mythology" (p. 300). They become a personalization based on a fantasy, and later, develop into a myth that plays a significant part in the person's psychic structure. The story that emerges is a continuation of a childhood fantasy, and it serves the function of undoing early traumas and narcissistic injuries, and assumes a role that is not obvious in the recounting of the patient's history. That story is recounted in ways that often contains reversal of facts, historical distortions, hidden facts, modified memories; all methods utilized in order to create a new drama, a new idealized parental complex, and /or a different idealized self-image. The dominant feature guiding this new creation is an attempt to undo unpleasant memories of the past and to re-establish the dominance of the pleasure principle as indicated by Freud in Family Romances. (1909 [1908]).

Perhaps of all the later theorists, it was Arlow (1969a,b) who brought into prominence the role of unconscious fantasies in mental life, and focused on the ubiquity that these fantasies exercise, both in normal development and in pathogenesis. Fantasy concerns an insistent libidinal or aggressive desire that seeks discharge in a variety of storylines, and in a variety of actions.

Memory, recording conflicts, traumata, vicissitudes of the drives and of development, is organized in terms of the pleasure-unpleasure principle into groups of schemata centering around childhood wishes [p. 43].

These contents, consisting of a continuous stream of fantasy thinking, remain a concomitant to all mental activity and exert an unending influence on the manner and means by which reality is perceived and understood (Arlow,1969a). He postulated that the ego's perceptual apparatus was driven from two direction—the external sensory sphere of objects and the internal world of inner stimulation that he called the 'realm of fantasy thinking'. Further, he indicated, "the most powerful influence distorting the image of the past and contributing to the misperceptions of the present is the intrusion of unconscious fantasy thinking" (1969a, p. 43). He indicated that in "keeping with the synthetic function of the ego and the principle of multiple function" the traumatic events of one's life and the pathogenic conflicts that develop from them "are worked over defensively by the ego and incorporated into a schema of memories and patterns of fantasy," and exert a powerful and unending dynamic effect (1969a, p. 42).

Theoretically, to differentiate fantasy from myth is not an easy endeavor. Myth, as I have indicated, has generally connoted the cultural expression of society's unconscious wishes, and serves a social purpose (Segal, 2015), while fantasies are expression of wishes that have a more temporal quality and are easily modified by the momentary experience. Yet, fantasies have also been considered to become solidified by the permanence of a specific wish, generally a childhood wish (Freud,1908a; Arlow,1969a, b; Baudry,1988; Erreich, 2003) that is subject to later modification. Myths, as I have stated, generally have assumed the universal. They function as a final organization of society's fairy tales, fables, and beliefs, and they are containers purported to tell a truth.

As psychoanalysis has begun to pay more attention to the role of myths in the individual, it has begun to recognize that they can also exist as a psychic structure, and that "at heart, myth is autobiography," and that by disguised modification, they can be molded into an acceptable, organized story in the individual (Segal, 2015).

Kluckhohn (in Segal 1999, p. 45) has indicated that myths provide a means of dealing with anxiety for both society and the individual, and Levi-Strauss posits that myths are humanity's means of "pairing impulses," that is, thinking in "pairs of opposition." Thus, myth "is distinctive in not only expressing oppositions which are equivalent to contradictions, but also resolving them" (in Segal, 1999, p.46). This concept is particularly pertinent to the thinking of individuals who are conflicted by contradictory impulses, wishes, and ideation. The individual mythical story may contain deeply repressed contradictory wishes, guilt, and a degree of failure of resolution, which can result in behavior that evidence doubtful thinking (see case of Mr. M), and still fall under the rubric of myth. Further, the myth, though not fully successful in allaying anxiety in its attempt at a compromise formation, still has all the functional elements that compose and structure a myth, such as fantasy, defense, denial, and a specific storyline that attempts to reflect realty and is fundamentally based upon hidden wish fulfillment. Segal (2015), in discussing Freud's oedipus complex, fortifies this concept in that this "key myth" of Oedipus: his (Oedipus') "destiny moves us only because it might have been ours—because the oracle laid the same curse upon us before our birth as upon him." (p. 82). The manifest level of the myth masks a latent meaning which is about the fulfillment of a wish in which the "myth-maker or reader" fulfills his own wishes. Myths, in Segal's constructs,

> constitute a compromise between the side of oneself that wants the desires satisfied outright and the side that does not even want to know they exist" (p.84). Myth provides the 'ideal kind of fulfillment', the true "meaning always lies at the level below ... but is always conveyed at the level above. [p. 84].

Since fantasies and the creation of the myth begin in childhood, we can observe how memory functions reflect the childhood mode of distorting memory and reality (Kris,1956). The failure to differentiate fact from fantasy is a natural consequence of childhood development. Thus, to establish the veracity of the past by means of reconstruction can be a Herculean task, since the life process is in "constant flux," subject to repeated re-organization and, more notably, that reality has been subsumed by defense, and distortion (Kris, 1956).

As I have already indicated, to distinguish fantasy from myth in the individual situation is no easy task, and may ultimately result in a sophist discourse that does not contribute significant clinical understanding. Yet, I believe, as Kris (1956) has stressed, that there is a significant difference between fantasy and myth, as exemplified by the degree to which the fantasy has been integrated into the ego structure, and forms the self-concept (Grossman,1982), and thus, may emerge as myth. The strength of the defenses, and the solidification of the story or "autobiographical screen," and the nature of the resistance indicate a difference in their dynamic aim. Fantasy is primarily an attempt at more momentary, narcissistic gratification, while the basic aim of myth is both gratification and the need to create a new reality not dependent on verisimilitude. Further, the degree of unconscious gratification of infantile wishes, and the difficulty in interposing the reality principle, poses the greatest source of resistance in undoing the myth.

Thus, I hope to show that the concept of myth as constituting a somewhat different dynamic structure than fantasy has frequently been overlooked in our clinical evaluation and treatment. Undoubtedly, fantasies surface as the predominant mechanism in the expression of unconscious wishes, and in the desire for pleasure. Richards, A. (1988) has indicated that "the complex tangle of fantasies constructed at various stages of development" each contain elements from "reality, myth, and personal fantasy... that may be altered at later stages of development to accommodate experience"

(p. 462). That fantasy assumes the dominant role in unconscious processes is not questioned, yet, the subtle role of the "personal myth" that frequently emerges as a pseudo-reality through the vehicle of autobiographical material and screen memories necessitates exploration, both as psychoanalytic theory, and in individual treatment cases. I juxtapose both myth and fantasy as both are explicatory processes in understanding that which has been concealed and denied to consciousness.

CASE OF MR. M. THE MYTH OF "THE BOY WITH THE BIG PENIS"

Mr. M.'s long standing oedipal myth emerged almost in a rather latent and obsequious manner, as it became increasingly clear that this myth had a significant influence on his affective state, his unconscious self-representation, object relations, and behavior patterns. I will focus on the basic myth as emblematic of certain developmental sequences that eventually characterized his character-structure, and unconscious conflicts.

The myth that he, as a young boy of 8–9 had a big penis—as big as his father's—emerged rather innocuously, never as a direct story, and only by circumstantial evidence was it established as an organized belief that influenced many of his ego functions. An exact derivative fantasy of his latency years and a surface manifest content was a memory of a childhood game played with his brother—"he was the owner of a large underworld city—he owned everything and was powerful." Any attempt to get more detail was met with resistance. The myth of the big penis emerged in relation to early sexual activity and its secret implications. I will also attempt to show the role of myth and ritual that Segal (2015) explicates in his discussion of how ritual underpins the functions of myth. The rituals for my patient emerged in the consistent patterns by which he interacted with his male employees by a repetition of the same actions and words. Raglan (1936 [1990]) indicated that "myth is really the story which the ritual enacts," (p. 95) and Sir James Frazer (in Raglan, 1936 [1990]) stated that "myths had once had their counterpart in magic; in other words, they are used to be acted as a means of producing in fact the events which they describe in figurative language" (p. 95). I believe, it became increasingly apparent that Mr. M exhibited repetitive ritualistic behavior as described by Frazer. Further, his repetitive doubting could also be explained by what Thompson (in Raglan, 1936 [1990]) stated as the necessity to get "the ritual exactly right (for the slightest deviation from the rules will ruin everything)" (p. 95). This concept of rites and its relationship to myth is very important and suggests further exploration in psychoanalytic theory. This is especially pertinent, since magical beliefs underpin ritualistic behavior, and is inherent in our conceptualizations regarding fantasy.

The patient, a 56-year-old man, self-employed as an architect, came for an initial consultation because of anxiety and doubts regarding his abilities, and fear of expanding his business. He was married with two children. Mr. M. had been in treatment with many different therapists over the years, all of whom were male. The treatments, primarily supportive psychotherapy, had been helpful, but the level of anxiety remained constant. He felt that he was ready for a more in-depth analysis. It was evident that his unconscious conflicts regarding his self-representation and the source of his anxiety had not been dealt with in depth. The patient began treatment three times a week, and though he welcomed an analytic approach, he did miss the direct advice and supportive approach of his former therapists.

Mr. M was a graduate of a prestigious architecture school and had secured an MBA from an equally prominent school. He disclaimed whatever success he had achieved, remembering the trauma of not being hired by one of the preeminent firms at the time of his graduation. He recalled being told that he was not assertive and lacked certainty in his ideas.

Mr. M. came from a well-to-do family of European ancestry. His father was a physician, and his mother a writer. There were two siblings, an older sister five years his senior, and a younger brother, three years his junior.

He was plagued with ruminations, repeating events and incidents that he felt he mishandled from years ago. He suffered doubts in almost every aspect of his life:

Was he being taken advantage of by his employees? Was he too miserly? Should he fire an employee? Did it make sense to take on a small job in order to please a client?

This would be repeated, session after session, even though he had already acted on many of these issues. In his repetitions, recalling events fifteen to twenty years earlier, he frequently, stated that he did not want to be "fucked" by anyone, yet, he felt that this is what had happened. The nature and pervasiveness of his doubts and fears of being "fucked" by men may certainly be understood as an underlying conflict over masculine and feminine identification. Yet, perhaps more pertinent to his conflicts was the creation and belief in his "myth" that as a young boy he had a big penis as big or bigger than his father's. I would suggest that the conscious myth of the big penis covered an earlier more latent unconscious belief that he had bested his father, was the chosen one—who had won his mother. Thus, an underlying oedipal myth. That doubts pervaded his psyche can be explained by the partial failure of the compromise formation and defense mechanisms to adequately sustain the myth. Yet, the underlying myth, though confronted by the reality that his penis was not bigger than his father's, or that he was not the owner of the underworld city (perhaps his mother), continued to exercise a dominant position in his characterological structure.

The patient was conscious of his wish to have a close relationship with a male employee on whom he could depend to help him make important business decisions, and to relate to clients. He would use this employee as a personal confidant, and at the same time expressed envy regarding his abilities to talk, gossip and relate freely to others. In relation to men, he was passive and conciliatory while in his relation to his wife and other women, he was quick to anger. He seemed surprised when I pointed out his anger towards women and his sadistic behavior towards his wife.

That his doubting of every action is evident in the consistent repetition of words, thoughts and ideas bears the impact of obsessive–compulsive ideation and behavior, it is also possible to suggest that the consistency in the way and manner in which he related to his employees had a ritualistic quality that does not deviate in practice. Segal (2015) had indicated that though myth is "taken to be words, often in the form of story, the theory of ritual and myth maintains that all myths have accompanying rituals and all rituals accompanying myths" (p. 49). Thus, the manner in which Mr. M. repetitively relates to his employees, seeks their advice and approval, appears to replicate the mode of a ritual. His behavior, spurred by the wish for approval (possibly the Gods), and sanction from retribution, resembles a preformed ritual, and can therefore conform to a form of myth and ritual "in coalescence" (Segal, 2015).

Further, this repetitive behavior of past events, session after session, also served a related purpose, in that in re-enacting the traumatic situation, he derived masochistic gratification, and added pleasure from "libidinizing anxiety" (Laforgue, 1930). These masochistic acts were a re-enactment of the oedipal drama of childhood; they were libidinized and, in spite of what appeared to be misery and distress, he unconsciously derived gratification from his suffering. Guilt and punishment were also retribution for his oedipal rivalry, the wish to destroy his father and siblings. Perhaps most pertinent in this repetition of doubts, which is in his compulsive behavior and obsessive thinking (Freud,1923), was the structurization of his latency-age myth—a reaction formation to guilt for wishing to best his father and all men. The myth of the big penis was his attempt to gratify both the id and the ego—a denial of the superego attacks on his ego, and punishment for his aggressive wishes. We observe that the structure of the myth is both a defense against the oedipal complex and a denial of the superego condemnation.

His repeated fear of "being fucked" could easily be reversed into its opposite—his wish to fuck the man or be fucked. This was another means of resolving his oedipal conflicts, the negative oedipal solution. His response to an interpretation that he was rivalrous with his sister, and wished to gain the attention of her boyfriend, was met with: "Perhaps, I want to be a girl, and be taken care of." He preferred to see himself as passive and dependent on the man rather than experience either his rivalry with the male or his more active sexual wishes regarding the male (Freud, 1919). Interestingly, he had had a strong identification with a neighbor who was a carpenter. He spent considerable time in his youth with this man and wished that he could be his father. This was both an identificatory figure and a homosexual object. This relationship could explain his interest in architecture and building rather than his father's profession. Contrary to more powerful parental images in family romance fantasies (Kris, 1956), Mr. M selected a less powerful figure in order to deny his unconscious wishes of besting his father.

It became apparent that Mr. M's repetitions, further, represented his attempts to deal with anxiety that stemmed from memories and traumatic events. He functioned similarly to a patient that Arlow (1969b, p. 44) described. The patient scanned "the data of perception of reality to discover reassuring evidence of the validity of the solution which he arrived at in fantasy." Unfortunately, Mr. M was unable to secure the desired reassurance, as the fantasy to dethrone his father aroused a sense of danger. I draw a parallel here to the mythical figure of Ulysses who, upon attempting to reach home after the Trojan Wars, encountered a series of life-threatening events, each that required his mastery or help from the "gods." Thus, it was that the patient always encountered a series of dangers from which he required rescue.

A second source of anxiety that preceded his oedipal conflicts resulted from a very early asthma condition. While he had memories of asthma attacks, visits to the doctor, and his mother's preoccupation with alternative health medications, he had very little affect, especially in recall of the asthma attacks. The lack of affect regarding them, and lack of relatedness to the condition itself, indicated that the disease—the attacks—had to be experienced as life threatening. The quality of his current anxiety, the repetitive fears of loss, his money, his home, his business, even his life is a repetition of the childhood trauma. The dangers to his life, the many hospitalizations, undoubtedly, aroused annihilation anxiety (Hurvich, 2007), and these annihilation fears are aroused by almost any event-large or small—that threatens loss.

Near the end of the first year of treatment, Mr. M related an incident that as a 9-year-old boy he was involved in sexual play with a 14-year-old girl. In describing the sexual activity, he recounted how the girl tried to stuff his 'soft little penis' into her vagina. He felt humiliated, and he then jumped to current perceptions of himself: "I am paranoid, I am a little man, I can't reach out to clients, I can't talk to them, they will see me as a fuck-up". Addressing his feelings of being paranoid, he associated it to his fear that other men would see him as a little boy, not a big powerful man. That was why he was afraid to contact them, he would appear as a fool. The idea of being a fool evoked memories of adolescent behavior where he played the fool. As a latency age boy, he teased and mocked his father. In this situation, the father was the fool. Thus, by identification with the father, the other men would mock him as he had once mocked his father.

When I pointed out that there was something strange about his still feeling humiliated by the memory of having a "small, and soft penis" as a nine-year-old, he was rather astonished. I indicated that nine-year-old boys have small penises; they aren't big enough to enter a vagina. I also wondered why he didn't see himself as a sexually precocious boy whom the girls liked, especially the older girls. He seemed surprised by this, and further, when I indicated that he must have had the idea or belief that he had a "big penis" like a man, and perhaps as big as his father's penis, he acknowledged this. Interestingly, about two weeks later in another session, when this material reoccurred, he denied that he had thought that he could enter the girl's vagina, that he was humiliated, and contrary to his earlier statements, he indicated that he really was pleased with his early sexual activity. I believe that this reversal in perception was an attempt to deny his illusory belief of what I address as his "myth" of the big penis as a child. Even now, he is always concerned about the size of his penis, and at the gym visually measures his penis against those of other men. He is frightened that men can see his shame—"see under my clothes—what a schmuck, I am."[1]

The theme of the child with the little penis or, in his unconscious, "the big penis," emerges in other session—he relates that what is "so glorious about sex—"you put the little stick in a little hole," this statement was about his mother and father having intercourse—an idea that he could not believe or tolerate very well. Thus, who has the little stick—he or his father whom he wishes to undermine? Perhaps, the myth of his having a big penis is constantly in danger of exposure as false. The wish became a true belief that he really had a big penis. But he is plagued by the reality that it was his father who had the big penis.

An additional factor that marks Mr. M's ambivalent relationship with men is the displacement from his father's penis to that of other men, the other men have the big penis—he is in doubt about his own penis. He wants the big penis from the other men, and the reassurance that there is a "big penis" to be gotten. His search for confidants, for powerful men, men with

---

1 Schmuck is a Yiddish word for penis, but used in a derogatory fashion.

money, men who seduce women, and even his former male therapists is driven by his myth to re-find the boy who had the "big penis." As Freud (1926 [1925]) indicated that the primary and immediate aim of reality testing is not to find an object in real perception that will correspond to the one presented, but to re-find such an object, and to convince oneself that it is still there.

I further, postulate that the compulsion that drove Mr. M was an almost hallucinatory sense (Gibeault, 2005) that the mythical big penis of childhood was not only experienced in thought but became a perception. It is this perceptual belief, followed by doubt, that further underlies his obsessive doubting—he had the big penis—but maybe he didn't.

Transference

How the myth plays out in the transference is quite interesting. I represented the oedipal mother—he does leave his male therapist to come into treatment with me. His former therapist was nice, supportive but not powerful; he did not provide him with insight or understanding, he appeased him, made him feel that all is well, and at times asked him for advice regarding real estate issues. I am the phallic woman, the psychoanalyst who gives him insight, makes meaningful interpretations, like his mother with whom he shared an intimate relationship, and to whom he turned to for advice, especially around sex. Yet now that he was considering moving his office and possibly expanding his business—that is, attempting to act on a realistic plan—the wishful ideas are immediately infused by his unconscious myth of the great and powerful penis, and he experiences doubt and panic. He is psychically dominated by myth, but also in doubt. I, the woman, phallic but also castrated, is too insignificant to grant him potency. He turns to a male, one of his former therapists who had been a professor at his university, to give him the "big phallus." His myth had become too dangerous for it created fantasies of omnipotence; he becomes the richest man, the most powerful—at which point, he is overwhelmed with anxiety, fear and doubt. Thus, his and the borrowed phallus are in danger of failing. It is not that he confronts reality; rather, he perceives the downfall of his fantasy world, and a world in which a great deal of libido has been invested.

Further, this act of turning to the male can also be understood as an act of undermining my strength; he had to make the woman less powerful by turning to the male and attempting to lessen any feminine influence over him. The danger at this moment of a too-powerful feminine identification undermines the mythical posture of a powerful male; all feminine identification, all passivity must be eradicated. He turns to the idealized male. We can observe in his behavior, the old unresolved oedipal conflict, and the role of his "personal myth," a multilevel of ego functions.

I was rather surprised, when Mr. M. returned from his session with Dr. R., to hear that he was disappointed. He indicated that the "magic" he sought was no longer there: "Maybe I wanted him to wave the magic wand. He appeared older, and tired, and acted more like a friend. He didn't charge me for the session."

No longer was the aura of the university so alluring, and the patient recalled his own successes at the university. He was thus left with a reality that he was finally beginning to tolerate. I, his therapist, a woman, could not give him the "mythical'" big phallus of childhood that he had been searching for; nor can any male supply it. There is no magic to phallic success, money, and power. No god-like savior in his ritualistic acts.

And yet, I wonder if on seeing his old therapist, Mr. M. felt a sense of victory—that he had the big penis—that he had stolen from this therapist and therefore, the myth unconsciously continues as a potent force? Or shall we postulate that as Freud (1909 [1908]) and Kris (1956) indicated, that the role of re-finding the lost heroic parental object remains the real quest behind the myth. By identification with his lost father of childhood, whom he both idealized and belittled, the patient is attempting to re-find both his father's big penis and his own mythological "big penis of childhood." The patient's doubts, reminiscence, and repetitions are further, attempts to reaffirm and establish the mythological "big penis" of the nine-year-old boy.

Though myths in general are concerned with establishing a heroic figure, this case presentation would appear as the very opposite of the heroic figure. His doubts, self-abnegations, passive wishes towards men, and sense of being found out that he is just a "little man"—all that would signify that he is the anti-hero. Yet, I am suggesting that autobiographical myths tell many different stories. Mr. M. has maintained an unconscious belief and fantasy that became a myth, a very specific organizing concept and ideation and story that he had a "big penis" as a young boy, and that he is constantly searching for this penis, much like the quest for the Holy Grail. Simultaneously, he must protect this 'big penis' against castration.

It is also, possible to conclude that, really at issue, is castration anxiety, and not the mythological big penis in a little boy, especially since he is now a grown man with a big penis. Furthermore, we could be dealing with issues of regression, and problems of self-representation. I believe that the above statements are also accurate as the conflicts are overdetermined. My point of reference is to the extent that his need to both re-find and maintain this mythological "big penis" of childhood has on his business dealings, interactions with people, and on his sense of self. The latency trauma of belief and doubt regarding his penis, the inability to accept that his father had the big penis, that his older sister had the man with the big penis, and that perhaps she too had a penis, continued to assault him.

That I have proposed a decided differentiation in this case between fantasy and myth is a result of the structurization and permanency of his belief in his "big penis'" as a nine-year-old boy. The difference between the two lay in the fact that his myth had taken on the form of a real story that continued in the present. His failure to accept the reality of his childhood state or to develop a fantasy that was more pliable such as daydreams (Winnicott, 1974 [1971]) that supply an immediate gratification without the belief that they are "true" has interfered with his current self-perception and a realistic perception of other men. That doubts persist in his unconscious and that, by displacement, effect major and minor decisions, does not preclude the existence of a myth (Freud, 1908a). I wish to stress that the ability to differentiate between myth and fantasy is both an important therapeutic and methodological task in our work.

THE MYTH OF THE UBER-WOMAN

In this case, that I have labeled as the "Uber-Woman," the myth was so successfully hidden by its disguise of a lack of a specific verbal construct that it may validly be questioned whether this can come under the rubric of a myth. And yet, this wordless story bears the structure of a consistent story. I realize that it may appear anomalous to present the concept of a myth whose unconscious ideational structure has no structured verbal story line, but rather presents a consistent theme by which the patient presents a fantasy and a self-image in a stable, repetitive fashion throughout her history. I suspect that in this case, most psychoanalysts would tend to describe this as unconscious fantasy in a narcissistic personality disorder. Yet the persistence, the same characterological behavior, and belief in this stable self-image, suggests to me an underlying consistent story line—a myth—that is the dominant psychological feature in her self-representation, rather than the function of unconscious fantasies.

That "personal myth" in our psychoanalytic constructs is so frequently subsumed under the aegis of fantasy is due in large part to regarding myths as part of literary and social history. Placing myth within the larger social and cultural orbit, and not recognizing that myths can be a significant factor in individual psychic structure, deprives psychoanalytic treatment of an important insight into many patients' disturbances. That unconscious fantasy is the predominant mechanism in the pleasure-unpleasure principle is a truism, but it need not negate that in some cases it is the personal myth that is the dominant defensive feature Freud (1909 [1908b], Klein, 1952, Winnicott, 1974). Segal (1999, 2015) has stressed the need for psychoanalysis to pay more attention to the role of personal myths in psychic structure. "At heart myth is—auto-biography," and that by disguise, myth can be molded into an acceptable, organized story in the individual.

Sara

Sara is a 37-year-old actress and playwright, unmarried at the beginning of treatment, quite beautiful, intelligent, and is very perceptive of the other's psychic functioning. Her writing reflects an in-depth understanding of character. Yet, she has been surprisingly defended against "knowing" her own unconscious wishes, conflicts, and acting out behavior.

Sara is the younger of two sisters. Her father was a very prominent professor of history, world renowned, and her mother was a college dean of students. Both eminent in their professions, and both came from wealthy families. The parents divorced when she was fourteen. Her father had numerous affairs during the marriage, which Sara denied any knowledge of until the divorce.

She was seen in psychoanalytic treatment, 4-times-a-week for 7 years, and then treatment was reduced to 3-times-a-week. In the first period of her analysis, the focus had been on the external environment, her parents, and sibling, their conscious and unconscious behavior patterns, her oedipus complex, her internal conflicts and acting out as it affected her development. She was a graduate student in academia at the onset of treatment, and thus, much of the focus was on her relationship with faculty and peers. While she had cordial relationships with peers, there were no real intimacies, and she tended to remain on the periphery of the social activity. With faculty, her relationships were ambivalent, some she idealized, and others she negated. She could accept intellectually her rivalry with other students, but the analysis at this time did not basically change the nature of her relationships. Her understanding was essentially cognitive. Dealing with her narcissism, her oral needs, and a need to become the center of attention was more successfully dealt with when she began to work as an actress in a small theatre company. Initially, her job began as a "honeymoon" but gradually deteriorated, due to her unawareness of the other person's basic existence and needs. In this narcissistic state, she could avoid dealing with her own rivalries and jealousies, and those of her co-workers. In her mind she became the center of the world, a prima donna, an only child, no siblings, and no other directors or authors existed, only "she." Sara had been adequately able to control this infantile narcissism while at school, but the moment she entered the work-world her narcissistic defenses became exaggerated. She demanded to be catered to, not explicitly, only implicitly, and the nature of this unconscious demand is what made it so difficult for her to grasp the meaning of her behavior. At work there was little acting out with anger; rather her narcissism took the form of negating others, unawareness of them, almost as though they had no existence or needs of their own. This behavior was so subtle that her co-workers had little awareness of why they disliked her and wanted to get rid of her. This aspect of orality, while indicative of her personality structure, also served a primarily defensive purpose of avoiding her deep unconscious oedipal conflicts; if people didn't exist, then they were neither rivals nor competitors.

Precisely, what was the myth that dominated Sara's affective beliefs and behavior? She was the Uber-Woman, the queen, the sole ruler of the "castle" (a euphemism); all were servants devoted to her. Thus, she had no need to recognize their existence outside of their caring for her. Only her needs mattered, and her authority. Whether acting or directing, the storyline was the same—her rule, her authority, her voice. She wrote the best plays, and only she was the consummate actress. Raglan (1990) indicated that words provide an entryway into the structure of the myth, but, unfortunately her words—the words of her mythical tale—never directly emerged. The resistance was powerful and the repression so pervasive that the manifest verbal myth did not emerge except in her behavior with other actors and directors.

Thus, again one may validly ask what makes this behavior a myth rather than a result of a fantasy or character structure? It was my impression that there was an unwritten storyline—I am the ruler in the home—the beautiful queen loved by my father; my mother and sister are maids to me. Wherever I go, the people bow down to me; I rule, I dominate, I am the greatest actress, the best director and writer, the most beautiful, the others are jealous of me. This is a consistent story line that is enacted in every situation. Fantasies may also be consistent, repetitive, and derive from the pleasure principle, but I would suggest that the fantasy that has a very permanent storyline, whether in words or basic beliefs, evolves into a more permanent story structure, therefore, a myth.

The major working through in this treatment occurred in the transference. It was as though the entire first part of the treatment was a prelude to the emergent transference neurosis; the symptoms now emerged in the treatment. Initially, I was a good object, held at a distance, who could be helpful and educational. Shortly, before graduating from drama school, I became the ambivalent transference object, the dramaturgic object. Initially, what seemed to be play at the onset of each session, was a nasty, teasing quality. She would enter the room and speak in various foreign languages as a greeting. If I did not respond in kind, she became offended and attacked me. "I was stiff, too formal, had no sense of humor." At other times, she berated

287

me for my interpretations; I did not use the correct words, and she would reword my statements. In truth, there were times when her rewording was more apt, and I would say so. At times she refused to speak simply because she didn't feel like it, and near the end of the hour she would yell at me for wasting the session. If she brought in a dream, I dared not interpret it, and when I would comment, she became very angry. At one point her regression took the form of wanting to draw. This lasted one session, and she gave it up, accusing me of interpreting her choice of colors. Her sister had been a rather good painter but had totally stopped painting.

I would characterize the transference as similar to what Goylan (2022) has described as "adolescent ruthlessness," a concept first defined by Winnicott (1964). It parallels the ruthless behavior of the attached infant to the caretaking object. The infant in the first year of life has the capacity to

> assume an ability to bring together the aggressive and erotic instinctual components into a sadistic experience, as well as an ability to find an object at the height of instinctual excitement. [p. 22–23].

Attachment to the object is fused with love, anger, ambivalence, and guilt. Winnicott will state that with development "ruthlessness gives way to ruth, unconcern to concern." (p.24). Goylan (2022) suggests that this duality of love and hate is repeated in adolescence during a period characterized by the "defense of ideality and splitting." Shane, Shane, and Gales (1997) have characterized this transference both in terms of Freud's transference neurosis, and in more modern self-psychological terms. Thus, transference in the treatment takes the form of a repetition of the "old-old" relationships, essentially the old parental relationship, to the old-new relationship of the patient to the analyst in the present, and to a more permanent state of old-new to a new-new state. Thus, experiencing the analyst as a new object that is neither assimilated nor accommodated to but seen as a separate, empathic object. It is in this state that enactments from the past to modification and a new development of the sense of reality and new affects emerge into a new self-state.

In this process, there were some very difficult hours. My interpretive focus at that time was to deal with separation anxiety. I had let her graduate; go out into the world, unprotected, like the way her mother had behaved. Her mother did not protect her from a school situation where faculty acted out sexually with other students, even though she told her about this problem that indeed, was a very frightening experience for her. Unconsciously, she experienced shame and humiliation as she too desired to be wanted sexually by the teachers. Furthermore, she could not trust that I, like her mother, had her best interests at heart. She recalled how her mother once told her that "it was too bad that her father preferred her sister to her." To the contrary, Sara was sure that the father preferred her. From the history and current behavior of the father, she appeared to be correct. Thus, how could she trust her mother who set up this competitive relationship? Much of this had been dealt with in the first part of the analysis, but now it became an important affective state in the transference. My interpretations were met with denials or confusion, or angry retorts that she did not understand me. I was accused of "not asking how she felt or what she thought." At this juncture of the treatment an important balance was necessary, i.e., affectively dealing with the disappointment and loss of a depressive mother, and helping her to maintain a realistic relationship with her mother in the present, while tolerating her rivalry and aggression towards the mother, the mother's rivalry with her, and the process of separation and individuation (Mahler, 1974).

If my words did not match exactly what she felt or reflect her image as a mirror, I again exposed her to separation from the object. Since words reflect sameness or difference, a word that did not resonate aroused too much difference, and thus, anxiety. Sara handled anxiety by a defensive use of anger. With anger she had control, and with anger she also had connection with me. (Jacobson, 1964) This need to be mirrored so insistently indicated an early deficit in the parenting. In the family constellation, a narcissistic father and a depressive, self-absorbed mother, Sara had to reflect their glory, especially the father. There was little room for the needs of the child. It is this demand to be mirrored that she makes on her adult relationships and ultimately, leads to failure with friends and lovers. Further, her need that I say the precise word or pose my interpretations as to reflect her feelings precisely, is also due to her attempts to ward off superego criticism. She is constantly on edge lest she be at fault or did not do the right thing. Any imperfection or sense that some episode would expose her to criticism would arouse an internal attack that immediately became externalized. Thus, words became the persecutor and the separator, both intolerable states for her. And yet, it is words that she uses to write plays, and to act.

Kris (1956) has referred to certain patients who, at a very young age, become very self-sufficient emotionally. They turn into themselves and construct a world in isolation while still retaining relationships with the outside world. They do not become withdrawn or schizophrenic, but remain somewhat insular. This is essentially the position of Sara. She built an internal world removed from the turmoil of the family—the father's sexual affairs, the mother's depression, and the rivalry with her sister and mother. In this world, she creatively constructed an image of herself based on fantasies that, with time, became firmly fixed as a "Personal Myth."

Sara felt morally and creatively superior; her work was inviolable. The difficulty in working through the oedipus complex underpinned her guilt and defensive structure. The fantasy of the oedipal victor evolved into a narcissistic personal myth that she was the Uber-Woman, powerful and superior to all women.

The behavior of her father, from a very early age, encouraged her oedipal rivalries and spurred the defensive oedipal myth of the Uber-Woman. The mutual enactments between father and daughter, trips to expensive resorts, hiking in the Alps, and traveling through Europe, reinforced her fixation on the infantile oedipus complex. His promises to give her money, support her career, and his demand for constant contact portended oedipal gratification. Yet, this closeness, and this fantasy with her father were always in danger of disappointment. As a defense against his own incestuous wishes, he would become involved repeatedly with younger women about the patient's age, looks, and body-type, at which time, he would withdraw emotional and financial support.

The ambivalent love relationship with her father was displaced onto her relationships with men. She was sexually frightened of men, frigid, and feared penetration. To my interpretations or more often attempts at clarification, she responded with a defensive reaction formation; "she was not fearful of men, she could have intercourse, could be penetrated and have orgasms." I believe that her so-called sexual freedom was a reaction to the transference; she had to retain her power over the mother, the other women, and especially me. Though, she unconsciously feared rejection by the man, she was argumentative, behaved aggressively, and was demanding of constant attention. In each relationship with a male, her myth of superiority over her mother, and over the succession of the father's girlfriends was in constant danger of destruction. What then happened to the myth? It became repressed, less accessible to the analysis, and the transference rage was accentuated. My interpretations, my words became an insult, a humiliation. Not only did my words accentuate separation issues, and failure to mirror her, but they had become a source of pain and insult. I then became the other woman, the more powerful woman, and her competitor who shattered her "myth," and took away her father.

In the transference she continued to enact her oedipal conflicts, vying with me, and her anger at me due to her dependency. She expressed fear that she would become "too dependent on me." My attempt to analyze this was again met with huge resistance. Her fear of dependency was due in large part to the danger of losing her unconscious "personal myth" of the Uber-Woman. This myth of the Uber-Woman had additional elements of early ego and superego development wherein a structural separation had not yet sufficiently occurred, and thus gave expression to a very high self-idealization, the grandiosity of early childhood fantasies (Segal, 2015). Further, her myth of the Uber-Woman had all the elements of a phallic woman, a fantasy derived from the idealization and identification with a powerful father.

Sara's myth is remindful of our literary history, derived from the wealthy source of Greek mythology. Can we not envision elements of the tales of Zeus, and his daughters, Aphrodite and Persephone? Thus, does not Sara experience herself as the goddess born of her idealized, powerful father?

In the treatment, I never directly referred to her actions or beliefs as a myth. I rather quietly recognized them, and analyzed her fears, oedipal conflicts, wishes, rivalries, jealousies, and frequently made note of her creative abilities. The transference was essentially positive despite her rivalry and criticisms of me, and so, I became both an object of incorporation and a separate object.

As I previously suggested, the transference took the form of what Shane, Shane, and Gales (1997) had theoretically postulated as a three-step sequence, differing somewhat from Freud's concepts of the transference neurosis, though still incorporating many of his ideas. Initially we encounter the "old-old," relationships to the parents—the transference neurosis. The second stage reflected changes in the self-organization, self-maturation, object attachment, object separation, and repetition of the old object patterns. We went through the stages as "Old-Old" to "Old-New," to "New-New," with fluctuations back to "Old-New." Thus, we repeated the old relationships and defenses with the parents, from a reenactment in the transference to a modification of self-image and object separation and development. The new self-image reflected a more independent self and object. The Myth was encapsulated in a new self-representation that was both creative and reality oriented. Though there still existed some qualities of primary narcissism, self-object cohesion became less incorporative and more assimilative and characterized by objectification and reality. Sara has successfully written and directed plays for regional theatre groups. She has married a loving and supportive man who is successful in his field. Her relationships with her family are both caring and separate.

CONCLUSION

To focus the role of the "Personal Myth" as a theoretical concept, and to distinguish myth from fantasy, has been a primary objective in this paper. That the "Personal Myth" in psychoanalytic theory as a construct has tended to be subsumed under the aegis of fantasy, has led to a failure to recognize myth as a significant factor in the individual's psychic structure. Fantasy has been considered the main and dominant process in the expression of warded-off id and ego wishes fueled by the pleasure-unpleasure principle. Yet, the subtle role of the "Personal Myth" in most cases can present as a basic, solidified component, and reflect unconscious conflicts that are a more difficult challenge in the treatment. The defensive structure of the myth is adhesive and encapsulating, and more resistant to interpretation and modification. Freud (1923) indicated that fantasy ideation is more readily accessible to consciousness, thus more accessible to analysis. The "Personal Myth," established as a fact, as a reality, primarily in the present, but possibly as a reality of the past (Kris, 1956), is more resistant to change or modification. To challenge the myth is to destroy a piece of ego structure. As one patient lamented, "What am I to do without my belief?"

Therefore, to focus on the "Personal Myth" is to present a nuanced template in psychoanalytic theory and treatment.

REFERENCES

Arlow, J (1969a). Fantasy, Memory, and Reality Testing. *Psychoanalytic Quarterly* 38:28–57.

_____ (1969b). Unconscious Fantasy and Disturbance of Conscious Experience. *Psychoanalytic Quarterly 38*:1–27.

Balint, M. (1959). *Thrills and Regression.* London: Hogarth Press.

Baudry, F. (1988). From Prophet to Poet: Jacob A. Arlow's Contributions to Applied Psychoanalysis. In *Fantasy, Myth, and Reality. Essays in Honor of Jacob Arlow,* Ed. H.P. Blum, M.D., Yale Kramer, M.D., A.K. Richards, Ed.D. & A.D. Richards, M.D. Madison, CT: IUP, 1988.

Beres. D. (1962). The Unconscious Fantasy. *Psychoanalytic Quarterly* 31:1–27.

Campbell, J. (1959). *The Masks of God: Primitive Mythology.* New York: Viking Press.

Erreich, A. (2003). A Modest Proposal: (Re)Defining Unconscious Fantasy. *Psychoanalytic Quarterly* 72(3):541–741.

_____ (2015). Unconscious Fantasy as a Special Class of Mental Representation: A Contribution to a Model of Mind. *JAPA* 3(2):247–278.

Frazer, J.G. (1922). *The Golden Bough.* London: Macmillan, (see Segal, R. (2015) *Myth: A Very Short Introduction.* Oxford University Press.

Freud, S. (1894). The Neuro-Psychosis of Defense. *Standard Edition* 3.

_____ (1908 [1907]) Creative Writers and Daydreaming. *Standard Edition* 9.

_____ (1908a). Hysterical Phantasies and their Relation to Bisexuality. *Standard Edition* 9.

_____ (1909 [1908b]). Family Romances *Standard Edition* 9.

_____ (1911). Formulation on the Two Principles of Mental Functioning. *Standard Edition* 12.

_____(1913 [1912–1913]). Totem And Taboo. *Standard Edition* 13.

_____ (1919). A Child is Beaten: A Contribution to the Study of the Origin of Sexual Perversions. *Standard Edition* 17.

_____ (1923). The Ego and The Id. *Standard Edition* 19.

_____ (1926 [1925]). Inhibitions, Symptoms and Anxiety. *Standard Edition* 20.

Gales, M.E. (1978). Mother-infant bonding. Grand Rounds presentation, University of California, Los Angeles. In Shane, Shane & Gales,1997.

Goylan, (2022). Ruthlessness and Transitioning of the Analyst's Mind. *International Journal of Psychoanalysis* 70:1–34.

Gibeault, A. (2005). Mr. A's Creative Adventure: Reflection on Drives and Psychic Conflict. *Psychoanl. Quarterly* 74:157–186.

Grossman, W. (1982). The Self as Fantasy as Theory. *JAPA* 30:919–937.

Hurvich, M. (2003). The Place of Annihilation Anxiety in Psychoanalytic. *JAPA* 46: 579–616.

Isaacs, S. (1948,1949). The Nature and Function of Phantasy. *Int. J. Psycho-Anal.* 29:73–97.

Jacobson, E. (1964). *The Self and the Object World*. Connecticut: International Universities Press.

Klein, M. (1946) Notes on Some Schizoid Mechanisms. In *Melanie Klein Envy and Gratitude and Other Works 1946–1963*. New York: The Free Press,1975.

_____ (1952). The Mutual Influences in the Development of Ego and Id. In *Melanie Klein Envy and Gratitude and Other Works 1946–1963*. New York: The Free Press,1975.

Kluckhohn, C. (1942). *Myth and Rituals: A General Theory*. Harvard Theological Review (see Segal, 2015).

Kris. E. (1951). On Preconscious Mental Processes. In *Organization and Pathology of Thought,* Ed. D. Rapaport. New York: Columbia Universities Press. pp.471–496.

_____ (1956). The Personal Myth: A Problem in Psychoanalytic Technique. In *Selected Papers of Ernst Kris.* New Haven, London: Yale Universities Press, 1975.

Laforgue, R. (1930). On the Eroticization of Anxiety. *International Journal of Psychoanalysis* 11:312–321.

Raglan, F.R.S. (1936). The Hero: A Study in Tradition, Myth, and Drama, Part II. In Otto Rank, et.al., *In Quest of the Hero.* Princeton: Princeton University Press, 1990.

Reik, T. (1957). *Myth & Guilt.* New York: Grosset & Dunlap.

Richards, A.K., (1988). An Object Choice and Its Determinants in Fantasy. In *Fantasy, Myth and Reality: Essays in honor of Jacob A. Arlow, M.D.* Madison, CT: IUP, 1988.

Segal, R, (1999). *Theorizing About Myth.* Amherst: University of Massachusetts Press.

_____ (2015). *Myth: A Very Short Introduction.* Great Britain: Oxford University Press.

Shane, M., Shane, E., & Gales, M. (1997). *Intimate Attachments: Toward a New Self Psychology.* New York / London: The Guilford Press.

Sharpe, E. (1940). Psycho-Physical Problems revealed in Language: An Examination of Metaphor. In *Collected Papers on Psychoanalysis* by E.F. Sharpe. New York: Brunner/Mazel, 1978.

Levi-Strauss, C. (1974). *The Structural Study of Myth; Structure and Dialectics in Structural Anthropology.* New York: Basic Books. Thompson, (1990). In Raglan,1990).

Winnicott, D. (1974 [1971]). Dreaming, Fantasying, and Living. In *Playing and Reality,* D.W. Winnicott. New Zealand: Penguin Books.

CHAPTER 14

FREQUENCY OF SESSIONS: THE PSYCHOANALYTIC CRUCIBLE

To discuss the issue of frequency of weekly sessions at this point in the history of psychoanalysis seems an onerous undertaking despite the fact that this subject should be rather straightforward. In the early years of psychoanalysis, frequency was axiomatic—simply taken for granted, either as a matter of custom, or based upon a theoretical premise that was automatically accepted. The early literature is marked by its absence of much discussion or dispute regarding the issue of frequency. The question arises as to what has occurred since the late 1960s, which makes this problematic in regard to psychoanalytic treatment, and, more importantly, disturbs our understanding of the parameters involved in the analytic process?

The decline of public interest in psychoanalysis (Galatzer-Levy, et. al, 2000) has affected the number of people who come for analysis and, perhaps, played a role in reducing the number of sessions per-week. Has this shift also affected the psychoanalyst's own thinking regarding the efficacy of frequent sessions, and has this, simultaneously, resulted in changed theoretical constructs (Ehrlich, 2010)? To examine the theoretical bases for establishing a certain number—i.e., five, four, or three sessions (that is still open for debate)—as to which is the best conduit for the voyage into unconscious conflicts and ego disruptions, is the major aim of this paper. The hypothesis will be made that without frequent sessions, we lose the basis for establishing those "...coordinates whereby it is possible to gain access to unconscious material more consistently, and in greater depth" (Schwartz, 2003 p.182).

The issue will be discussed from two perspectives: one, societal, and the second, from the perspective of psychoanalytic theory. When Freud stated that the aim of psychoanalytic treatment was the resolution of transference and resistance, and that

> ...any line of investigation which recognizes... [transference and resistance] and takes these as the starting point of its work has a right to call itself psychoanalysis [1914, p.15].

one may surmise that he was outlining a process that required a time-frame. A time-frame is not a technique any more than attending four years of college, or needing a certain amount of class hours in order to adequately learn. Rather, it is the parameter by which learning can occur; it is methodological error to equate frequency with technique, for frequency is the realm wherein technique can be utilized.

A further presumption will be made, that one of the difficulties in discussing frequency of sessions is due to the role of external influences, that is, the political and economic forces that arise from our cultural ethos. Some of theses forces are only subliminally experienced, and therefore, give rise to an undercurrent of discomfort within the psychoanalytic community. The advent of insurance coverage for mental health has also changed the discourse between the patient and analyst, to a discourse among patient, analyst, and insurance company. Psychoanalysis has increasingly come under the purview of a third party whose concerns are more monetary than treatment-bound. A shift occurred from that of the analyst's judgment and treatment concerns for the patient to a new set of judges, the insurance companies, who became the supervisors of treatment and method. (Lionells, 1999). Many years ago, at a meeting of The New York Psychoanalytic Society, Kurt Eissler warned of the dangers that insurance companies, as third-party judges, would pose for psychoanalysis, and, unfortunately, his prediction has come about. The issue of the number of treatment sessions per-week tends to be made by these companies rather than by the analyst. Thus, an area for valid research and continued discussion within the discipline has unwittingly been tampered with by an outside source. These third-party persons are ill equipped to understand the process and treatment aims of psychoanalysis, and more to the point, their judgments regarding the quality of disturbance and conflict in the patient are limited. Thus, the arbiter of psychoanalysis as a method of treatment, the aim and the frequency of sessions, is no longer made solely by patient and analyst, but by those outside the analytic parameters. Further, the changes in our mode of living, the distances of travel to work and then to the analyst, the consuming work and social demands, all, conflict with intensive time for psychoanalytic treatment. The promise of quick cures, from medication to short-term treatment methods, certainly has its claims, in contrast to the longer and more intensive psychoanalytic process.

I do not want to underestimate the theoretical issues that were developing within the psychoanalytic community, and that also led to the question of frequency of sessions per-week. Major theoretical differences regarding theory, treatment methods, and aims resulted in a plethora of new ideas and training institutes. The differences, such as environmental factors versus instinct theory, the prominence of self theories, the role of the transference interaction, countertransference, intersubsectivity, etc., appears to have accelerated the psychoanalytic discourse, and to have created a more equivocal attitude in the public, the scientific community, and even among analyst's themselves regarding the fundamental constructs of psychoanalysis. These theoretical differences would lead to different conclusions, particularly regarding the role of the analyst, the mode of interpretation, the analytic dyad, the place of personal history, and, I believe most significantly, the number of sessions per-week.

On the surface the various Training Institutes seem to have made satisfactory decisions as to the most efficacious number of sessions that constitute effective treatment, in spite of the fact that there is a good deal of theoretical disagreement as to what number really constitutes an effective psychoanalysis. Research has not been able to give a definitive or quantifiable answer to the necessary number, except to emphasize that more is better than less. Unfortunately, theories and research studies regarding the number of sessions per week for an analysis appear to many to lack the weight of truth. Glatzer-Levy, et, al. (2000) indicated that without adequate research, there is not a good answer that can provide a surety of method or that can establish a universal standard. They further, stated:

> We rely on subjective experiences, clinical evaluations that are not easily replicable, and are subject to numerous divergent theories and hypotheses as to goals and methodology, each claiming to meet the demands of objective validity.

Thus, they maintain,

> ...without basic statistical analysis that provides verifiable evidence, it is not possible to postulate a methodology that defines the parameters of treatment, provides proven explanatory evidence for the tenets of psychoanalytic theory, and criteria of outcome [p. 11].

Yet, Frosh (2011), has indicated that a number of studies would confirm the reliability of frequent sessions as deepening and achieving better results in the analysis. Still, it is difficult for many to resolve the question of frequency of sessions, and, further, many ask: Does frequency of sessions provide the *sine qua non* without which psychoanalysis cannot occur? A 1996 Panel at the American Psychoanalytic Association meetings raised the question as to what, if any, are the significant qualitative differences among the differing frequencies of one-, two-, three-, four-, five-, and six-times-a-week psychoanalysis and, if so, with what kinds of patients? And what, they asked, is the optimum requirement of the time-intervals for the psychoanalytic process to prove itself as the effective method of analytic treatment?[1] Underlying and perhaps fundamental, to this question is the relation between frequency of weekly sessions, and the differentiation between psychoanalysis and psychotherapy—a topic beyond the scope of this paper.

We can posit, though, that a certain number of sessions are invariable to the psychoanalytic process. Can we, however, establish with certainty, that there is an intimate co-dependence between frequency and the development of transference? Does the working through of resistance, the unfolding of psychic structures, and defense, the repetition compulsion, and regression (Schwartz, 2003) also necessitate a certain level of frequency without which an in-depth understanding and modification cannot be achieved? If frequency is a cognate with psychoanalytic treatment, the question that plagues us is: How can we measure the correct amount, and its effectiveness? And Why, in our research, have we not established this factor with sufficient evidence (Galatzer-Levy, et. all,2000)?

Since psychoanalytic theory has been influenced by a plethora of varying constructs, classical Freudian, object relations, early- and post-Kleinian, environmental, intrapsychic, interpersonal, relational, intersubjective, and social constructivism, How are we to measure the validity of the various treatment modalities, their success, or failures (Twemlow, 2002), as well as the numerous variables that constitute psychoanalytic practice? Psychoanalytic practice, like all disciplines that involve treatment modalities, must rely on

---

1 Refer to The Psychoanalytic Review: 90, No.2, April 2003 that published a survey and papers on the question of frequency of sessions. Also, refer to the panel of the meetings of the American Psychoanalytic Assn. 1996 and published in JAPA , 1997.

elastic theories. Since practice is constantly influenced by pragmatic issues that refer to both theoretical constructs and practical factors, it is incumbent upon the practitioner to modulate theory to practice and practice to theory. Alexander (1950) indicated that

> Between theory and therapy there is a reciprocal relationship: observations made during treatment are the main source of our theoretical knowledge, and we apply our theoretical formulations to improve our technique [p.1065].

This is not to imply a *laissez faire* attitude in the treatment process; rather, we consider that there is an inherent correlation between theory and practice (Schafer,1983). The variability of character structure, modes of defense, intactness or weakness of ego structure, and the force of the drives are so multi-varied in individual patients that even those within the same diagnostic category require flexibility of method within the treatment parameters. It is this variation that has often led many to consider psychoanalysis as an art rather than a science, i.e., an ability to creatively utilize basic analytic theory along with flexible methodology. Certainly, the nuances of treatment and the variables among patients also contribute to the difficulty in research. Yet, if we regard art from the perspective of creativity, skill in procedures, inventiveness in technique, and imaginative understanding, then from this perspective, science also falls under the aegis of art. Schapin (June 2010, reviewed in *The New York Review of Books* by Jenny Uglow) indicated

> Science itself is not above the prejudices of its time, is not transcendent, is discovered, not made placeless, timeless, objective, [or] unsullied by the conditions or the personalities and prejudices of its makers.

Solano (2010) indicated that the

> emotional impact of discoveries made in the positivist era was such as to give medicine a very high level of social credit, while the underlying paradigm lost its historical connotation and became permanent, absolute, the only true science.... Western medicine appears oblivious to Heisenberg's uncertainty principle—which long ago recognized that data obtained always depend on the method of observation—and seems to believe itself in possession of definite, objective truth [p.1447].

This appeal for a more open mind, by implication, would apply to all schools of psychoanalytic theory, for it is a call to both practitioners and theorists to pursue their quest for truth without absolutism.

Was frequency of sessions defined by a too-close reading of classical psychoanalytic theory and practice, binding them in a binary complex, and frequency becoming the *sine qua non* of classical psychoanalysis? Did frequency define the parameters of what constituted proper psychoanalytic practice? One of the difficulties in psychoanalytic practice has been a rarified relationship between method and theory. Clearly, theory does proscribe methods or at best defines the parameters of method. Greenberg (1999 [1996]), a relational theoretician, indicated, "few issues in psychoanalysis are quite so muddled, or generate quite so much confusion in the mind of the clinician, as to the relationship between theory and technique" (p.133). In an earlier critique of classical psychoanalytic practice, he indicated that the "classical clinical approach was excessively theory driven, and thus, precluded a freer, less technique-laden practice."

Despite the above-mentioned caveats, I hope to make a case for the validity of frequent sessions. While studies on the role of frequency are generally inconclusive, a study by Freedman, et al, (1999) found that there was an incremental gain from the treatment as it increased from one to two to three times a week. Frequency was related to specific symptomatic relief, and to satisfaction with the treatment received. The authors also found that studies in Scandinavia and England indicated that increased session frequency "exerts a persistent and even long term impact on patients' "mental health" (p.769). More specifically, the Scandinavian studies (1993) indicated that the benefits from psychoanalysis had a more lasting effect than those achieved from psychotherapy (quoted from Schwartz, 2003). A study by Gedo and Cohler (1992) also indicated that increased frequency led to an increase in the quality of clinical material, and an improvement in the capacity of the patient to use the insights gained.

Historically, frequency of sessions-per-week seemed to have automatically underscored the assumption as to what constituted psychoanalysis. Clearly, numbers do not automatically ensure a psychoanalytic process; rather they provide a basic frame for the effective utilization of the psychoanalytic method. The number of sessions per-week have unobtrusively declined from six times a week, in the early days of psychoanalysis to five, four then three and, quite recently, the number one seems to have achieved some legitimacy. Gill (1979), who in his early years, represented a very classical drive/ structural orientation, shifted from his early position and became convinced that frequency is an irrelevant and a "non-essential tool" for the analytic process. Does this change in the role of frequency represent a change in our theoretical understanding of the psychoanalytic process? Have we added a different dimension to our understanding of the goals of psychoanalysis and, more significantly, to our concepts of working through the transference and the resistance that evaded Freud? Or, as has been indicated: Have some recent, external forces impinged upon psychoanalytic theory? Has a new dialectic arisen in the culture that has so imperceptibly influenced our thinking? Or have we convinced ourselves that new theoretical constructs, and not extraneous forces, are responsible for changes in our attitude toward frequency of sessions?

CURRENT THEORETICAL INFLUENCES

The theoretical constructs of the Relational and the Intersubjective schools may also have subtly influenced the issue of frequency. Unfortunately, there is almost no literature coming from these theoreticians and institutes as to frequency of weekly sessions. Thus, conjecture is our only means of approach. The increased focus on countertransference and the analytic dyad (Greenberg & Mitchel,1983) a focus, that views drives, conflict, and defense as secondary, and at times of minor import within the context of the transference-countertransference configuration, may from a theoretical perspective changed the importance of session frequency. Since the transference-countertransference dialectic is more dependent on the dynamics of the therapeutic relationship, it is possible to assert that an intensity of relationship is less dependent on time factors—i.e., quantity— and more dependent on quality. Renik (1997), in describing the work from these perspectives, indicated that the requirement by both analyst and patient consists of "co-creating the past truths, and co-creating the present truths." The focus in this conceptualization of the transference is on the "here and now," and assumes the dimensions of the "real relationship." Benjamin (1998) asserted that the "reciprocity constituted in relation to the other, depending on the others recognition, [and] ... acted on by the other in a way that changes the self" (p.79) presents us with a transference conception that focuses on the "real relationship," rather than an "as if" transference relationship (Greenson,1967).

From this theoretical perspective, it is possible to assume that intensity of the therapeutic relationship is not co-dependent on time factors and, in fact, time is not imperative. Quality, not quantity, is the framework to determine frequency, and that can be a variable factor more dependent on the patient and analyst's evaluation.

Yet, as we examine the role of countertransference as a vehicle for knowing the patient, and the mode by which the analyst interacts with the patient, the subtlety of response and interpretation, and the empathic reactions (Hirsch,2001), all of this would seem to indicate that a rather frequent time frame is necessary for both participants to develop the capacity for deeper understanding. Hirsch indicated that here, we are not referring to a general understanding, but a "moment-to-moment" emotional and cognitive reaction to latent meanings. Further, the process of free association, the quest for unconscious conflicts, and the fears and anxieties that hide behind the patient's defenses, and the obfuscation in the analyst's unconscious, all would indicate that an intensity of quantitative time was required to achieve these goals. Can we make the assumption that frequency of sessions is an enabler to the process of knowing on the various psychic levels, i.e., conscious, preconscious, and unconscious? Hirsch has also alluded to the goal of establishing the reality principle, a process, that he indicated depends on the quality of transference to the analyst. Does "time" play some role in this development?

Bleichmar (2004), in examining the factors involved in psychic change, postulated a motivational system that appears either superordinate or contingent to the tripartite structure of id, ego, and superego. His motivational systems comprise "hetero/self-preservation, sensual/sexual, attachment, narcissistic, psychobiological regulation, etc." Thus, any interpretation, transference enactments, even co-constructions must address the system or systems that are dominant factors at a particular time in the treatment. Making a motivation conscious is only a first step, albeit an important component in modifying the unconscious motivational systems. Further, Bleichmar indicated that the movement from declarative memory to procedural memory, as a basic component in the analytic work, requires an extensive working through on both the levels of conscious and unconscious memory. It is these changes within the various motivational systems that will culminate in fundamental psychic change. It is unfortunate that in presenting a clinical vignette of an analytic patient seen three times a week, he does not discuss any theoretical basis for frequency of sessions.

In "Working Through and Its Various Models," Roussillon (2010) indicated that working through is an integral part of the psychoanalytic process, even the "epitome" of the process. He presented three forms or models of working through: the first involves insight into a repressed representational complex; the second stresses the work that has to occur in bringing into consciousness drive-related impulses or mental experiences that until now have not been represented; and the third, when the integration of representation and symbolization of the subjective experience and drive-related issues are metabolized.

This work occurs "piece by piece" working its way back through the preconscious structures to the issues behind the earlier repressions, to the earliest 'primal' repressions. Further, in the work of co-construction necessitated by the working through, the "analyst cannot avoid revealing something of how they themselves function and of their own ideals." Roussillon pointed to a coupling relationship between patient and analyst and then the necessary and sometimes difficult task of "uncoupling." Again, I want to stress that the working through, as outlined by Roussillon as a central and crucial technique, requires enough intensity of emotional and cognitive involvement by analysand and analyst that the question is raised: Can this be achieved on a once or twice a week basis? Otherwise, as Roussillon has indicated, we have all the elements of a suggestive therapy rather than psychoanalysis.

FREUD'S WRITINGS

In this section, the focus will be upon the classical theories, that is, the constructs of Freud, as a basis to indicate the relationship of frequency of sessions to psychoanalytic theory. From a historical perspective this approach provides a progression of theory and practice that may help us to better define what belongs to theory and what may simply belong to custom. Further, an examination of these constructs, and their relation to the number of psychoanalytic sessions per-week, is pertinent in order to judge whether frequency has a significant relationship to achieving the goals of psychoanalysis or, at best, providing the best possible conditions for psychic change from a theoretical and clinical perspective.

It is difficult to ascertain the theoretical basis or the *raison d'être* upon which Freud determined session-schedules of six times per week. In his 1913 paper on "Beginning the Treatment," he simply stated that:

> I work with patients every day except on Sundays and public holidays—that is, as a rule, six days a week. For slight cases or the continuation of a treatment which is already well advanced, three days a week will be enough. Any restrictions of time beyond this bring no advantage either to the doctor or the patient; and at the beginning of an analysis they are quite out of the question. Even short interruptions have a slightly obscuring effect on the work. When the hours of work are less frequent, there is a risk of not being able to keep pace with the patient's real life and of the treatment losing contact with the present and being forced into by-paths [p. 127].

Since the above paper followed the 1912 paper on transference, it is useful to read these remarks within the context of his treatment goals of resolving the transference and overcoming resistance. Thus time, that is, intense time, meant for Freud the means by which an in-depth transference relationship could be established, in which significant remembered events would emerge. Further, the intensity of time encouraged the "transference neurosis," a fresh re-enactment of the earlier neurosis (1925). He also, indicated that the patient is "obliged to repeat the repressed material as a contemporary experience instead of, as the physician would prefer to see, remembering it as something belonging to the past" (p.18). This compulsion to repeat provides an understanding for both patient and analyst as to the source and mode of the representational complex of unconscious conflicts. There is a *quid pro quo* relationship to the intensity of the transference in which "time" is an important factor. Time is my metaphor for the special context in which an intensity of affect, and emotional tie to an object is aroused, established, and maintained. This is certainly an arguable assumption, in that emotional ties can occur very quickly, retreat just as rapidly, and not occur despite frequent association.

FREUD'S POSTULATES ON PSYCHOANALYTIC GOALS

Freud gave a number of explanations, in regard to the goals or aims of psychoanalysis, some cryptic, such as, to resolve the transference and overcome the resistance (1912–1914), and after the introduction of the structural theory where "Id was there Ego shall be" (1933). In the *Introductory Lectures* (1916–1917), and the *New Introductory lectures* (1933), he gave a much more detailed account, yet, a precise, that is, *ipso facto* relationship between goals and the number of sessions-per-week can only be ascertained and understood from the meanings of such fundamental therapeutic concepts as working through the resistance, achieving alteration of the ego by modifying defenses, lifting repression, and resolving the "transference neurosis." It is important to note that when Freud modified his view of the psychic structure from the dichotomy between the conscious and unconscious to a tripartite structure, i.e., id, ego, and superego, the goal did not essentially change.

TRANSFERENCE AND RESISTANCE

Freud (1912) stated that

> each individual, through the combined operation of his innate disposition and the influences brought to bear on him during his early years, has acquired a specific method of his own in his conduct of his erotic life- that is, in the preconditions to falling in love which he lays down, in the instincts he satisfies and the aims he sets himself in the course of it [p. 99].

This produces a stereotype plate that is constantly repeated in the person's life, and it is this plate, this prototype, that will emerge in the course of psychoanalytic treatment. Freud referred to this plate as the transference, and it is in the transference that the battleground for either health or illness occurs. The task of the analyst is to find the "hiding places," the regressions and fixations, and to bring to consciousness the "subject's infantile imagoes" that have been displaced onto the analyst. In our attempts to undo the unconscious repression of the instincts, we encounter our most noteworthy opponent—the resistance. Resistance, Freud (1917 [1916]) indicated, "puts up a struggle in the interest of his illness against the person who is helping him" (p. 288). Further, he indicated that

> resistances determine the sequence of the material which is to be repeated, [and in the process the] patient brings out of the armory

of the past the weapons with which he defends himself against the progress of the treatment—weapons which we must rest from him one by one [1913, p.151].

Further, Freud (1917) felt that the overcoming of the resistance "is the essential function of the analysis and is the only part of our work which gives us the assurance that we have achieved something with the patient" (p. 291). He also stated that the patient develops a "resistance against uncovering of resistance" (1937). A negative transference may arise due to the influence of unpleasurable impulses that the patient experiences as a result of the "fresh activations of his defensive conflicts.... They are resistances not only to the making conscious of contents of the id, but also to the analysis as a whole, and thus to recovery" (p. 239).

Can this process of reclamation of memories, filling gaps in memory (Freud, 1916), and changing affective memory states (Rapaport, 1942), modification of defenses, and undoing of the transference and the resistance really occur in one- or two-times-a-week sessions? Or have we seen emerging different affective experiences, and therapeutic goals in once- or twice-a week-treatment from that which we aimed for in "old fashioned" Freudian psychoanalytic treatment?

THE EGO AND THE ID

In elaborating on another of Freud's definitive but terse statements, that the goal of psychoanalysis is to establish ego where id reigned (1933,1937), we also, find ourselves facing another difficult task in working once or twice a week. What we are asking of the patient is to modify and control the force of the drives, the wishful impulses—in essence to relinquish the pleasure principle for the reality principle. This has enormous implications for changes in psychic structure, and for strengthening of the ego (Lansky, 2007). The balance between gratification and frustration was a significant factor in Freud's methodology (1913), and he indicated that it was important to consider these valences in the treatment process.

Furthermore, one may validly inquire whether frequent sessions, inadvertently, provide a source of gratification in the object relationship with the analyst. Does it encourage the hope for love, succor, and relief from inner frustration by the intensity of the time spent together?

We can assume that, initially, most transference expectations, in all modes of treatment, evoke images by the patient of protection and some form of love. Thus, was the selection of six-times-a-week analysis a covert message to the patient that, in this analytic environment, some expectation of gratification would be granted. After all, closeness in time may metaphorically invoke early body memories of closeness or desires of such to the mother. Can we assume, without full clarification from Freud, that he acted on the theory that the individual patient could better release the cauldron of id forces, the ego's unconscious defenses, and the superego's strictures in an analytic setting that Winnicott (1960) would refer to as the "holding environment," an environment that established a closeness—yet, without physical contact in a closed space?

The tasks of resolving the transference with simultaneous modification of the ego's pathogenic defenses, strengthening the ego against the id, and of establishing the primacy of the reality principle may provoke the opposite of a positive transference: that of a strong negative feeling. As the transference increases in intensity, we encounter the full force of the aggressive and sexual drives in a more direct fashion. It is not only the ego's relationship to the drives that require containment, moderation, and management, but also, the transference and countertransference relationship is sorely tested and must be managed. A negative transference may arise due to the influence of unpleasurable impulses that the patient experiences as a result of the "fresh activation" of the defensive conflicts. There are resistances not only to making conscious the conflicts of the id, but also to the "analysis as a whole, and thus to recovery" (p. 239).

> Freud (1933 [1932]) further, indicated "wishful impulses which have never passed beyond the id, but impressions, too, which have been sunk into the id by repression, are virtually immortal; . . . . They . . . can only lose their importance and be deprived of their cathexis of energy, when they have been made conscious by the work of analysis, and it is on this that the therapeutic effect of analytic treatment rests to no small extent" [p. 74].

He had also, made this same point in the first of the *Introductory Lectures* (1917) where he said that the "sole task of therapy" is to bring both combatants to meet on the same ground, i.e., to bring the unconscious to consciousness. This work of making that which is unconscious conscious has its antecedents in Freud's first therapeutic methods, that of finding the underlying meaning of the patient's symptoms and then relating to the patient the latent meaning of his symptoms and conflicts, i.e., making the unconscious conscious. This was soon modified by his recognition that merely making conscious the latent material by the analyst had little effect. He realized that there were levels of knowing; one can know and not know due to the mechanisms of defense, e.g., splitting, isolation and denial. Therefore, the analytic method of making conscious what was unconscious required a different procedure, that of working through the transference and the resistance. The interpretations required both intellectual and affective experiences that revived childhood memories, impressions and the "early efflorescence" of the drives. It is the analytic task to not only undo repressions but to modify and understand "affective memory states," states that have, according to Rapaport (1942), frequently been altered by distortions and drive wishes.

If we accept these goals as intrinsic to the analytic process, to healing, and if not total cure, then at least to significant changes in personality structure, then the question of frequency of sessions becomes a major issue for analytic practice. Is it reasonable to conceive that the resolution of transference and resistance, even, modified resolution of the transference, essentially, the "transference neurosis," can be accomplished in once- or twice-a-week therapy?

In listing such a formidable array of tasks for psychoanalytic treatment, one could conceive that not only intensity of weekly sessions was required, but also years of treatment. Yet, in Freud's era, the length of treatment was approximately one year or less, and two to three years for a more troubled patient. In a study by Silver (2003), it was found that four to five years of psychoanalytic treatment was the average, currently, for the analytic patient population at large, and ten to twelve years for psychoanalysts. Sessions ranged from three to four times a week; though, three was the average number. While this is a topic for another paper, it is important to draw attention to these significant differences i.e., to shorter length of treatment in the early years of psychoanalysis, with greater weekly frequency, to less weekly frequency, but greater length in the present. It is also significant to note that the length of sessions has decreased from sixty minutes–to fifty minutes, and now we have the forty-five-minute hour. Does this effect psychoanalytic treatment in any significant manner?

OTHER THEORISTS AND THEORIES

In examining Klein's (1921–1945) theoretical position and psychoanalytic goals, we observe a theoretical parallelism between drive and object at a very early stage, a goal to undo the destructive drive in the interaction with the object. For Klein, the fundamental task of the analysis was to shift the paranoid position to a depressive position, and achieve a more reparative relationship with the object, to create a mutative shift in the internalized object. Though Klein did not address frequency of sessions, it was clear from her clinical practice that four or five times a week was a prerequisite. Glover (1955) indicated that the course of psychoanalytic sessions, of six times a week, as practiced on the continent, 'was modified by the English habit of rest on weekends, though, sometimes for select patients a sixth session was provided on Saturday mornings'. He does not provide any rationale or theory except to outline procedures in his introductory suggestions to the beginning of treatment.

Fenichel (1945, 1953, 1954) whose work has achieved the status of a basic theoretical reference book in the United States, and Greenson (1967), who is also acclaimed as a basic source for psychoanalytic technique, make no significant reference to frequency. One can only speculate as to why an issue as fundamental as time-investment in the analysis, and the probable impact that time, i.e., frequency of sessions has on the transference and countertransference, is not addressed by these eminent psychoanalysts.

The theories of Alexander and French (1946) and Lacan (1977) add another dimension to understanding the use of the time frame and frequency of sessions. These theorists focused on the use of transference to manage the margins of pleasure–unpleasure, the levels of regression and unconscious affect in the transference necessary for both the unfolding of the transference, and an impetus for psychic growth and development. Alexander and French (1946) were concerned that there was a pernicious danger in frequent sessions, and that it could foster a too dependent relationship to the analyst. Thus, frequency became an important tool in weaning the patient from the dependency on both the analyst and the treatment. Alexander (1950) indicated that treatment, rather than resolving transference could become the goal in and of itself. French and Alexander (1946) and Lacan (1977) utilized variances of sessions, intervals between sessions, and length of sessions as an important technique in the psychoanalytic process. We may regard this as a manipulation or as a systematic regulatory mode in the analytic procedure. Though, each had different concepts of working through the resistance, analyzing transference, and the nature of the unconscious processes; they very consciously utilized a time frame in their work.

CLINICAL VIGNETTES:

I will present three cases; two, of which are a four-times-a-week treatment, one of which is a psychoanalytic case, and the other, a psychodynamic psychotherapy case. I hope to show *in vivo* some of the issues raised in this paper. The third case is in twice weekly psychotherapy. In this case, I intend to illustrate how increased sessions could have enhanced the working through of fundamental conflicts that were merely touched upon or dealt with intellectually in the treatment. I am proposing that a change from psychotherapy to psychoanalysis is based not only on frequency of sessions, but also, on the analytic process of working through the character defenses, the resistances and the transference, and ultimately structural change.

CASE 1

The patient is a 52-year-old man who has been in psychoanalytic treatment for the past three years, and was seen four times a week. Mr. M is owner of a small manufacturing firm, divorced, and has three adult children. He is very knowledgeable regarding psychoanalytic theory, and had been in treatment previously with a male therapist for four years, on a twice-a-week basis, along with, once-a-week group therapy. Mr. M. left that treatment in anger; feeling that the therapist did not help him, and had betrayed him in the group by revealing some sexual information. He entered treatment in a rather hostile state at all around him though he was initially conciliatory towards me. But that quickly changed, and he could readily become angry. He railed against his life, his deceased parents, his aloneness, shallowness of people, their narcissism, and their immaturity. Mr. M views himself as smarter, more mature, a more "humane helper." Simultaneously, he feels frightened of interaction with people, particularly with women. Mr. M. complained about his "passivity." He had never made overtures toward women, they reach out to him; they initiate the sex.

His anger is pervasive—at his employees, his friends, and his siblings, and his language is infused with frequent "fucks." I am a good target for his rage, particularly, when I make an interpretation that he experiences as a "humiliation." Thus, when he speaks about his need to control people or situations as a means of self-protection, and I add to this "that this need to control is also, a means by which you reinforces the ideal of being very powerful," he first responds that this is "defensive," and engages in a theoretical discussion.

But, when I point out that he is using an intellectual discussion so as to not let himself feel his wish for power, or to feel his anger at me for making such an interpretation, he bursts out with "You are fuckin' right, you are not gentle, you have no empathy. I am not like you, I am soft and gentle, you cut in, and you fuckin' penetrate me!"

I respond, after a few seconds of silence, that "I guess I am like your mother, chasing you with a hypodermic needle to penetrate you."

"Yes", he states softy, "I wish I could cut off my head."

And I reply, "So, you will castrate yourself." This then is one source of his shame and humiliation: the passive oedipal wishes, submitting to both an incestuous and, also, to a phallic, penetrating mother; in the transference, I am that mother who both seduces and humiliates him. Yet, another source of humiliation is his identification with his mother, his feeling feminine.

In one session, he stated that he recalled that he had been accused by his former wife of "touching himself" in company, and that others had commented on this. He was furious. "How dare they gossip about me, a bunch of stupid people." And when he asked, if I believe that this happened, and I responded in the affirmative.

I stated that perhaps, in a state of anxiety he touches himself to make sure his "penis was still there," he exploded at me.

"You are like everyone else, 'stupid,' an interpretation that goes by the book, you don't understand me, even though I try to help you."

The next day, though, I had decided to deal with the meaning of his compulsive behavior in public, and to point out the self-destructive consequences, and the unconscious motivation that his "need to scratch his scrotum and touch his penis," was to make sure that he is a man, not a woman, i.e., his mother. The patient had already reflected on these issues, and calmly, and in soft tones, he tells me that he remembers that he has touched himself before, at other times when with groups of people. He gets very anxious in a group—he is aware of the behavior only after his hand is on his penis—not when the compulsion hits him. We then could go on to analyze his castration fears, an early operation on his testicle, his feeling of being deformed, and his uneasiness with women. He does not know what to do with women, how to please them. I point out that maybe as a twenty-year-old he didn't know what to do sexually, how to please, but as a fifty-two-year-old of man, he does know what to do.

"Yes, he states, I do know what to do, but maybe, I don't want to; I am too angry at my mother."

Then the defenses emerge again—"How could I be different—be like others—I was always too afraid—to leave the house. I was my father's helper—everyone has a life, has women, has friends, go on vacation, and etc...." And thus, he again leaves the session in anger. However, the next session, the next day, he relates that he feels calmer, he has never fully understood before that he has a "gender identity problem."

What I want to explicate in this session is that his material, his associations, these remembrances and affect were made possible by the intensity of frequent treatment sessions, the day after and the day after—when the pain, the sadness, the anxieties, the humiliation, and the rage could be affectively tapped in the analytic space of interpretation, self-awareness, defense, and transference. I believe that this transference material, his defense against affects and drive, and his defensive intellectualizations and isolation (Eissler,1959) could not have been worked through sufficiently on a once- or twice-a-week basis. Many interpretations regarding his identification with his mother, his taking on the wife's role with his father, his passivity, his rivalry with his siblings, and his enactments with me, were given early in the treatment. These interpretations, contrary to Strachey's (1934) recommendation that we interpret at the "point of affective urgency," were made to set the tone and the parameters of the analysis. I realized that they served primarily as a cognitive recognition of his conflicts and defenses. They represented the initial phase of the treatment, but could in no way change the defensive meaning of his associations or provide real insight at that stage of the treatment.

It is the intensity of the treatment, the developing object relationship, the object distortions via the transference, and the closeness of frequent emotional contact that provides the patient with the ability to "work through," and to tolerate the pain of insight. Modell (1990) indicated that what occurs in the analysis is a retranslation of the patient's memories and experiences. Memories are not isomorphic, they require a new categorization, and within this new/old object relationship, memories are modified, contextualized, shifted from displacements, and infused with affect. This retranslation of memories leads to a cojoining of affect with ideation that is primarily responsible for psychic change within the transference relationship. What occurs is a removal from the infantile situations that were experienced as dangerous, a modification of the defenses, and a strengthening of the ego, resulting in an increased sense of reality.

Case of Mrs. C.

The patient is a very pretty, thirty-four-year-old, blonde-haired and blue-eyed, who has the appearance of a "woman/man." Her facial looks and hairstyle are feminine, while her dress, tee shirts, and gait (a swagger) are very masculine. She is married with two children, has a PhD in history, and has a part-time position as an Adjunct Professor. She comes from a strict Catholic background. Mrs. C. had presented with a serous depression, and she had been bed-ridden for approximately a month with what was diagnosed as a "bad back." But she quickly indicated that the depression was a result of her ending an affair with a woman. While there was no genital sex there was kissing and hugging. She mourned the loss of the "hugs, the warmth, and understanding," she had received from her girlfriend.

My initial impression was that Mrs. C. would be an excellent psychoanalytic patient. We began treatment at four times a week.

I am presenting this case to show that frequency of sessions does not *ipso facto* imply psychoanalysis. It soon became very clear in the treatment that she was unable to tolerate frustration and separation from the analyst. Her desire for a real relationship, despite her intellectual understanding that this would interfere with the ultimate goals of the analysis, was very powerful. She wanted "hugs" from me, and expressed distress when this was not gratified; her insistence on wanting me in her life, to come to her house, and the unrepressed fantasies of wanting to make love to me, all indicated difficulty in functioning within the parameters of the "psychoanalytic reality," a reality that Modell (1990) refers to as an inherent paradox in psychoanalysis, in that the real object relationship exists in parallelism with the "as if" relationship, and thus, creates a duality for both the patient and the analyst. This "as if" aspect of the relationship caused confusion and anxiety for my patient.

Statements, regarding "how difficult it must be to understand this relationship," and how fearful she was of separation from me were made, but Mrs. C. received them essentially, as words of wisdom. At times she was hurt by my interpretations, but she could idealize them by proclaiming their "brilliance." She insisted on bringing me gifts: food, expensive items, and sent invitations to celebratory parties. Interpretations, such as that she needed to appease me, to bring me offerings like the ancient pagans asking for the gods' favor, or to show love for me by giving me presents lest I kick her out or—become angry at her if she showed any anger—could not stop these enactments. Her explanation for her gift-giving and wanting me in her nontherapeutic life was that I did not understand the culture from which she came. One gave presents to doctors, and even to hairdressers; since in her mind, I did not understand the appropriateness of her behavior, she was able to make her peace by indicating that we could disagree.

I believe there were two primary reasons that account for this persistent behavior: one, a powerful impulsion from the Id—"what I want, I want," and "I will do what I want"—a defiance that had genetic roots in her early childhood relations with her parents and siblings. Second, I became a self/object, an object to incorporate, to devour. Interestingly, I felt that it was not I that she devoured, but her/self in me. I was the projected self, her idealized self/object. I was to become her in body and mind. After ten years of treatment, this wish is still very powerful; though recently, she had the insight that, like her relationship with her mother, with whom she could not separate, so it was with me, she had to "swallow me so as not to separate."

In regard to changes that occurred in relationships, and with work that proved successful, she would claim that it was all due to me. Sometimes, I introduced that "we" did this together, rather than her "you," in order to pave the path for ego growth and separation-individuation. When she used the "we," it generally meant that we were interchangeable—she would often say, "we did this" or "we achieved this," and she would quote me with statements that actually represented her own thinking and words. Her need was to fill the psychic hole in her ego structure, a structure that was dominated by powerful id forces, and a demanding and punitive superego structure. She often stated that I was her conscience, "sitting on her shoulder like Jiminy Cricket." Yet, this conscience was also easily corruptible; for example, during Lent, if she went out to dinner with friends, she would eat meat, but if her husband or children broke the rule, she became upset. The issue was not hypocrisy, but rather a sense of loss of control of ego boundaries, a sense that her world would collapse if others disobeyed the rules.

In the transference, I was also a homosexual object, the mother/object , whom her father had desired. She had a strong masculine identification with her father, and an idealized image of men. It was also with men with whom she was in competition. In parallelism with the father identification and male idealization, there existed an identification with the powerful phallic mother. It was this gender ambivalence that created havoc for her. The inability to adequately synthesize these identifications was largely responsible for her "self" deficits, and the motive force for the oral incorporative transference enactments.

A good deal of change has occurred in the treatment: vast improvement in her mothering skills, and unleashing of her genuine creativity; she has written two books. The question that I shall raise is: Is this a "transference cure," a result of her incorporation of me, the self/object? Am I a homunculus within the ego, and the benign non-abstract superego? Is it possible that eventually, a different ego synthesis can develop, if separation from the transference object evolves into an "as if" transference object?

A second question arises regarding the frequency of sessions. Did four-times-a-week treatment represent a transference gratification and, therefore, result? Or will it result in the ultimate failure in working through the separation process that Modell (1990) has indicated is a primary goal for successful treatment? Did the frequency of sessions increase the "Id forces," thus interfering with ego functions, and higher-level defenses such as identification rather than introjection and imitation?

Would once, or at most, twice a week, have been a more efficacious mode of treatment?

Case of Mrs. B.

In presenting this case of twice-a-week therapy, I want to show what I believe to be the differences between less and more frequent sessions. I recognize that we are dealing with different character structures, different defenses, and perhaps, different motivations or aims by a patient within a similar nosology. Yet, I believe that this material can make a valid case for increased frequency.

Mrs. B is a thirty-five-year-old very attractive woman whose looks and manner are quite seductive. Her makeup, hairstyle, and dress are trendy and very feminine. What then is rather startling is to hear her speak—her expletives, her language. If one closed one's eyes, the sounds would resemble a construction site, exactly the business her father had established. She has three children, is separated from her husband, and works as an educator. Though separated for the past year, she and her husband, R, are in daily contact, and they share what has occurred in their individual therapy sessions (they have different therapists).

During a session, I commented to Mrs. B as to "what is all this language about?"—"fuck, and hell and asshole and shit," etc. She replied curtly, "I told you my father wanted a boy. We know that, so what? I was closer to my father." Her sister, three years her senior, was closer to her mother, though

Mrs. B had begun to wonder if this was really true. I asked, "In what way were you closer to your father?"

She replied, "He understood me. I liked to play in the dirt, to ride the tractor, I didn't have to do the 'girly' stuff."

In the following session, she stated that "I can't stand my husband's softness, his wanting too much attention, his talking all the time about his needs, and crying too much." To my comments, that he seemed to her too much like a woman, she agreed. She can't stand it; he gets on her nerves. If she spends any time with him, within "five minutes," she can't tolerate him; she feels like an "electric rod" has gone through her body; she has to get away or she will suffocate; she gets choked up in his presences.

"Like last night, I had lesson plans to do, and he kept talking and talking, and I just sat there without saying a word. It was then too late to do anything. I can't live with him."

My thoughts at that moment were conflicted—what to pursue—her masochism or her stereotype image of male and female roles—or both? And underlying these issues are incestuous wishes regarding her father, her rivalry with her mother and sister, and her male identification. I decided to make the point that her sitting for hours and not saying that she had work to do, was her attempt to act like a good woman who listens to her husband—to get up would be too much like a man—men are assertive—they do what they want."

She stated, "I was paralyzed; I couldn't move."

At the next session, four days later, the issues of her passivity, masochism, and homosexual conflicts were suppressed. Had she thought about them, even in a preconscious state? These were my thoughts—not spoken aloud.

She began the session talking about her husband wanting to go to mediation around divorce proceedings. It would cost a thousand dollars; that annoyed her. I wondered why she didn't want to go. "For what purpose? Since he wants to move back in with me—what is the point?" The session revolved around her conflicts of whether they should go for mediation, could she let him move back in, it would help to have him there to help with the children, she would not have to get up so early to get them ready for school; she doesn't want to have sex with him—he would sleep in another room, etc.

To my asking of why no sex, her reply was "I can't stand him—his whining and crying—he doesn't let me have any space!" Until recently, she was having sex with her husband, but she is now seeing another man who is a better lover. This man is married and does not intrude upon her space.

Could I get to at least some of the material in this session that had begun to emerge in the previous two sessions? Her identification with her father, her conflicts over identity, her wishes to be a man, her idealization of the male that her husband does not live up to, and her wish to incorporate the man's penis, all that, lay beneath the external issues that preoccupied her. It would have been a futile exercise, for the "crust" had already covered over whatever conscious acknowledgements had been achieved in the former sessions. I suggest that had there been a session the following day, or even the day after, it would have been possible for me to deal with some of this material—to point to her resistance over dealing with such conflictual and painful affects regarding her identity and how it influences her evaluation of her husband. But four days later, the material is too far removed; it is suppressed.

Yet, three weeks later, the issues of her sexual identification came up again; you would think that it had never been talked about! "I am so unsure of myself—who am I?" I could then say how doubtful she is about everything, and that she probably was always doubtful, and that these doubts had to do with her wondering if she was a woman or a man. If she got too close to a man, then these doubts about her femininity or masculinity would torment her; perhaps she would be found out.

Four days after this session, she arrives in a rather excited state and exclaims, "Am I crazy or not?" She wants to take the kids to Disneyland, and she wants her husband to come with them. "It would be wonderful for the kids … I would feel terrible if he took the kids and didn't take me." She feels she can't handle them alone; they are too wild. I enquire about the sleeping arrangements, and she informs me that they will all share the same room. I say, "she and R would sleep in the same bed but no sex."

"Of course," she replied, "we have slept together recently in the same bed without having sex." Her husband said he doesn't think that he can do it: "he wants to live with me and sleep with me." The session goes on about Disneyland—the fun she had as a child—she had gone there with her father (to my question—she replies that it was with the entire family). She still has fond memories of the visit. It is increasingly evident that her incestuous oedipal conflict and sadomasochism are enacted with her spouse. She pushes him away and then wants him back; and if he should see another woman, she rages.

One of her defenses against her incestuous wishes is to turn to women. She recently took a weekend trip with a woman to Puerto Rico, and now is contemplating having another woman friend move in with her instead of her husband. I decide at this point to make an interpretation that is distant from her conscious awareness. I tell her that she is like an "oedipal child;" then I ask if she knows what I mean. "Yes" she responds, and then I point out that she sees her husband like a daddy who should take them all to Disneyland—repeating her childhood experience—and she doesn't understand why this is so difficult for him. Is it that she can't let go of him (like her tie to her father)? I think that she feels guilty towards him. Further into the session, I indicated that I think she is also, guilty because of her rivalry towards her sister and her mother, and that because of her rivalry, she can't let another woman have her husband, even though she doesn't want him.

She responded that "I had feelings of guilt while I was in Puerto Rico," and that she had texted her husband saying that they should all go to Disneyland—she felt so bad that she had left the kids. There is silence and she appeared despondent. I ask what she is feeling? "You broke my bubble—now I can't go to Disneyland."

I am somewhat surprised by this, and exclaim that "it seems strange that you are not troubled by my talking about your tie to your father and your guilt feelings, but rather, that you can't go to Disneyland'—she smiles at this—and leaves the session.

Why do I interpret when she is far away from the oedipal issues that motivate much of her enactments? Am I hoping to pave the way for psychoanalytic treatment by stimulating an intellectual awareness, and letting her know that her decisions and conscious conflicts are determined by her unconscious conflicts? And that there is a need for her to know what lies beneath the surface?

In my mind, more frequent sessions would have made it possible for her to understand the unconscious meaning of her behavior, such as sleeping with various married men rather than her accepting glib statements that she just liked sleeping with them, because it made her feel good. That, her relationships with men represented acting out her wish for a penis, and that the intense jealousy of other women—women, whom her husband might sleep with—indicated her underlying homosexual conflict. All of this requires an intensity of working through in the treatment that cannot be achieved without frequent sessions. Perhaps, you might say that years down the road this material could become part of her affective and symbolic understanding, but given the quality of her defenses, I doubt if this recognition could be deeply synthesized in twice-a-week sessions.

CONCLUSION

The ability to claim verity regarding the absolute impact of frequent sessions, i.e., three, four, or five times a week, still remains one of the conundrums of psychoanalytic practice. Yet, the inability to provide conclusive statistical reliability does not preclude the reliability of objective clinical experience, for even statistics have their relativity, and remain a cloudy vehicle besides long and labored clinical experience. I have tried to show that there is an inherent logic to our hypotheses that is reliable within the clinical context, and that is borne out by both the patient and the analyst's experience. I make the claim for both the subjective, and objective evaluations of both partners in the analytic experience. I contend that there is an inherent observable consistency to human development, i.e., zonal phase drive organization, object constancy, and object relationships. Based upon this psychic organization, that is modified by social and cultural experiences, and by the specific role of the external object, our theories regarding psychoanalytic treatment, its mode and process, belong within the parameters of the natural sciences. That we can establish a dictum to frequency of sessions for the psychoanalytic process without pure statistical corroboration is a given for the continued practice and validation of psychoanalysis as a theory and a treatment method.

I would, therefore, suggest that we sustain the value and beneficial aspects to frequency of sessions. It is not essential to change basic hypotheses or postulates in order to modify treatment methods. We can adhere to the rigors of our hypotheses, alter technique due to the realities of our patients and their internal conditions, and still hold to theoretical propositions that enhance knowledge and practice. However we modify our theories, it must be based upon knowledge and theoretical consistency, and not by insurance companies.

REFERENCES

Alexander, F. (1950). Analysis of the therapeutic factors in psychoanalytic treatment. *Psychoanalytic Q.* 19:482–500.

_____ & French, T.M. (1946). *Psychoanalytic Therapy Principles and Application*. New York: Ronald Press.

Barnet. J.E. & Holmes, K. (2016). The Practice of Tele-Mental Health, Ethical, Legal and Clinical Issues for Practitioners. *Practice Innovations* Vol.1:53–66.

Benjamin, J. (1998). *The Shadow of the Other*. New York and London :Routledge.

Bleichmar, H. (2004). Making conscious the unconscious in order to modify unconscious processing. *International Journal of Psychoanalysis* 85:1379–1400.

Ehrlich, L.T. (2010). The analyst's ambivalence about continuing and deepening an analysis. *New York Review of Books,* Review by J. Uglow. *JAPA* 58:515–532.

Eissler, K. (1959). On Isolation. *Psychoanaly. St. Child* 14:29–60.

Fenichel, O. (1953). *The Collected Papers of Otto Fenichel*. New York: David Lewes, Inc.

Freud, S. (1912). The Dynamic of Transference. *Standard Edition* 12.

_____ (1913). On Beginning the Treatment (Further Recommendations on the Technique of Psycho-Analysis, *Standard Edition* 12.

_____ (1914). Remembering, Repeating and Working-Through (Further Recommendations on the Technique of Psycho-Analysis) *Standard Edition* 12.

_____ (1916–1917). The Introductory Lectures on Psychoanalysis [1915–1917] *Standard Edition* 15.

_____ (1917[1916–17]). General Theory of the Neurosis. *Standard Edition* 16.

_____ (1925 [1924]). The Resistance to Psycho-Analysis. *Standard Edition* 19.

_____ (1933 [1932]). New introductory Lectures on Psychoanalysis. (lectures XX1X –XXXV) *Standard Edition* 22.

_____ (1937). Analysis Terminable and Interminable. *Standard Edition* 23.

Freedman, N. Hoffenberg, J. Vous, N. & Frosh, A. (1999). The effectiveness of psychoanalytic psychotherapy, the role of treatment duration, frequency of sessions, and the therapeutic relationship. *JAPA* 47:741–772.

Frosh, S. (2011). Framing Pictures, Picturing Frames. Visual Metaphors in Political Communications *Research Journal of Communication Resear*ch 35(2):91–114.

Galatzer-Levy, R. (2000). *Does Psychoanalysis Work?* Yale University Press, New Haven, Conn.

Gedo, G. & Cohler, B.J. (1992). Session frequency, regressive intensity and the psychoanalytic process. *Psychoanalytic Psychology* 9:245–249.

Gill, M. (1979). The analysis of the transference. *JAPA* 27(suppl):263–288.

Glover, E. (1955). *The Technique of Psychoanalysis.* New York: IUP.

Greenberg, J. (1999 [1986]). *Theoretical Models and the Analyst's Neutrality. In Relational Psychoanalysis: The Emergence of a Tradition* ed. Mitchel, S.H. & Aron, L. Hillsdale, NJ: Analytic Press, pp.131–152.

_____ & Mitchel, S.A. (1983). *Object Relations in Psychoanalytic Theory.* Cambridge, MA: Harvard University Press.

Greenson, R. (1967). *The Technique and Practice of Psychoanalysis, Vol. 1.* New York: IUP.

Hirsch, I. (2001). A note on two common assumptions about interpersonal psychoanalysis: commentary on Jeanne Wolff-Bernstein's "Countertransference: Our new royal road to the unconscious." *Psychoanalytic Dialogues* 2:115–126.

Klein, M. (1975). *Love, guilt and reparation and other works 1921–1945.* The Free Press: New York

Lacan, J. (1977). *Ecrits: A Selection: Function and Field of Speech and Language.* United States: Tavistock Publications Limited.

Lansky, (2007). Unbearable shame, splitting and forgiveness in the resolution of vengefulness. *JAPA* 55:571–593.

Lionells (1999). Thanatos is alive and well and living in psychoanalysis. In *The Death of Psychoanalysis*. ed. Prince, R.M. Northvale, NJ & London: Jason Aronson, pp. 1–24.

Panel: American Psychoanalytic Association (1996). (published by *Journal of the American Psychoanalytic Association,* 1997).

Modell, A. (1990). *Other Times, Other Realities.* Cambridge, MA, London, England: Harvard University Press.

Rapaport, D. (1942). *Emotions and memory. The Collected Papers of David Rapaport.* ed. Gill, M. New York: Basic Books, 1967, pp.120–127.

Renik, O. (1997). Intersubjectivity, therapeutic action, and analytic technique. *Psychoanalytic Quarterly* 76:1547–1562.

Roussillon, R. (2010). Working through and its various models. *International Journal of Psychoanalysis* 91:1405–1417.

Schafer, R. (1983). *The Analytic Attitude.* New York: Basic Books.

Uglow, J., (2010). The other side of Science: Review of S. Schapin *New York Review of Books,* June 24, 2010.

Schwartz, C. (2003). A brief discussion on frequency of sessions and its impact upon psychoanalytic treatment. *Psychoanalytic Review* 90:179–192.

Silver, C. (2003). A survey of clinicians' views about change in psychoanalytic practice and theoretical orientation. *Psychoanalytic Review* 90:193–224.

Solano, L. (2010). Some thoughts between body and mind in the light of Wilma Bucci's multiple code theory. *International Journal of Psychoanalysis* 91:1445–1464.

Strachey, J. (1934). The Nature of the Therapeutic Action of Psychoanalysis. *International Journal of Psychoanalysis.* 15:127–159.

Twemlow, S.W. (2002). Hidden influences on success or failure in clinical psychoanalysis. In *Failures in Psychoanalytic Treatment.* ed. J. Reppen, & M.A. Schulman. Madison CT: International Universities Press, pp. 63–80

Winnicott, D.W. (1960). The theory of the parent-infant relationship. In *The Maturational Processes and the Facilitating Environment by D.W. Winnicott.* New York: International Universities Press, pp. 37–55.

BOOK REVIEWS

Intrapsychic and Interpersonal Dimensions of Treatment: A Critical Dialogue. by Robert Langs, MD & Harold Searles, MD New York: Jason Aronson, 1980.

[(1981) *Psychoanalytic Review* (68)(3):460–462.]

Robert Langs has attempted to redress what he considers a failure of the psychoanalytic community to concern itself with the "gradual development of a basic clinical psychoanalytic methodology." Since his book *Technique in Transition* was published in 1978, Langs could not refer to the *JAPA* Supplement (1979) on "Psychoanalytic Technique and Theory of Therapy." The issues of transference, the role of genetic interpretation versus the focus on the "here and now," curative aspects of insight, and the working alliance were discussed.

However, I am inclined to think that this would in no way alter Langs's evaluation of what he regards as the current clinical "orthodoxy" in psychoanalysis. To read Langs, especially his recent two volume interviews with Stone and Searles, is to be impressed not so much with the "orthodoxy" of the International Psychoanalytic Community as with the "orthodoxy" of Langs. He has the zeal of a messiah and the rancor of a prophet in his critical assumptions that both analysts have deviated from the psychoanalytic "frame" and ignored transference reactions.

The "frame" is a basic structure emanating from the "primary adaptive context" of the analytic situation. The patient's communications in the analysis derive not simply from the derivatives of unconscious conflicts, infantile wishes, memories, and fantasies, but are stimulated by the specific interactional context in the analytic exchange. Borrowing from Freud's theory of the role of the day residue in the dream, Langs has extended this concept of the day residue to an even more primary role in the psychic structure. The day residue consists of those reality precipitates that either elicit an adaptive-reality response from the patient or set off a sequence of unconscious fantasies and memories related to the patient's "pathology, inner anxieties, and conflicts." The most significant of the day residue content is aroused from the analyst's responses to the patient. Langs views these responses as pivotal to the analysis and attributes to them responsibility for provoking pathological reactions in the patient. Since the reality-adaptational mode is primary in the interactional context, a maladaptive response by the analyst, that is, non-therapeutic behavior, will result in a maladaptive response in the patient. If this is not recognized and properly analyzed, the patient who has introjected the anti-therapeutic response creates a negative introject of the analyst. The results lead to pathological behavior or regressive states. The frame for Langs, therefore, becomes the critical focus of the analytic situation and all interpretations or verbalizations are reflected through this adaptational interactive prism of the transference experience. Genetic material, affective states, and drive derivatives projected in the transference pale before the introjective sequence.

Langs is correct when he states that his theories "are not extensions of the prevailing orthodoxy" but constitute more of a departure. Here, we may reflect upon Freud's (1913) recommendation that the theme of transference should be left untouched so long as the patient's communications and ideas run on without any obstruction. When the transference becomes a resistance, then transference becomes the focus of treatment.

Langs's dialogue with Searles in *Intrapsychic and Interpersonal Dimensions of Treatment* is an admirable attempt to improve and expand discourse in the analytic community. It is regrettable that Langs did not exhibit more appreciation for Searles's willingness to provide clinical sessions through which technique and theory, based upon empirical evidence, could be investigated. Langs was unable to refrain from donning a supervisor's role, indeed an irritant to both Searles and the reader. A stance of inquiry rather than pedantry would have brought into sharp relief a number of issues and questions inherent in the presentation. What, for example, motivates Searles to treat a psychotic woman for more than eighteen years, a woman who has already been psychotic for over twenty-seven years, and to present this case as an example of psychoanalytic technique with schizophrenics? That Searles continues to hope that she may "become enduringly non-psychotic" when already reaching the age of 60 is indeed an amazing example of the plasticity of hope. Was Searles presenting to the audience some portion of his own psychic motivations or is there a more profound intellectual problem that he is after—some painstaking method to reclaim the libido for the object world?

An interesting transference problem is presented. After all these years of treatment, the patient, with some perception of the reality of Searles's professional relationship to her, wishes to pay for the sessions; a few nickels are left on the desk. Searles rejects the payment without any discussion or even a simple "thank you." At the end of the session the patient expresses suicidal thoughts. Certainly, the suicidal threat was a transference response. Unfortunately, it was not possible to investigate the unconscious content. Langs immediately understood the patient to have introjected a negative therapeutic behavior and the suicidal expression emanated from the presence of the negative introject of Searles that must be destroyed. The rather compulsive and uniform application of a theoretical interpretation leaves no room for the specific investigation of meaning in behavior or thought.

The technical applications of analysis are not always within the conscious grasp of the analyst. Technique consists of the synthesis of skill, knowledge, and intuition. The capacity to conceptualize the "why" or "when" of a particular interpretation or methodical approach requires time and associative thinking. Searles had some difficulty with the critical approach utilized by Langs. Since Langs appeared less interested in understanding Searles's conceptualizations and countertransference responses, the reader was denied an opportunity to explore with the analyst why he chose a particular response. We can postulate that Searles's refusal of the payment without investigation was preferred to an approach that may further humiliate the patient or intensify the transference wishes and thereby induce a more regressive psychotic defense. It is possible that Searles's choice at times of genetic material over transference issues was to preclude the emergences of fantasies and conflicts that could overwhelm the already tenuous ego functions. To preclude errors in judgment and countertransference problems, all of which Searles was quite receptive to consider, would be a kindness no analyst can be spared.

In spite of Langs's difficulty in pursuing a more impartial investigation of Searles' theories, it is to his credit that he has focused upon issues of technique and methodology.

CHAPTER 16

Infantile Origins of Sexual Identity
by Herman Roiphe and Eleanor Galenson. New York: International Universities Press, 1981, xv + 301 pp.

[(1986). *The Psychoanalytic Review* (73)(4):223–227.]

If this is the age of large-scale revolutions in the field of psychoanalysis, then Roiphe and Galenson in their latest joint work have created only a *"petite revolution"* The phallic-genital phase, according to the authors, occurs much earlier than has heretofore been considered. Heretofore, it has been thought that the onset of castration anxiety and penis envy have always followed an approximate 36-month time clock; not so, say the authors. Their observations indicate a much earlier beginning, a 15- to 19-month period spanning through the 24th month. They regard this early genital phase not as a precocious development or pathological condition but as a normal process due to the "heightened narcissistic valence as a consequence of the regular genital arousal." A preoedipal sexual identity quite different from gender identity is achieved in this period with the parent of the same sex. The authors distinguish between pleasurable genital sensations and genital play which Spitz first described in *The First Year of Life* and a specific focused genital sensitivity with an ideational content. Their observations reveal affective and erotic components of "flushing," facial expressions of excitement, rapid respiration and perspiration: The children display an "inward gaze" expressive of fantasy feeling; this "state had become a regular concomitant of genital self-stimulation." The authors believe that this early fantasy formation includes a partial memory of the earlier maternal contact, since the genital manipulation so often involves these typical "mother-me" objects. Concrete objects are then gradually discarded, and masturbation approaches the adult model.

Since, the authors note, this genital specificity occurs during the height of the anal phase of libidinal development, the confluence of the two drives, the anal and genital derivatives, calibrate in a very specific manner.

The period of anal libidinal development exudes, in a sense, two distinct forces; one that increases the libidinal cathexis of body parts and body functions due in part to the maturation of the motoric and perceptual systems, and zonal cathexis. The second extends to the world of objects and the wish for mastery over the external environment. The excreta or the process of excretion assumes a highly symbolic function. On the one hand it is a valued body possession, a narcissistic investment; and on the other hand, the function is a source of great pleasure and satisfaction for the discharge of the libidinal and aggressive drives. Language development is accelerated, and the symbolic process further provides an avenue for drive gratification. The excreta itself and the function of elimination characterize the attention cathexis of the child.

For the authors, this is a phase of rapid ego development and the phase of nascent object constancy. The problem as they view it is to maintain the internal representations of the object in a phase of volatile fluctuations of aggressive drive energy. The ego's capacity to manage the aggression is limited due to the constitutional weakness and susceptibility to rapid regression. The capacity to obliterate the object either by indifference or hate presents the ego with a precarious position. The loss of the object or the object's love threatens the infant with "annihilation" and disintegration of body integrity. The object in this phase is viewed by Roiphe and Galenson as a "stool-object," an object that symbolizes the self-body cathexis and part other. The "stool" as an anthropomorphism takes on the characteristics of a "transitional object," and the authors develop Winnicott's concept of transitional objects in regard to the meaning of the "stool-object."

The concomitant development at the anal-urethral phase of an early genital phase complicates the ego's tasks. The awareness of the sexual difference is responsible in both the male and female for the traumatic state that gives rise to castration anxiety. In girls, the authors note a "shock-like reaction which consisted of a denial of the genital difference with displacement of interest to the mother's breast, umbilicus and buttocks." They claim that this aroused in the girls a fear of object loss and self-disintegration that was then countered by a developmental advance into fantasy play and graphic representation, a defensive effort against anxiety. The absence of a penis in the girls heightened their aggression to the mother and resulted in a phase of hostile ambivalence. It is this aggression that endangers the child's internal representation of the mother and threatens the object loss.

For the male child, knowledge of the absence of the penis in the female initially resulted in an increase of masturbatory activity, and then a sharp decline, followed by an increase in motoric activity, and a turn to hard toys, cars, and engines. An avoidance of looking at the female genitalia, notably the mother, was observed; this was an attempt at denial of the sexual difference. The authors hypothesize that the recognition of the female without a penis implied a "threat of castration and regression to the more symbiotic type of passive attachment to the mother."

Roiphe and Galenson observe that there is a decided difference in the play between the female and male child with the male displaying far less elaboration of fantasy elements. In both sexes, there is a turning away from the mother to the father. The female turns to the father as an erotic choice, rejecting the castrated object; while the male turns to the father as an object for identification.

The subjects of the study ranged in age from 10 to 13 months upon entering the nursery. The final study population consisted of 66 infants, 33 girls and 33 boys. Two thirds of the infants came from upper-middle-class families, the remaining one third came from lower-middle-class families. Most of the fathers were employed in some aspect of a medical program or a related field. Each group was studied from September through June and attended the nursery four mornings a week.

The authors present us with clinical findings that are indeed surprising and seem to conflict with previous findings in the infant observation studies of Mahler, Provence, Kestenberg, and even Winnicott's individual case study. They refer in the literature to statements by Anna Freud and Phyllis Greenacre that indicate some cases of an early genital development, though this was considered as a pathological condition or a precocious phase development indicating serious impediments for ego development. It is hoped that continued study and research on infant development will clarify these issues and possibly enrich our knowledge of libidinal phase development, zonal dominance, and the organization of object relations.

Perhaps a major issue of contention is the authors' theoretical revision of the classical concept of "castration anxiety." If the early genital phase occurs prior to or without the parallel oedipus complex, which is the ego's response to the libidinalization of the genitals, then what is the *raison d'être* for castration anxiety? The castration threat in the male results from his rivalry with the father for the possession of the mother, and in the female it is the castration fantasy that ushers in the oedipal phase. In the male, the hostile, aggressive wishes toward the father are what threaten the child with retaliation. The sexual difference, the female without a phallus, becomes a source of danger, a reminder that this might happen to him. Without the oedipal conflict and rivalry, castration, in the dynamic sense, is not a danger.

Freud states that the differences between the sexes are noted but the expectation is that the mother will grow a penis. There is no danger nor distress until the oedipal phase when the rivalry with the father is intensified.

Only then does the sexual difference spell danger for the oedipal boy and gives rise to castration anxiety.

If Roiphe and Galenson subscribe to a formulation that the absence of a penis in the female represents a narcissistic injury and assault to the integrity of the body, this would assume that a body schema, is clearly established in the cognitive sphere. This would represent a rather unusual level of abstraction requiring the establishment of long-term memory and a level of perceptual integration that is questionable for a 15- to 20-month-old child. One would ask for more corroborative research.

Psychoanalytic theory regarding the female's development of castration anxiety also differs from the authors' views. That genital stimulation exists is not the issue. Freud also made note of clitoral and genital sensations in two-year-old girls. The question is not one of genital sensations but of genital dominance—the zonal importance and increased cathexis with the establishment of defenses, sublimations, and ego patterns regarding the aims of earlier libidinal phases. In the female this genital phase dominance is accompanied by cognitive ego development (this applies likewise to the male) that takes account of the functions of the male organ, particularly as the progenitor of babies. Previously, the female in her preoedipal attachment acted as if she could make a baby for mother or have a baby with mother. The genital phase has to shatter this infantile sexual theory. The anger at the mother is not simply due to a narcissistic body injury but a deprivation of a wished-for function to make a

baby. It is this frustration of the wish and the failure to gain a penis that makes the girl turn away in anger from the mother and turn to the father. The initial wish for a penis, thus the template of penis envy, changes to a wish for a baby from the father. Castration then is responsible in the female for the introduction of the oedipus complex.

Roiphe and Galenson neglect in their study the consideration of the nature of the ego's response to function, role, and identity. The penis for them is a highly valued body part, an aspect of body schema, a narcissistic investment, but what they ignore is that the value of the penis is due in large part to the function and role in procreation and the sexual act. It is certainly open to question whether the 15- to 20-month-old has attained this level of cognitive integration to thus postulate an early genital phase. Certainly, their case studies do point to a surprising precocity in language development, symbolic thought, and organized structured play less random than we are accustomed to observe in this age group. It is possible that the continued research in infant development will one day concur in their findings.

Roiphe and Galenson must therefore be credited for their analytic investigation of child development.

CHAPTER 17

Sexual Subjects: Lesbians, Gender and Psychoanalysis. by Adria E. Schwartz. New York: Routledge Press, 1998, 200 pp.

[(2001). *Psychoanal. Review* (88)(4):585–587].

In *Sexual Subjects*, Adria Schwartz has presented a series of essentially political essays on lesbians, gender, and psychoanalysis. She is a good writer, but, unfortunately, her claim that this books deals with lesbian sexuality within a psychoanalytic frame of reference is overstated. Schwartz's admixture of declaratory statements and theoretical hypotheses represents the dicta of postmodern feminism without, however, an in-depth psychodynamic theory.

The first paper, titled "Resistance," accuses society in general, and the psychoanalytic establishment specifically, of rejecting and pathologizing lesbianism. One cannot quarrel with this claim, nor escape her accusation that many analysts have been responsible for intensifying the internal conflicts and self-abnegation of lesbians. She reminds us that it took twenty years for the American Psychoanalytic Association to accept the American Psychiatric Association's position that homosexuality is not a pathological condition. Her accusations against psychoanalysts, both past and present, are a distressing reminder of our prejudice and rigidity.

Schwartz continues this critique in relation to what she views as the patriarchal and phallocentric aspects of psychoanalytic theory. She states that within the "spectrum of women resisters, there is a refusal of phallic primacy that has to do not solely with desire, but, also with issues of agency, subjectivity, and their worldly manifestation in the form of power" (p. 3).

Later she indicates that "the spirit in which I discuss resistance carries within it the seeds of de(con)struction for any identity that fixes a parameter of sex/gender in place" (p. 5). These examples highlight the manifesto-like quality of her book rather than the creation of a psychologically informed theory regarding human development that reflects internal psychic structure interacting with the social structure.

Schwartz has deconstructed classical psychoanalytic theory in accordance with postmodern feminist theorists, specifically in regard to sex and gender. She postulates that feminism informs "psychoanalysis within a context of political/cultural and historical reality and delineates ways in which that reality is transmitted and interiorized within the individual" (p. 9). The problem, according to the author, is that psychoanalysis uses sex and gender to "reify experiences." In her view, the male-female binary delineation of anatomical differences serves the function of perpetuating masculine hegemony. Lesbian, gay, and heterosexual identities reflect historical and cultural influences rather than "endogenous psychic structures." That social factors leave a qualifying mark on sexuality, and are used to create dominance of one sex over another does not, however, negate the role of biology in human development. Schwartz further disclaims the role of gender as a central organizing factor in the developing sense of self. She subtracts "generative" factors from the body equation, and questions whether generativity equates with femininity and, thus, heterosexuality. She refers to this as "generativity redux" (p. 68). In Schwartz's view, we are not the children of nature but, rather, the children of sociocultural factors; the body and anatomy are transcendental. In posing the question "Does the gendered sense of self have to correspond to some objective reality about the sexed body?"

She widens the divide between the externalization of the body ego and anatomical internalization. She views internalization as totally dependent upon cultural discourse; there is no room in her theory for the influence of biological systems interacting with psychological development.

As a treatment mode, Schwartz finds the interrelational school most appealing. The interactional therapeutic mode that defines both past and present in terms of the interaction between patient and analyst also defines gender identity. For Schwartz, gender identity is partly a function of who we are in relationship to "that other object," a relationship subject to interaction, interpretations, and fantasies. The sense of self and the internalized ego identifications are isolated from gender identification, and the sense of self and core gender do not necessarily equate with sexual object choice. To the contrary: The sense of belonging to one sex or another is not compromised by cross-sex identification and behaviors.

When Schwartz turns to clinical material, we are faced with a paradox. From her theoretical framework, she concludes that the mother/child dyad has been incorrectly "reified." Yet her case presentations uniformly underscore the problem as between mother and daughter. From her writings we can almost anticipate that the infant girl will have a prescient sense of phallic hegemony, and already view her mother as powerless. In each case, the author presents a narcissistic mother with whom the daughter is unable to identify. In some cases, the fathers are unsupportive, and in others the fathers are loving. Does the loving father provide an identificatory object and, thus, the homosexual object choice? Schwartz warns against bifurcating the choice of a love object and gender identity. Yet in her schema we have no way of arriving at an understanding of how gender identity and sexual object choice develop. If we should not conflate core gender identity, identifications, and sexual object choice in some interactive relationship with each other, how then are we to understand psychological development? Unfortunately, Schwartz's clinical presentations do not offer much insight into her patient's fundamental conflicts. We are, therefore, left with a lacuna in understanding her conceptions regarding lesbianism.

CHAPTER 18

The Temptation of Biology: Freud's Theories of Sexuality. by Jean Laplanche. Translated by Donald Nicholson-Smith. New York: The Unconscious in Translation, 2015.

[(2017) *Psychoanalytic Review* (104)(2):263–266].

Jean Laplanche, the French psychoanalyst renowned for his writings on Freud, often tests the comprehension of the American reader in his book *The Temptation of Biology: Freud's Theories of Sexuality.* Laplanche's theoretical perspective is intellectually challenging, and while "revising" Freud, despite his disclaimer, he also provides an important exegesis into certain aspects of Freud's thinking that warrant evaluation, reevaluation, and support. As he states, "there is no question of revising Freud"; the task is to "discern the false equilibria within it" (p. 6). The book is essentially a compendium of a series of lectures delivered from 1991 to 1992 at the University of Paris, along with one given in 1997 in Buenos Aires, Argentina.

Laplanche, who is both critical and admiring of Freud, presents an interesting paradox regarding Freud, whom he feels "may have gone astray," but whose strayings nevertheless led to a "clearer picture of fundamental problematics often difficult to discern in [a] conceptual labyrinth" (p. xii). This should not surprise us, as Laplanche (1970) had indicated in an earlier paper, "Life and Death in Psychoanalysis," that

Freud's "dialectical approach, entailing an evolution through reversals and crises, mediated by contradictions whose status will not be immediately apparent in any attempt to situate them, are all "deserving of the same 'free floating' attention. No doubt, in practice, certain contradictions may prove to be relatively 'extrinsic' or adventitious, the results of polemic or of hasty formulations; but even in such cases, they cannot be discarded without a certain loss [p. 1].

Thus, Laplanche's major criticism of Freud in this book provides an opportunity to follow his interpretation of Freud's first drive theory in the *Three Essays* (1905) in light of Freud's second drive theory, enunciated in *Beyond the Pleasure Principle* (1920). Laplanche asserts that by "biologizing" sex, Freud was "straying" from himself. This has a confusing quality, for we assume that sex is a biological factor, and that no concept can remove it from its basic root, that is, biology. Laplanche sets out to examine Freud's use of the words *Instinct* and *Trieb*, and concludes that Freud's frequent use of *instinct* is closer to biology, while *Trieb* is more psychological and adheres to what occurs in mental life. *Instinct* has the quality of purposeful, specific actions that are predetermined by heredity, whereas *Trieb* is a force, a "pressure," that is somewhat further removed from biology. As Laplanche notes, Freud used the two words interchangeably, though in German the two words *Instinkt* (instinct) and *Trieb* have distinct meanings. Laplanche claims that when Freud used *Instinct*, he was referring to an action or condition biologically inherent in specific acts, whereas when Freud used *Trieb*, he was referring to pressure removed from the strict categorization of the instinctual.

This distinction between the two terms is more evident in the January14 and January 22 lectures of 1992, in which Laplanche discussed Freud's developmental stages: oral, anal, and genital. Essentially, Laplanche did not regard infantile sexuality as biological or as hereditarily based. He preferred a seduction theory more suggestive of what Freud referred to in the *Three Essays*. There, seduction of the infant occurs as a result of the mother's care and administration, which results in the sexualization of the infant. It is important to point out that Freud indicated this only in passing, and as an adjunct to the inherent instinctual drive in infancy. Laplanche suggests that Freud's refuting of the Aristophanes' myth in the *Three Essays*—which attributed the origins of sex to God's original splitting of a unified being into two parts, male and female, implying their persistent drive to reunite—was a far better position than his later 1920 paper, which established the second drive theory, the Death Instinct. By exhuming the Aristophanes myth from the ashes, Freud was again biologizing sexuality. I assume that in Laplanche's view, this myth—in explaining a basic hereditary, instinctual act—correlates sex with biology, a theoretical position he opposes.

The primary question is this: How does Laplanche view sexuality? In his final lecture we are able to discern a clearer exposition of his position. Laplanche preferred Freud's concepts regarding *Trieb*, which convey the idea of pressure, to *Instinkt* (the German spelling), which is too close to a static and inherited view of behavior. He takes issue with neuroscience for what he regards as an attempt to co-opt psychoanalysis under a different aegis. Psychoanalysis is no more an adjunct to neuroscience than is aesthetics or logic. He thus places psychoanalysis outside the orbit of any biological endeavors. He also feels that modern biology, neurobiology, and neurophysiology have little to offer psychoanalysis, and he questions the validity of the relationship of psychoanalysis to genetics. He does not believe that neurophysiologists can expect, even in the future, "to identify the mathematical distinction between quadratic and cubic equations in a given localized process in the brain," concluding that these sciences have little to offer psychoanalysis. Psychoanalysis is concerned with the mental, the universal phenomena of conflict, for which there is no specific gene or localization in the brain.

Further, Laplanche questions Freud's using the terms auto-eroticism and narcissism to designate stages of development. He regards both terms, rather, as "repeated macro-sequences" that arise in a multitude of situations and relationships. Freud's division of libido into ego libido and object libido (recall that "libido" for Freud emanates from the sexual instincts) also comes under scrutiny, as Laplanche questions the legitimacy of their derivation from sexuality. In a rather complex and somewhat confusing discourse, he forces us to reconsider the meaning of homosexual and heterosexual libido, narcissistic libido, and others. Are we dealing, he implies, with instincts per se, qualities of instincts, a descriptive nomenclature, or a mode of libidinal function in regard to the object?

Throughout the essays, Laplanche questions Freud's biologizing of sexuality, particularly in regard to the sexual nature of the oral, anal, and phallic stages. Laplanche stresses that an adult caretaker does not function in accordance with oral, anal, or phallic stages presumably undergone by the infant in his or her care. These appellations of sexual stages, therefore, are not reasonable and belie the reality that it is the caregiver who eroticizes these zones by the very fact that inadvertent stimulus is an inevitable product of tending to the child. That Freud viewed the oedipus complex, castration fantasies, anxieties, and even primal-scene fantasies as inherited—that is, as aspects of instincts—is, in Laplanche's view, a gross error. He is critical of Freud for these depictions and characterizes these complexes and behaviors as myths that human culture has devised as a means to control behavior. Thus, for Laplanche, Freud's acceptance of these myths was indeed a falsification of sexuality.

Laplanche felt that Freud's first seduction theory, in which "the genetics of sexuality must be confronted with the following paradox, as illuminated by the general theory of seduction" (p. 130) was preferable to his later theories. Laplanche's basic claim is that "in the history of the human individual, acquired sexuality precedes innate sexuality, this on account of the young human's contact with adult sexuality" (p. 130). Certainly, Laplanche supported the concept of drive, that is, *Trieb*, as sexual, but asserted that the pressure of the drive is activated by the relationship with the mother. Even the self-preservative drive that Freud placed in conjunction with the sexual drive is considered by Laplanche as "open to the other person; it involves the other" (p. 68). Further, Laplanche indicated that the "self-preservative relationship fosters seduction" (p. 68). He stated that the more obvious sexual drives and self- preservation are latent states activated only by the "other."

This is an interesting point, and one is reminded of René Spitz's work with children in foster care and foundling homes, who, without the care of a consistent object, tend to become ill and die. Though Spitz never questioned the instinctual or biological nature of sexuality, it is possible to raise the question, namely, that if the sexual drive in infancy exists in a passive or quiescent state and requires a human object to activate its force, why can this not be considered an inherent quality of biology? There is a categorical quality to Laplanche's evaluation of Freud's instinct theories that seems to neglect the modulation of instinct in respect to environmental and human relationships. Even in science the environment plays a role in activating certain biological conditions that, though latent, have fundamental invariant qualities.

Laplanche, who died in 2012, raised many thought-provoking points and issues about Freud's work, which continue to require clarification, discussion, and further research. His praise for Freud, despite his disagreements, is steady throughout, and he viewed himself as a loyal Freudian.

www.ingramcontent.com/pod-product-compliance
Lightning Source LLC
Chambersburg PA
CBHW062114020426
42335CB00013B/963